CW01303183

INSIGHTS

General Editor: Clive Bloom, Senior Lecturer in English, Middlesex Polytechnic

Editorial Board: Clive Bloom, Brian Docherty, Gary Day, Lesley Bloom and Hazel Day

Insights brings to academics, students and general readers the very best contemporary criticism on neglected literary and cultural areas. It consists of anthologies, each containing original contributions by advanced scholars and experts. Each contribution concentrates on a study of a particular work, author or genre in its artistic, historical and cultural context.

Published titles

Clive Bloom (*editor*)
JACOBEAN POETRY AND PROSE: Rhetoric, Representation and the Popular Imagination
TWENTIETH-CENTURY SUSPENSE: The Thriller Comes of Age
SPY THRILLERS: From Buchan to le Carré

Clive Bloom, Brian Docherty, Jane Gibb and Keith Shand (*editors*)
NINETEENTH-CENTURY SUSPENSE: From Poe to Conan Doyle

Gary Day (*editor*)
READINGS IN POPULAR CULTURE: Trivial Pursuits?

Gary Day and Clive Bloom (*editors*)
PERSPECTIVES ON PORNOGRAPHY: Sexuality in Film and Literature

Brian Docherty (*editor*)
AMERICAN CRIME FICTION: Studies in the Genre
AMERICAN HORROR FICTION: From Brockden Brown to Stephen King

Rhys Garnett and R. J. Ellis (*editors*)
SCIENCE FICTION ROOTS AND BRANCHES: Contemporary Critical Approaches

Robert Giddings (*editor*)
LITERATURE AND IMPERIALISM

Robert Giddings, Keith Selby and Chris Wensley
SCREENING THE NOVEL: The Theory and Practice of Literary Dramatisation

Dorothy Goldman (*editor*)
WOMEN AND WORLD WAR I

Graham Holderness (*editor*)
THE POLITICS OF THEATRE AND DRAMA

Paul Hyland and Neil Sammells (*editors*)
IRISH WRITING: Exile and Subversion

list continued on next page

continued from previous page

Maxim Jakubowski and Edward James (*editors*)
THE PROFESSION OF SCIENCE FICTION

Mark Lilly (*editor*)
LESBIAN AND GAY WRITING: An Anthology of Critical Essays

Christopher Mulvey and John Simons (*editors*)
NEW YORK: City as Text

Adrian Page (*editor*)
THE DEATH OF THE PLAYWRIGHT? Modern British Drama and Literary Theory

Frank Pearce and Michael Woodiwiss (*editors*)
GLOBAL CRIME CONNECTIONS: Dynamics and Control

John Simons (*editor*)
FROM MEDIEVAL TO MEDIEVALISM

Jeffrey Walsh and James Aulich (*editors*)
VIETNAM IMAGES: War and Representation

Gina Wisker (*editor*)
BLACK WOMEN'S WRITING

Series Standing Order

If you would like to receive future titles in this series as they are published, you can make use of our standing order facility. To place a standing order please contact your bookseller or, in case of difficulty, write to us at the address below with your name and address and the name of the series. Please state with which title you wish to begin your standing order. (If you live outside the United Kingdom we may not have the rights for your area, in which case we will forward your order to the publisher concerned.)

Customer Services Department, Macmillan Distribution Ltd
Houndmills, Basingstoke, Hampshire, RG21 2XS, England.

From Medieval to Medievalism

Edited by

JOHN SIMONS
Senior Lecturer in English
King Alfred's College, Winchester

M
MACMILLAN

© Editorial Board, Lumiere (Co-operative) Press Ltd 1992

All rights reserved. No reproduction, copy or transmission of this publication may be made without written permission.

No paragraph of this publication may be reproduced, copied or transmitted save with written permission or in accordance with the provisions of the Copyright, Designs and Patents Act 1988, or under the terms of any licence permitting limited copying issued by the Copyright Licensing Agency, 90 Tottenham Court Road, London W1P 9HE.

Any person who does any unauthorised act in relation to this publication may be liable to criminal prosecution and civil claims for damages.

First published 1992 by
THE MACMILLAN PRESS LTD
Houndmills, Basingstoke, Hampshire RG21 2XS
and London
Companies and representatives
throughout the world

ISBN 0–333–53273–2 (hc)
ISBN 0–333–53274–0 (pbk)

A catalogue record for this book is
available from the British Library.

Printed in Hong Kong

Contents

	Acknowledgements	vii
	Notes on the Contributors	viii
1	Introduction: From Medieval to Medievalism **John Simons**	1
2	Manuscript Studies: New Directions for Appreciating Middle English Romance **Murray J. Evans**	8
3	Medievalists and Deconstruction: *An Exemplum* **David Aers**	24
4	Traces of Romance Textual Poetics in the Non-Romance Works Ascribed to the 'Gawain'-Poet **Barbara Kowalik**	41
5	Structure and Meaning in *Guy of Warwick* **Maldwyn Mills**	54
6	Women and Chaucer's Providence: *The Clerk's Tale* and *The Knight's Tale* **Catherine La Farge**	69
7	Popular Reading Tastes in Middle English Religious and Didactic Literature **John J. Thompson**	82
8	*The Double-Armed Man*: Images of the Medieval in Early Modern Military Idealism **Simon Barker**	101
9	Romance in the Eighteenth-Century Chapbook **John Simons**	122

10	'The Paths of Virtue and Early English': F. J. Furnivall and Victorian Medievalism **Peter Faulkner**	144
	Index	159

Acknowledgements

Murray Evans gratefully acknowledges the generous financial assistance of the Social Sciences and Humanities Research Council of Canada in aid of his research. I would like to thank my colleagues Simon Barker, Howard Cooper, Martin Pumphrey and Carol Smith for their helpful comments on parts of the manuscript.

Notes on the Contributors

David Aers is Professor of English Literature at the University of East Anglia. He has published on English literature and culture from Langland and Chaucer to Blake and Wordsworth, and his most recent book is *Community, Gender and Individual Identity, 1360–1430*. He is currently writing a book on versions of the self and communities in the new Arnold series 'Literature in History'.

Simon Barker is a Senior Lecturer in English at King Alfred's College, Winchester. He was educated at Stirling University and University College, Cardiff. He has taught at the Welsh College of Drama. He has published on military theory in the early modern period and is currently editing *'Tis Pity She's a Whore* and an international collection of papers on Shakespeare.

Murray J. Evans is an Associate Professor at the University of Winnipeg, Canada, where he teaches medieval literature, children's literature, and rhetoric. He has published on Malory and the Malory MS, Chaucer and C. S. Lewis's Narnia books. He has recently completed a book-length study of Middle English verse romance in its manuscript contexts.

Peter Faulkner is Reader in Modern English at the University of Exeter. His interest in Furnivall arose from work on William Morris. His publications include *William Morris: The Critical Heritage*, *Humanism in the English Novel*, *Modernism*, *Robert Bage*, *Angus Wilson*, *Against the Age* and *Yeats*. He is currently working on literature of the British Empire.

Barbara Kowalik is a Lecturer in English Language and Literature at the Maria Curie-Skłodowska University in Lublin, Poland. She was awarded her doctoral degree – on *Man and the World in the Works of the 'Gawain'-Poet in Relation to his Concept of the Text* – by the University of Łódź. In 1985–6 she was a visiting scholar at St Hilda's College, Oxford. She has published a number of articles on medieval English literature and literary theory. Her interests include the Bible and literature.

Catherine La Farge studied at Harvard and Oxford; she has taught at Cork, Belfast and Oxford and is now a Lecturer in English at Birkbeck College, London. Her work on Malory includes 'The Hand of the Huntress' in *New Feminist Discourses*, ed. I. Armstrong (forthcoming).

Maldwyn Mills has a personal Chair in English at the University College of Wales, Aberystwyth. He was educated at University College, Cardiff, and Jesus College, Oxford. His research and teaching has been predominantly in the field of Middle English romances, also in Chaucer, eighteenth-century poetry, film studies and crime fiction. Major publications include editions of *Lybeaus Desconus*, *Six Middle English Romances*, *Fragments of an Early Fourteenth-Century 'Guy of Warwick'* (with Daniel Huws) and *Horn Childe and Maiden Rimenhild*.

John Simons is a Senior Lecturer in English and Co-ordinator of American Studies at King Alfred's College, Winchester. He was educated at the University College of Wales, Aberystwyth, and the University of Exeter where he was Tutor in English Medieval Studies. He has published numerous articles on English and American literature from the fourteenth century to the present day and also on popular culture. Major publications include editions of Henry Porter's *The Two Angry Women of Abington* (with Michael Jardine), *The Poems of Lawrence Minot* (with Thomas Beaumont James) and *New York: City as Text* (with Christopher Mulvey).

John J. Thompson is a Lecturer in English at the Queen's University of Belfast. He is the author of *Robert Thornton and the London Thornton Manuscript* and a contributor to the volume *Book Production and Publishing in Britain, 1375–1475*. He has published a number of articles on different aspects of the literary implications of manuscript study and has two books in progress, one on the Middle English *Cursor Mundi* (for the Medium Aevum Monographs Series) and the other a collaborative work on 'Late Medieval English Courtly Lyric Anthologies'.

1

Introduction: From Medieval to Medievalism

JOHN SIMONS

The purpose of this book is manifested in the range and scope of the contributions which are collected between its covers. It presents both examples of new directions in the literary criticism of the medieval text and surveys the ways in which the idea of the Middle Ages has been used as a cultural token or as a cultural heritage between the reign of Queen Elizabeth I and that of Queen Victoria. This latter project is also intended to serve as a guide to the ways in which medievalism – considered broadly as the study and use of medieval culture in the post-medieval period – can be seen as a key to understanding the culture of those periods in which it is pursued. The motivation behind the collection of the essays here presented is a desire to counteract the prevailing tendency by which the study of medieval literature, as part of the general discourse of 'Eng. Lit.', has been marginalised.[1]

As early as 1964, A. C. Spearing was exploring medieval literature's potential for canonisation according to the then dominant Leavisite techniques of close reading: 'One of the aims of the present book will be to see how far the technique of close reading can be of service in a critical approach to medieval literature.'[2] By 1977, however, N. F. Blake gave a strong, if occasionally splenetic, reminder of the linguistic specificity of the medieval text and called for a return to forms of study which were becoming increasingly uncommon:

> The new fashion of reading literature 'as literature' has had its impact on the medieval period so that many critical theories have been imported from later periods of English and applied indiscriminately to the medieval period. Few have bothered to consider how suitable such theories are in the early period, though this may have been for lack of time because critical fashions have come and gone so rapidly. The result is that many students read medieval literature without having any feel for or understanding

of the language in which the works were written. Teachers often deplore this lack of a language basis in modern teaching and scholarship, but as philology is considered so outmoded they have not known how to satisfy this felt need.[3]

The reason for rehearsing this old argument here is that it illustrates most effectively the dilemma which has faced medieval literature since the establishment of the modern English degree in higher education. Medievalists navigate between the Scylla of a philology which is seen (in England at least) as increasingly arcane and irrelevant and the Charybdis of a literary criticism which seems often capable of little more than the bombastic commonplace. The result of this difficult passage has been to leave medieval literary studies in an isolated position. They are perceived as a specialist activity hedged around by sub-disciplines such as phonology, palaeography and codicology which are seen as outside the normal range of literary critical skills or they are briefly tacked on to the course as a compulsory element done as a chore, an option which only a small number pursue, or as a curious ahistorical element which sets the scene for the Renaissance. The combined effects of these perceptions have been to put the medieval text almost outside the categories which are normally seen as literature: I frequently encounter students who tell me that they have done no poetry at 'A' level when they have, in fact, read one or two of the *Canterbury Tales*.

The Middle Ages also pose problems of periodisation which are more extensive than for other areas of literary studies: and it is surely periodisation above all else that facilitates the construction of courses. The specialist in, say, English Romanticism might reasonably be expected to be competent in the literature of a period covering 70 years, for example, 1780–1850, at most. When we speak of eighteenth-century specialists and nineteenth-century specialists the hundred years which the appellations imply often turn out to cover only a section of the century, for example, 1830–1890. It is not rare, on the other hand, to find medievalists covering periods of almost 1000 years from the earliest Old English texts to Malory. As a teaching profile this is by no means unknown but even more profound specialism in the Middle English period alone implies a familiarity with three centuries of literary production. This problem of periodisation has also contributed to the marginalisation of medieval studies. However, the problem has been made worse because of a tendency among medievalists and non-medievalists alike to homogenise the period. Attempts have been made to segment the Middle Ages in various ways, the most interesting and successful being found in *Ricardian Poetry* by J. A. Burrow.[4] This book, which is now 20 years old, made a laudable attempt to identify within the later fourteenth century a set of cultural concerns which were articulated commonly across a varied range of texts: whatever one may think about the exclusivity of Burrow's canon the fact remains that his attempt has not been widely repeated. All too often medieval texts are not debated within historical limitations and insufficient distinctions are drawn between texts which are years apart.

The contributions in the present collection constitute, in their entirety, an attempt to remedy the problems outlined above. The first essays show modern approaches to medieval texts at work. There can be little doubt that, over the past decade, the most exciting progress in the field has been made in the development of the significance of manuscript studies. This has had some important effects on literary critical work, not least in the growing recognition that it is useful to read texts in the contexts in which they were available to at least some of their medieval audience. One popular textbook which exemplifies this trend is S. A. J. Bradley's *Anglo-Saxon Poetry* which is an extensive anthology of translations.[5] In this book the groupings of well-known poems are determined not by subject matter or ethos (for example, religious/secular) but by codex. In spite of this manuscript studies still appear as part of the arcana of the medievalist. In his essay Murray J. Evans provides a valuable service with a survey of the field as it currently exists. In particular, he is concerned to point out the value of manuscript studies in literary criticism. Evans demonstrates that codicological research is not a dry relic from the days when philology was dominant but a vibrant scholarly activity which facilitates insight.

The next five essays show medieval studies in its engagement with a range of modern critical positions. David Aers's polemical and topical essay provides an entertaining and engaging correction to the blind adherence to critical dogma which he finds in a number of modern medievalists. In addition he exposes some of the grave epistemological problems which appear to be structural to much post-structuralist and New Historicist writing. What is important about this contribution is that it is based on the firm foundation of a knowledge of the tendencies against which it struggles. Over the past five or six years hostile reactions to contemporary literary theory have become not uncommon but it is important to separate bad-tempered conservatism from rigorous evaluation such as that produced by David Aers.

Barbara Kowalik and Maldwyn Mills both demonstrate different techniques of reading. Dr Kowalik refers us to fine linguistic detail and shows how the interpretation of medieval narrative can proceed through the integration of contemporary concerns with language and the categories of medieval philosophy without an extreme trial of both historical decorum and the reader's patience. She shows that the process of integration need not operate through the pulling together, by violence, of two heterogeneous theories without any regard for their historical determinations: the action can be achieved elegantly and fruitfully. In his approach to *Guy of Warwick* through narrative structure Maldwyn Mills takes the reader into the area which, so far, has provided the most productive union between medieval studies and modern literary criticism. Since the value of Vladimir Propp's work was perceived, narratological study has flourished especially perhaps in the field of the Middle English romances and has provided new and useful ways of classifying a notoriously protean mode of writing. In addition, narratological work has added fresh insights to our attempts to understand the complexities of the relationship which exists between the identification of a highly traditional set of narrative possibilities and the need to explain critically the differentiation, at a range of levels, between texts which share a common type. The medieval period is increasingly attracting research into the history of women and into feminist literary criticism. In her essay Catherine La Farge explores the treatment of women in two well-known Chaucerian texts. Here we again see how responsive the medieval text can be to detailed and sophisticated linguistic analysis where this is combined with a subtle grasp of the position of readers in history. A volume of essays on medieval literature without a contribution on Chaucer would be difficult to imagine and in Catherine La Farge's work – and, in particular, in her close attention to the encoding of power in the text – we find another example of the rich possibilities of the encounter between the medieval author and the modern critic.

One aspect of the problem of periodising the Middle Ages which I did not deal with above has to do with the difficulties of identifying the literary audience. This is a problem which plagues scholars working in all periods, but for medievalists it is particularly acute because of the relative paucity of good information. The problem is exacerbated by the peculiar structure of medieval literacy and the

Introduction 5

role that oral performance may have played in the dissemination of culture. My own view is that medieval culture as representative of a world view or, more accurately, a set of world views exists sporadically and discontinuously across social classes. Thus, for the majority of English people (again the specificity is deliberate) the Renaissance did not happen in the sixteenth century and while the Reformation brought about changes in mentality which were relatively broadly based, at least among urban communities, the transition from the medieval period to the early modern period appears to have taken place over perhaps two centuries. This is clear from studies of popular culture among early modern rural communities but it is also plain that during the early modern period and up to the Enlightenment there was a progressive dissemination of medieval court culture to social groups of lower status.[6] This means not only that the difficulties encountered in canon-formation are magnified in the early modern period as it becomes hard to exclude the popular and the medieval without significantly distorting the literary–historical model but also that medievalists themselves have tended to ignore the rich layers of medieval texts which are to be found from the sixteenth century onwards not as survivals but as living and meaningful cultural artifacts. John J. Thompson shows something of what can be done towards establishing the parameters of popular taste from the slight evidence which is generally available and also underlines Murray Evans's point that manuscript studies are an invaluable aid when making judgements about the social composition and cultural preferences of the medieval audience.

The volume then turns its attention to the question of medievalism. I referred above to the Middle English romances as protean: cultural history, on the other hand, is procrustean and the Middle Ages have been stretched in many directions in order to provide a ideological space in which a society can explore and articulate concerns which are otherwise repressed. The *locus classicus* for this is, of course, the Gothic literature of the eighteenth and nineteenth centuries – study of this has been deliberately excluded from the present volume because of its relative familiarity as, for the same reason has work on the Pre-Raphaelites. Similarly, ideals of chivalry have been periodically revived to validate activities as diverse as imperial conquest and fair cricket.[7] The current vogue for 'sword and sorcery' novels and role-playing fantasy games such as 'Dungeons and Dragons' which derives from the great Tolkien enthusiasm of the 1960s and 1970s and, to a lesser extent, from the novels of another eminent medievalist C. S. Lewis, is another example of the way in which the medieval is used to provide a play space. Why else did subject matter as unpromising as that in Umberto Eco's *The Name of the Rose* achieve international best-seller status and spawn a host of imitators?

Simon Barker shows how, in the field of early modern military discourse, the Middle Ages were constructed as a period to which commentators could look in order to castigate present abuses and to find practices from which the present could learn. It must be said that this construction of the Middle Ages as a form of Golden Age is one of the most common uses to which the period is put. By the nineteenth century the Middle Ages had become a Gothic dystopia (at least in part) which provided a measure of the March of Intellect and industrial progress. In the early modern period this perception was often, though by no means always, reversed and the medieval facilitated the operation of a range of cultural interests. These ranged from the adaptation of narrative structures drawn from the medieval romances in order to articulate the achievements of the citizen heroes of prose fiction aimed at non-courtly urban audiences, to the nostalgic residues manifested in the Accession Day tilts or the neo-chivalric shows which were used to promote the cult of Prince Henry at the beginning of the seventeenth century.[8]

In the eighteenth century attitudes to the medieval were more complex and my own contribution, on chapbooks, attempts to survey these attitudes as they manifested themselves in different social groups. The last essay, which takes us up to the turn of the twentieth century, is Peter Faulkner's study of the extraordinary F. J. Furnivall. Furnivall's work shows how self-conscious some scholars can be in their own construction of the Middle Ages as a usable discourse. Furnivall made huge contributions to scholarship but in his radical politics and in the explicit connections he made between them and his academic activities he appears strikingly modern. His work may, in this sense, be seen as to some extent analogous to the contribution made by J. P. Collier to the development of modern approaches to Elizabethan drama.[9]

It is appropriate to end the collection with an account of Furnivall because his attitudes do pre-empt many of the concerns which connect the diverse topics which are considered here. The state of medieval studies which I surveyed at the beginning of this brief introduction will not be changed overnight. Nevertheless, the relegation of medieval texts to special options or, worse, the 'compulsory medieval course' which undergraduates follow pragmatically while they pine to get back to 'real literature' is a situation which must be remedied. These essays show that that the study of medieval texts is viable as an integral part of the modern English course especially when we move from medieval to medievalism and begin to open up large sections of cultural history to inspection from otherwise unavailable perspectives.

NOTES

1. The best commentator on this process of marginalisation is probably Lee Patterson. See his *Negotiating the Past* (Madison: University of Wisconsin Press, 1987).
2. A. C. Spearing, *Criticism and Medieval Poetry*, 2nd edn (London: Edward Arnold, 1972) pp. 5–6.
3. N. F. Blake, *The English Language in Medieval Literature* (London: Dent, 1977) p. 8.
4. J. A. Burrow, *Ricardian Poetry* (London: Routledge & Kegan Paul, 1971).
5. S. A. J. Bradley, *Anglo-Saxon Poetry* (London: Dent, 1982).
6. See, for example, P. Burke, *Popular Culture in Early Modern Europe* (London: Temple Smith, 1978) and B. Reay (ed.), *Popular Culture in Seventeenth-Century England* (London: Routledge, 1988).
7. On this see M. Girouard, *The Return to Camelot* (New Haven, Conn.: Yale University Press, 1981).
8. See, for example, F. Yates, *Astraea* (London: Routledge & Kegan Paul, 1975), especially 'Elizabethan Chivalry: the Romance of the Accession Day Tilts', on pp. 88–111.
9. On Collier see D. Ganzel, *Fortune and Men's Eyes* (London: Oxford University Press, 1982).

2

Manuscript Studies: New Directions for Appreciating Middle English Romance

MURRAY J. EVANS

Recent years have seen a marked increase in scholarly attention to Middle English (ME) romance manuscripts and their relevance to our literary-critical and historical-critical appreciation of the romances which they contain. The effect of much of this attention has been codicological, that is, concerned with the study of manuscripts as wholes, rather than merely with particular items in their contents or some one aspect of their make-up, such as script or watermarks. Thus the sometimes disparate approaches of textual scholarship and literary criticism concerning ME romance have had more exchange, and there now exists a considerable body of scholarly literature which combines the two approaches, or closely bears on their combination. Surprisingly, there is no analytical survey of these studies yet in print. As a result, those interested in investigating the subject need themselves to expend some effort in assembling a working bibliography. My essay is meant to facilitate this process by providing an overview of recent work on the subject. I shall deal first with conceptual background for the field and some other foundational material, then with three influential scholars for the combination of romance manuscript studies with literary criticism, and finally with examples of the two predominant directions of recent studies to date.

A key aspect of the conceptual backdrop for discussions of the productions of ME romance manuscripts appears in Malcolm Parkes's article 'The Influence of the Concepts of *Ordinatio* and *Compilatio* on the Development of the Book'.[1] In his article, Parkes describes the development of *compilatio* in the thirteenth century 'both as a form of writing and as a means of making material easily accessible' for the reader; the compiler 'was free to rearrange', to impose 'a new *ordinatio* on the materials he extracted from others' by 'disposing the material into clearly defined books and chapters, or other recognizable divisions based on the nature of the subject-matter'.[2] Readers and librarians by the fourteenth century would insert the by then popular features of *compilatio* into manuscripts, if they were not already there. A case in point is Troyes MS 718 of Ockham's commentary on the second book of Peter Lombard's *Sentences* where subsequent readers have added paragraph marks, marginal headings, running titles, and the underlining of citations.[3] Notions of *compilatio* also influenced vernacular literature, such as Gower's *Confessio Amantis* and Chaucer's *Canterbury Tales*.[4] Parkes identifies the Ellesmere MS of the *Canterbury Tales* as a 'spectacular example' of *compilatio*, having 'almost all the trappings' of the new *ordinatio*:

> sources and topics are indicated in the margins, and the word *'auctor'* is placed alongside a sententious statement. The text is well disposed in its sections, and each section is carefully labelled by means of full rubrics. There are running-titles, and the final touch is the introduction of pictures of each of the pilgrims (the basis of the division of the work) in order to assist the reader to identify them with the General Prologue. Last but not least is the way in which *Sir Thopas* has been laid out: the bracketing serves to emphasize the 'drasty' rhymes and the stanza division is carefully followed.[5]

Parkes identifies 'divide and subordinate' as the central principle of *compilatio*:[6] what new readers found unmanageable in existing manuscripts was divided into and subordinated as more intelligible parts. Inasmuch as this approach of rearranging existing books also became 'a form of writing'[7] for the making of new books from exemplars, *compilatio* was also a constitutive procedure for these new books such as the Ellesmere MS, as well as a method of rearrangement of already existing books such as Troyes MS 718. Presumably, then, *compilatio* and its attendant devices can be as much a matter of making a whole book from individual parts (multiple exemplars, for example), as 'dividing and subordinating' the parts of existing books. It is this former, constitutive sense of *compilatio* which appears in many recent studies of ME romance MSS.[8]

The first category of studies which invites our attention is useful foundational works for further textual and literary-critical studies of ME romance. Chief amongst these are the Scolar Press facsimiles of many important romance manuscript collections, notably the Lincoln Cathedral 'Thornton' MS 91, the Auchinleck MS, and Cambridge University Library MS Ff.2.38.[9] These facsimiles allow for the portable study of many features of the MS collections without the inconvenience of microform or of travel to the holding institutions, unless examination of the originals is necessary for attention to quiring, coloured decoration, watermarks and, in some cases, script. These facsimiles also include valuable introductions on the literary-historical context and physical description of the MSS. For example, Derek Pearsall underlines in his introduction to the Auchinleck MS that it is a very early miscellany (1330–40) which includes, as three-quarters of the surviving volume, eighteen romances (if we count *The Seven Sages of Rome* and the sections of *Guy of Warwick* as three items): eight of these are in unique copies, and all the rest (except *Floris and Blauncheflur*) are in their earliest copies.[10] His introduction goes on to describe the collaborative compiling activity of the six Auchinleck scribes, particularly regarding the MS's romances. Then follows Ian Cunningham's able discussion of physical description (on material, page layout, item numbering and so on), collation (disposition of folios in gatherings), script, ornament and binding. A bibliography and catalogue of contents completes the introduction.

Frances McSparran's section of the introduction to the facsimile of the Cambridge University Library MS Ff.2.38, a late fifteenth- or early sixteenth-century manuscript,[11] is also noteworthy for two reasons. First, her piece usefully discusses not only the manuscript's eight romances gathered at the end of the MS – 'pious, lively and full of incidents and marvels'.[12] She also attends to the collections's different kinds of religious items, fairly consistently grouped in distinct earlier sections of the MS: penitential/meditative items (for example, William Lichfield's *Complaint of God*), pieces of basic doctrinal instruction (on the ten commandments, the seven deadly sins and so on), 'edifying narratives' (including saints' lives), and noticeably more secular exemplary narratives, such as *How the Goode Man Taght hys Sone*.[13] Her categorisation and discussion of such religious items provides a useful reference point for those interested in whole ME romance collections, who attempt to take into account the numerous non-romance items which often accompany romances there. Secondly, McSparran's speculative inferences from Ff.2.38's contents about its original audience are also noteworthy:

The result is a one-volume library varied in contents but strikingly homogeneous in tone and quality; it seems ideally suited to the instruction, edification and entertainment of well-doing, devout readers of modest intellectual accomplishment. One can easily imagine it serving for family reading in a pious middle-class household, some items serving for 'edification and profit', others 'for edification and delight'.[14]

While admittedly somewhat circular in argument[15], these comments taken in their detailed context are an example of necessary kinds of speculation on audience when we know, as in this case, nothing about the early history of the MS.[16]

The introductions to these two facsimiles thus orient readers to pertinent historical-critical and textual information and issues; the latter are often so debatable (as in McSparran's reflections on audience) or controversial (as in Pearsall's view of Auchinleck's compiling)[17] as to be invitations to further research and scholarly exchange.[18]

Also valuable as foundational works are volumes published in the Manuscript Studies series by Boydell & Brewer, which provide the benefit of more amplified analysis of particular MSS, sometimes with a generous number of photographic plates of important MS contexts. The first of this series, Julia Boffey's *Manuscripts of English Courtly Love Lyrics in the Later Middle Ages*,[19] while not about romance MSS, is an excellent introduction to manuscript studies and its application to another genre of ME literature. Her book includes a survey of pertinent MSS and their presentation of courtly love lyrics, as well as chapters on authorship and composition, currency and transmission, and readers and owners of the MSS. Her first chapter on the MSS is particularly valuable as a fund of information on manuscript compilation: on the place of lyrics amongst other kinds of items in collections, for example as fillers between longer items or on flyleafs; the influence of fifteenth-century scribe and bookseller John Shirley on manuscript compiling particularly in the London area;[20] and distinctions among various kinds of MSS – the planned anthology, the household miscellany, manuscript as small library, the compendium or 'hold-all' and so on. Appendices list individual lyrics according to their MSS, and summarise the contents of each of the pertinent MSS. Much of the material and methodology of Boffey's book can serve as a model for similar discussions of other medieval works in manuscript. Happily Boydell & Brewer are continuing their series by publishing commentary-discussions of significant MS collections, which are also in effect partial facsimiles with selected but numerous plates of their key folios. John Thompson's book on the London Thornton MS (Brit. Lib. Additional 31042) is a recent example.[21]

Finally, in this category of foundational studies are recent scholarly articles which describe individual MSS. One excellent article is Timothy Shonk's on the Auchinleck MS.[22] Shonk's detailed and persuasive view of the process of compilation of the MS parts company with previous scholars on the topic. He recalls that Laura Hibbard Loomis's London bookshop theory of the MS[23] is based on the 'close parallels among the major romances of the codex', resulting from the collaboration of several authors and scribes in one location. While accepting Loomis's theory, Pamela Robinson argues that the MS results from a 'booklet' or fascicular production, the later binding together for a customer of its twelve previously independent booklets earlier produced on speculation; Pearsall in his introduction to the Auchinleck facsimile concurs with Robinson's view.[24] Shonk instead adapts Doyle and Parkes's theory that by the early fifteenth century there is no convincing evidence for the existence of London bookshops such as Loomis envisages; instead, patrons ordered books from a bookdealer 'who then farmed out the parts of the examplar to independent scribes for simultaneous copying'. Unlike Doyle and Parkes's scribes who were merely copyists, Shonk asserts that Auchinleck's Scribe 1 directed the organisation of the MS.[25] Shonk thus argues that the Auchinleck is neither produced in an organised bookshop of collaborative scribes, nor is the MS piecemeal or fascicular in production and structure. Rather, a buyer commissioned a dealer, perhaps Scribe 1 who copied out most of the items, farmed out some gatherings to other scribes elsewhere with instructions about format, compiled the gatherings into a codex, sent the completed MS to a decorator, then finally inserted titles and item numbers. The whole procedure, Shonk argues, proceeded according to Scribe 1's plan and instructions for the production of the MS as a preconceived whole.[26] Shonk's article not only offers valuable description of physical features of the MS, then, but also contributes to the ongoing debate concerning the conditions under which such MSS were produced.[27]

The path from manuscript studies to literary criticism of ME romance had its recent significant beginnings in the work of Dieter

Mehl, Pamela Robinson, and Derek Pearsall. I should like to discuss the importance of each in turn.

First, Dieter Mehl's *Middle English Romances of the Thirteenth and Fourteenth Centuries*,[28] in the course of classifying romances by length and proposing many excellent close readings of individual romances, comments on the relevance of whole manuscript context to his concerns. Mehl writes thus of the London Thornton MS, for example, which includes together with several romances excerpts from the *Cursor Mundi* (a versified sacred history of humankind), verse by John Lydgate, the debate poem *Winner and Waster*, and other religious/moral works:

> The few romances it includes are chiefly works of a decidedly militant Christian character, above all *The Sege off Melayne*, *Rowlande and Ottuell*, and *Richard Coeur de Lion*, as well as the poem *The Siege of Jerusalem* which can hardly be called a romance at all. It is clear that the romances in this collection were chosen mainly for their homiletic and religious qualities and do not stand in any contrast to the purely religious poems. The order of the items seems rather casual and does not reveal any significant design. . . . This is an anthology of a clearly religious and devotional character.[29]

Here and elsewhere in his book, Mehl attends to possible groupings of different kinds of romances (homiletic, courtly, and so on) with other kinds of items (religious, moral-didactic, chronicle). He considers such groupings or their absence as evidence of the shaping, or lack of shaping, of larger MS collections. While Mehl's comments on MS collections in relation to individual romances thus remain general, his book significantly combines literary criticism of individual romances, generic discussion of ME romance, and attention to whole MS collections.

This kind of approach to romance manuscripts continues more extensively and systematically in the work of one of Mehl's former students, Gisela Guddat-Figge's *Catalogue of Manuscripts Containing Middle English Romances*.[30] The larger part of her book is invaluable descriptions of most ME romance MSS (Chaucer, Lane, Lydgate and Malory are excluded)[31]. In entries for each of the 99 MSS (including fragments) dealt with, there are sections according to the following headings: date, material and size; number of folios and collation if discernible; manuscript condition, decoration, scribe(s), script, and page layout; origin, type, and contents of the MS; and finally, synthetic interpretation of previous information, history of the MS (if known), and a short bibliography.[32] Besides gathering this information on specific MSS, the catalogue is also 'an attempt to establish certain types of romance manuscripts, and a discussion of the relevance of the manuscripts for the romances as a literary genre, for their audience, and for the regional distribution of the romances'. For example, Guddat-Figge classifies her manuscripts according to 'the professional or amateur status of their scribes'; and according to their contents – mixed miscellanies, religious miscellanies, secular miscellanies (including commonplace books), and romance manuscripts proper. She is particularly interested in the extent to which different romance MSS have concentrations of romances in sections of the MS or exhibit groupings of romance with religious/didactic, historical or other kinds of items.[33] Like Mehl's, these comments often remain general, as one might expect in an introduction to a detailed catalogue. Nevertheless, the scope of their context, detailed attention to so many MSS, is a valuable advance on Mehl's concentration on the major romance MS collections.[34] Most importantly, Guddat-Figge's catalogue proper of ME romance MSS is itself a crucial foundational work for both examining original manuscripts and also writing about them.

The second important influence for relating romance MSS to literary criticism of ME romance is Pamela Robinson, a former student of Malcolm Parkes. Her B. Litt. thesis is both an exploration of how the compiling of selected ME romance MSS might influence our reading of their contents, and also a catalogue of descriptions of many romance MSS.[35] Here Robinson first discusses her notion of 'booklet', a definition probably better known in a subsequent published article. A 'booklet' is a gathering or collection of gatherings self-sufficient in terms of content: it contains a complete text or group of texts (except in the case of loss or damage). A booklet has also often existed separately before being bound with other booklets into a composite manuscript book.[36] Robinson's notion of the booklet as composite literary unit has certainly had its detractors, notably Ralph Hanna who argues that the booklet is primarily a production unit reflecting the exigencies of a compiler's stages of physically assembling a manuscript book piecemeal: booklets so defined allow the compiler to delay 'any step which would absolutely determine the shape of the resulting codex'.[37] None the less, 'booklet', even if in looser and other senses than Robinson's, has become a significant part of the vocabulary for discussing the compiling of ME romance and other MSS. Her thesis is also noteworthy for its discussion of groups of romances which, reflecting the growing role of the compiler in manuscript preparation, recur wholly or in part in a large number of romance MSS. One such recurring group is comprised of *Octavian*, *Sir Isumbras*, *Sir Eglamour*, *The Earl of Tolous* and *Libeaus Desconus*, romances which she argues all exemplify the virtue of (often Christian) patience rewarded, often in the context of the separation and reunion of families.[38]

A third and, I think, the most important influential figure in the relation of manuscript studies and literary criticism of ME romance is Derek Pearsall. One of his early essays outlines the development of non-alliterative ME romance from 1240 to 1400; a second essay continues the outline for ME romance through the fifteenth century and beyond, predominantly for prose romance so much in vogue in the later period.[39] Besides situating romance chronologically and generically in the two essays, Pearsall describes individual romances, or versions of romances, and places them in their particular MS collections, sometimes with brief characterisations of the individual MSS. The following comment on *King Horn* in the first essay is a case in point:

> *Horn* seems to us of crucial importance, for it embodies, partly by derivation from Layamon, a conventional technique and conventional phraseology in unalloyed form, like crude ore, from which later romances such as *Guy* or *Richard* drew extensively. Where they modify the metre of the oldest text, the two later manuscripts of *Horn* (Laud 108 and Harley 2253) always move towards four-stress regularity but the clipped, short-breathed lines of the Cambridge *Horn*, with their sparse, abrupt syntax and lack of articulation, are the perfect complement of the narrative's lyric quality and may be considered a deliberate choice.[40]

Pearsall continues this attention to MS collections in his *Old and Middle English Poetry*, notably in a chapter entitled 'Some Fourteenth-Century Books and Writers' in which he discusses ME romances with special reference to the Auchinleck MS.[41] These essays not only illuminate the historical development of ME romance with helpful generic considerations, but are also significantly responsible for establishing manuscript collections, not merely modern editions of often individual romances, as a necessary locus for discussing romance. This, Pearsall's bias for studying romances in their original MS contexts, has had a marked influence, not only through his own publications, but also through those of his former students, and through the biannual York Manuscripts Conferences first organised by him in 1981 and succeeded by published proceedings. The first of these volumes, *Manuscripts and Readers in Fifteenth-Century England: The Literary Implications of Manuscript Study*,[42] includes a number of essays bearing on ME romance. Carol Meale's 'The Compiler at Work: John Colyns and BL MS Harley 2252' is an examination of 'the literary, social and historical conditions'[43] underlying the compilation of this early sixteenth-century MS which contains the *Ipomydon* (B version) and the stanzaic *Morte Arthur*, as well as works by John Skelton, and other assorted items. George Keiser in a review of the whole Pearsall collection recommends Meale's essay as 'an exceptional example' of the codicological approach.[44] In the same collection, Thorlac Turville-Petre's article, 'Some Medieval English Manuscripts in the North-East Midlands',[45] proposes a north-east Midland provenance for National Library of Scotland Advocates' MS 19.3.1, a miscellany including three romances – *Sir Gowther*, *Sir Isumbras* and *Sir Amadace*; courtesy items such as *Stans Puer ad Mensam* on children's table etiquette, major religious items such as *The Vision of Tundale* (of heaven and hell), and numerous shorter pieces of nonsense, piety and practical wisdom. Turville-Petre discusses: evidence for the manuscript's ownership by a local family, the Sherbrookes; the probable derivation from a local village of the name of the main scribe Richard Heege, possibly also a local household scribe; and the inclusion of a number of local place-names in a burlesque poem in the manuscript's first booklet. This evidence and the miscellaneous nature of the manuscript's contents suggest, Turville-Petre argues, that the MS was a library for a small provincial household, even the Sherbrookes'.

One other essay in Pearsall's collection, John Thompson's 'The Compiler in Action: Robert Thornton and the "Thornton Romances" in Lincoln Cathedral MS 91',[46] is also noteworthy for its emphasis on Thornton's problems in constructing his romance book, and scepticism of his literary shaping of it. Thompson highlights the *ad hoc*, progressive nature of Thornton's compiling of the romance section of his MS: Thornton did not have a grand plan from the outset, but copied items in separate gatherings, belatedly cobbling them together. Thompson finds it puzzling that Thornton's romance section, including items such as the alliterative *Morte Arthure*, *Sir Isumbras* and *Sir Degrevant*, also includes a number of what he sees as generically intrusive items: 'a text telling of a miracle of the Virgin, a[n antimendicant] satirical text ostensibly about an old grey horse, and a text containing a series of political prophecies'.[47] Thompson finds the explanation for this apparent anomaly in two pieces of physical MS evidence in the pertinent gathering or quire. First, there are two soiled leaves now at the middle of the quire, rather than as its outer leaves where one would expect grime to accumulate on a gathering lying around unbound. Secondly, the gathering's folios have disintegrated into singletons, apparently from excessive folding. These conditions, Thompson argues, result from Thornton's originally taking a partially used quire whose opening folios were already filled with *The Awentyrs of Arthure*, and folding the quire outside inwards. Thus the filled folios now began at the middle of the gathering, and the previously final folios of the gathering were now opening and closing blank folios in the refolded quire. On these now opening blank folios, Thompson argues, Thornton completed copying an unfinished item, *Sir Eglamour*, from a preceding gathering. This still left blank inner folios before *The Awentyrs* on which the apparently generically dissonant items in the romance section were copied as fillers. Thornton also began copying *Sir Perceval* on final blank leaves of the gathering.[48] While Thompson's reading has been contested as being too 'ingenious' and dismissive of generic similarities between the 'intrusive' and romance items,[49] his argument represents one broad approach to MS studies which is sceptical, often with good reason, about arguments for the literary shaping of MS books. (The echo of Robinson vs. Hanna on 'booklets' is noticeable here in this instance of that larger question.) Thompson's approach is similar in his subsequent book, already mentioned above, on Thornton's other miscellany, Brit. Lib. Add. MS 31042.[50] Here he succeeds the late Sally Horall and Ralph Hanna[51] in drawing particularly on a close examination of watermarks in the MS, as part of his comprehensive discussion of its physical makeup, compiling procedures, and decorative features. Thompson's careful, and often carefully speculative, examination of the London MS means 'to characterise the final results of Robert Thornton's book-compiling activities as an intriguing mixture of obvious and sometimes happy accident, and occasional careful design'.[52]

While the pull in Thompson's work is thus clearly away from the search for much intentional literary-critical shaping in Thornton's MS books in favour of a focus on the exigencies of book production, other recent studies find warrant in manuscript studies, or at least the study of particular MSS, to make more confident literary-critical extrapolations from the manuscript evidence. Regarding the Malory MS, for example, my examination of layout, decoration and the wording of the *explicits* ('Here endyth the tale of . . . ') has led me to disagree with Malory editor Eugène Vinaver's view of *Le Morte Darthur* as eight separate tales. MS evidence rather suggests five linked blocks of narrative in Malory: the initial tales of King Arthur; tales of Arthur and Lucius, Lancelot, and Gareth; the Tristram section; the Grail quest; and final tales of Lancelot and the Morte Arthur.[53] Thus, we can establish, in my opinion more accurately, the actual tales, that is, the 'what' of Malory, and then go on to examine how Malory deliberately uses narrative linkage of these tales so as to create the impact of his 'hoole book' on readers.[54]

Another essay of this sort, this time not on a MS by one author, but on one with works by many different authors, is Phillipa Hardman's article on Natl. Lib. of Scotland Advocates' MS 19.3.1.[55] Hardman argues persuasively from the booklet structure of the MS that it contains nine booklets according to three kinds: the romance-followed-by-courtesy-item(s) booklet, the thematic anthology, and the volume of 'favourite religious narratives'[56] – in all, a miniature medieval library. She sees, moreover, the three tail-rhyme romances of the MS – *Sir Isumbras*, *Sir Gowther* and *Sir Amadace* – as having similar plots, a similarity heightened by the compiler Richard Heege's changing of details in his versions of the three romances so as to heighten their similar preoccupation with 'simple values: perseverance and physical strength; . . . despite a conventionally pious ending, [the three romances] reveal a deeper interest in the rewards of this world than in those of the next'.[57] In this way, Heege renders more similar not only the three romances, but also the three romance-cum-courtesy-piece booklets themselves. In all, Hardman thus uses the physical evidence of MS booklets to argue, in effect, that Heege exhibits a noticeably high degree of literary-critical sensibility: he produces different genres of MS booklets themselves in the MS as a whole.[58]

My own preference, worked out in a completed booklength discussion of 25 MS collections, is for this latter kind of study which explores the significance of romance MSS for our appreciation of both individual romances and also ME romance as an admittedly problematic genre. The future path of whatever sort of studies using textual and literary-critical approaches, however, must combine the careful, factual attention of the textual scholar with the generic and literary sensibilities of the critic, whether or not both impulses are coincident in the same persons. There are two broad dangers in this cross-disciplinary field: either that some observations remain inappropriately merely textual, sceptical of literary-critical significance where the evidence might warrant it; or else that literary critics make facile observations on the literary shaping of manuscripts, which ignore the compiling processess that enrich, or perhaps undercut, the patterns they propose. Certainty comes with very great difficulty in the field; there is lots of work yet to be done, and it will need a combination of all kinds of intelligent scholarly and literary-critical approaches. In the words of manuscripts scholar Ian Doyle, 'the jigsaw puzzle we are all working on is so big that it may need the help of every eye to try to fit a piece in it'.[59]

NOTES

1. M. B. Parkes, in J. J. G. Alexander and M. T. Gibson (eds), *Medieval Learning and Literature: Essays Presented to R. W. Hunt* (Oxford: Clarendon Press, 1976) pp. 115–41. On this and related material, see also A. I. Doyle and M. B. Parkes, 'The Production of Copies of the *Canterbury Tales* and the *Confessio Amantis* in the Early Fifteenth Century', in M. B. Parkes and Andrew G. Watson (eds), *Medieval Scribes, Manuscripts and Libraries: Essays Presented to N. R. Ker* (London: Scolar Press, 1978) pp. 163–210; A. J. Minnis, *Medieval Theory of Authorship: Scholastic Literary Attitudes in the Later Middle Ages* (London: Scolar Press, 1984); and Judson Boyce Allen, *The Ethical Poetic of the Later Middle Ages: A Decorum of Convenient Distinction* (Toronto: University of Toronto Press, 1982). One useful introduction to paleographical terminology and kinds of medieval script is in Anthony G. Petti, *English Literary Hands from Chaucer to Dryden* (Cambridge, Mass.: Harvard University Press, 1977) pp. 1–41.
2. Parkes, in Alexander and Gibson (eds), *Medieval Learning and Literature*, pp. 127, 128 and 130.
3. Ibid., pp. 135–6.
4. Ibid., p. 130.
5. Ibid., p. 134.
6. Ibid., p. 129.
7. Ibid., p. 127.

8. See, for example, John J. Thompson, 'The Compiler in Action: Robert Thorton and the "Thornton Romances" in Lincoln Cathedral MS 91', in Derek Pearsall (ed.), *Manuscripts and Readers in Fifteenth-Century England: The Literary Implications of Manuscript Study* (Cambridge: D. S. Brewer, Biblio, 1983) pp. 113–24, where he infers the processes by which Thornton as 'compiler' brought about the final form of his 'romance *unit*' (p. 114, emphasis added) which includes nine romances and additional items. Carol M. Meale, 'The Compiler at Work: John Colyns and BL MS Harley 2252', in Pearsall (ed.), *Manuscripts and Readers*, pp. 82–103, also argues that, while the contents of Brit. Lib. MS Harley 2252 are varied, nevertheless its compiler Colyns 'did, however, visualise the book *as a single entity*' (p. 93; emphasis added). On Meale's and Thompson's articles, see also below, pp. 16–17.

9. *The Thornton Manuscript (Lincoln Cathedral MS 91)*, intro. D. S. Brewer and A. E. B. Owen (1975; rpt. with revised intro., London: Scolar Press, 1977); *The Auchinleck Manuscript: National Library of Scotland Advocates' MS 19.2.1*, intro. Derek Pearsall and I. C. Cunningham (London: Scolar Press in assoc. with the National Library of Scotland, 1977); *Cambridge University Library MS Ff.2.38*, intro. Frances McSparran and P. R. Robinson (London: Scolar Press, 1979).

10. Pearsall, *Auchinleck Manuscript*, pp. vii–viii. Pearsall's figures on the Auchinleck romances relate to that larger caveat concerning romance manuscript survival raised, among numerous other noteworthy caveats, by A. S. G. Edwards in 'Middle English Romance: the Limits of Editing, the Limits of Criticism', in T. W. Machan (ed.), *Medieval Literature: Text and Interpretation* (State University of New York, Binghamton: Medieval and Renaissance Texts and Studies, 1991) note 1: 'Of the ninety-four separate verse romances recorded in the revised *Manual of the Writings in Middle English*, ed. J. B. Severs, vol. 1 (New Haven, CT: Connecticut Academy of Arts and Sciences, 1967), nearly fifty survive in only a single manuscript'. Pearsall adds in his essay on fifteenth-century romance (see note 39 below) that on his own count of 95 ME verse romances, 'only 30 occur in copies that pre-date the Thornton manuscripts (c. 1440), even though 61 at least would be regarded as of fourteenth-century provenance' (p. 58).

11. Robinson, in McSparran and Robinson, *Cambridge University Library MS Ff.2.38*, p. xii.

12. McSparren, in ibid., pp. x and vii. McSparran does not include *The Seven Sages* and *Robert of Sicily*, two other final items, in her count of romances (p. x).

13. Ibid., pp. vii–x.

14. Ibid., p. vii.

15. See also Manfred Görlach, 'Recent Facsimile Editions of Middle English Literary Manuscripts', *Anglia*, vol. 105 (1987) p. 126.

16. Robinson, in McSparran and Robinson, *Cambridge University Library MS Ff.2.38*, p. xvi. See also Derek Pearsall, 'Middle English Romance and its Audiences', in Mary-Jo Arn and Hanneke Wirtjes, with Hans Jansen (eds), *Historical and Editorial Studies in Medieval and Early Modern English for Johan Gerritsen* (Groningen: Wolters-Noordhoff, 1985)

pp. 37–47. Happily we occasionally have information about manuscripts' scribes, which can help investigations about original audience. Regarding Robert Thornton, for example, scribe of Brit. Lib. Additional MS 31042 and Lincoln Cathedral Lib. MS 91, see George R. Keiser's articles: 'Lincoln Cathedral Library MS 91: Life and Milieu of the Scribe', *Studies in Bibliography*, vol. 32 (1979) pp. 158–79; 'More Light on the Life and Milieu of Robert Thornton', *Studies in Bibliography*, vol. 36 (1983) pp. 111–19; 'The Nineteenth-Century Discovery of the Thornton Manuscript (Lincoln Cathedral Library MS 91', *Papers of the Bibliographical Society of America*, vol. 77 (1983) pp. 167–90.

17. A critique of Pearsall's view may be found in Timothy Shonk, 'A Study of the Auchinlek Manuscript: Bookmen and Bookmaking in the Early Fourteenth Century', *Speculum*, vol. 60, no. 1 (1985) pp. 71–91.

18. For useful reviews of these and other recent MS facsimiles, see A. S. G. Edwards, '"The Whole Book': Medieval Manuscripts in Facsimile', *Review*, vol. 2 (1980) pp. 19–29; and Görlach, 'Recent Facsimile Editions', pp. 121–51.

19. Julia Boffey, *Manuscripts of English Courtly Love Lyrics in the Later Middle Ages* (Woodbridge, Suffolk: D. S. Brewer, 1985).

20. For her more recent overview of Shirley, see Julia Boffey and John J. Thompson, '12. Anthologies and Miscellanies: Production and Choice of Texts', in Jeremy Griffiths and Derek Pearsall (eds), *Book Production and Publishing in Britian, 1375–1475* (Cambridge: Cambridge University Press, 1989) pp. 284–7. This whole collection is invaluable in its programme to 'make clear what has been done in particular areas, identify the questions that need further to be asked, and thus point the way for future research' (Pearsall, 'Introduction', p. 1). Particular areas covered include materials, manuscript decoration and illustration, different aspects of book production (e.g., London, Lollard); patrons, buyers and owners; the contents of books (e.g., major poets, scientific and medical books), and 'manuscript to print'.

21. John J. Thompson, *Robert Thornton and the London Thornton Manuscript: British Library MS Additional 31042* (Cambridge: D. S. Brewer, 1987).

22. Shonk, 'A Study of the Auchinleck Manuscript'. For other examples, see also Karen Stern, 'The London "Thornton" Miscellany: A New Description of British Museum Additional Manuscript 31042', *Scriptorium*, vol. 30 (1976) pp. 26–37, 201–18; and Philippa Hardman's description of Natl. Lib. of Scotland MS Adv. 19.3.1, which is discussed later in the chapter.

23. Laura Hibbard Loomis, 'The Auchinleck Manuscript and a Possible London Bookshop of 1330–40', *PMLA*, vol. 57 (1942) pp. 595–627.

24. Shonk, 'A Study of the Auchinleck Manuscript', pp. 72–3, is citing P. R. Robinson, 'A Study of Some Aspects of the Transmission of English Verse Texts in Late Mediaeval Manuscripts', unpub. B. Litt. thesis, University of Oxford (1972). See also my comments on Robinson later in the chapter; and Pearsall's qualification of his view in *The Auchinleck Manuscript*, in A. S. G. Edwards and Derek Pearsall, '11. The Manuscripts of the Major English Poetic Texts', in Griffiths and Pearsall (eds), *Book Production*, particularly pp. 257–8 and 260–3.

25. Shonk, 'A Study of the Auchinleck Manuscript', p. 73. Shonk is referring to Doyle and Parkes, 'Production of Copies of the *Canterbury Tales*', pp. 163–210; but see P. R. Coss's argument for the earlier existence of bookshops in 'Aspects of Cultural Diffusion in Medieval English: the Early Romances, Local Society and Robin Hood', *Past and Present*, vol. 108 (1985) pp. 60–62.
26. Shonk, 'A Study of the Auchinleck Manuscript', pp. 90–1. See I. C. Cunningham and J. E. C. Mordkoff, 'New Light on the Signatures in the Auchinleck Manuscript (Edinburgh, National Library of Scotland Adv. MS 19.2.1)', *Scriptorium*, vol. 36 (1982) p. 291, for the suggestion that Scribe 1 may not initially have conceived of the MS as a whole.
27. For a recent overview of such conditions and related matters, see the essays in Griffiths and Pearsall (eds), *Book Production*.
28. Dieter Mehl, *Middle English Romances of the Thirteenth and Fourteenth Centuries* (London: Routledge & Kegan Paul, 1968).
29. Ibid., pp. 259–60.
30. Gisela Guddat-Figge, *Catalogue of Manuscripts Containing Middle English Romances* (Munich: Wilhelm Fink, 1976).
31. Ibid., p. 65.
32. Ibid., pp. 67–8.
33. Ibid., pp. 7–8, 17, 22–9 and 37–42.
34. Guddat-Figge's discussion is also superior to the abstract and general observations in Harriet Hudson, 'Middle English Popular Romances: the Manuscript Evidence', *Manuscripta*, vol. 28 (1984) pp. 67–78.
35. See note 24 above.
36. P. R. Robinson, '"The Booklet": a Self-contained Unit in Composite Manuscripts', *Codicologica*, vol. 3 (1980) pp. 46–69.
37. Ralph Hanna III, 'Booklets in Medieval Manuscripts: Further Considerations', *Studies in Bibliography*, vol. 39 (1986) p. 105 and *passim*.
38. Robinson, 'A Study of Some Aspects of the Transmission', pp. 57, 42 and 56.
39. Derek Pearsall, 'The Development of Middle English Romance', in Derek Brewer (ed.), *Studies in Medieval English Romances: Some New Approaches* (Cambridge: D. S. Brewer, 1988) pp. 11–35 (originally appearing in *Mediaeval Studies*, vol. 27 (1965) pp. 91–116); 'The English Romance in the Fifteenth Century', *Essays and Studies*, vol. (1976) pp. 56–83.
40. Pearsall, 'Development of Middle English Romance', p. 26.
41. Derek Pearsall, *Old and Middle English Poetry*, Routledge History of English Poetry, vol. 1 (London: Routledge & Kegan Paul, 1977).
42. Meale, 'The Compiler at Work'.
43. Pearsall, *Manuscripts and Readers*, p. 83.
44. George R. Keiser, review of Pearsall, *Manuscripts and Readers*, in *Publications of the Bibliographical Society of America*, vol. 79 (1985) p. 242.
45. Pearsall, (ed.), *Manuscripts and Readers*, pp. 125–41.
46. Ibid., pp. 113–24.
47. Ibid., p. 120.
48. Ibid., p. 123.
49. Keiser, review of Pearsall, ibid., pp. 244–5.

50. Thompson, *Robert Thornton and the London Thornton Manuscript*.
51. Sarah M. Horrall, 'The London Thornton Manuscript: a New Collation', *Manuscripta*, vol. 23 (1979) pp. 99–103; Ralph Hanna III, 'The Lincoln Thornton Manuscript: a Corrected Collation', *Studies in Bibliography*, vol. 37 (1984) pp. 122–30; 'The Growth of Robert Thornton's Books', *Studies in Bibliography*, vol. 40 (1987) pp. 51–61.
52. Thompson, *Robert Thornton and the London Thornton Manuscript*, p. 69. Like many areas of MS studies, the significance of watermarks and compilers' uses of paper stocks is a matter of incipient understanding and sometimes considerable disagreement. For further investigation, Thompson's case study, including its references and bibliography, is one possible starting-point. Another more general one is R. J. Lyall, '1. Materials: The Paper Revolution', in Griffiths and Pearsall (eds), *Book Production*, pp. 11–29.
53. Murray J. Evans, 'The *Explicits* and Narrative Division in the Winchester MS: a Critique of Vinaver's Malory', *Philological Quarterly*, vol. 58 (1979) pp. 263–81; 'The Two Scribes in the Winchester MS: the Ninth *Explicit* and Malory's "Hoole Book"', *Manuscripta*, vol. 27 (1983) pp. 38–44.
54. See Murray J. Evans, '*Ordinatio* and Narrative Links: the Impact of Malory's Tales as a "Hoole Book"', in James W. Spisak (ed.), *Studies in Malory* (Kalamazoo, Mich.: Medieval Institute Publications, Western Michigan University, 1985) pp. 29–52. For a different approach to Malory using ME romance MS collections to illuminate the variety of his themes, see Felicity Riddy, *Sir Thomas Malory* (Leiden: E. J. Brill, 1987).
55. Phillipa Hardman, 'A Mediaeval "Library *in Parvo*"', *Medium Aevum*, vol. 47 (1978) pp. 262–73.
56. Ibid., p. 272.
57. Ibid., p. 269.
58. For further discussion of Heege's role by Boffey and Thompson, see Griffiths and Pearsall (eds), *Book Production*, pp. 295–7.
59. A. I. Doyle, 'Retrospect and Prospect', in Pearsall (ed.), *Manuscripts and Readers*, p. 146.

3

Medievalists and Deconstruction: *An Exemplum*
DAVID AERS

'Flee fro the prees and dwelle with sothfastnesse'
                              Chaucer, *Balade de Bon Conseyl*

'Nontruth is the truth'
Derrida, 'Play: from the Pharmakon to the Letter and from Blindness to the Supplement', in *Dissemination*

'Whan alle tresors arn tried truthe is the beste'
                               Langland, *Piers Plowman*

During the postwar period the work of those specialising in medieval literature, normally employed in semi-autonomous departments of Middle English language and literature, habitually assumed a thoroughly complacent resistance to any theoretical and political self-reflection. The paradigms determining teaching and research remained invisible to practitioners who took pride in their scholarly objectivity. When major currents of modern philosophical, historical, cultural, psycho-analytical, political and theological inquiry entered adjacent domains of literary studies, professional medievalists remained confident that there was no need to engage with such currents. It was simply assumed that such engagement could not improve either self-knowledge or knowledge of the past. This mistaken belief continued to prevent medievalists from making their own paradigms topics for critical reflection, even though these paradigms carried absolutely decisive theoretical and political views. A mixture of naïve positivism and varieties of distinctly *modern* political conservatism, these paradigms inevitably shaped the version of the past handed out to students as well as the version of medieval texts approved in the respectable professional journals. This history needs recalling but needs no further elaboration here since it has been told and documented by Lee Patterson in recent studies which are themselves outstanding models of critical historiography and which deserve to become major reference points for those working in medieval studies.[1] The fact that Patterson's works, published in 1987 and 1990, include well-informed attention to contemporary theory and an admirably clear grasp of the ideologies informing the dominant scholarly paradigms is itself a sign that the intellectual forces evident everywhere else in the literary academy during the 1970s and 1980s had begun to enter what Patterson called the 'ghetto' of medieval studies.[2] To those who had been rather unsuccessfully seeking to bring some of the insights of critical theory (Horkheimer, Adorno, Marcuse), Marxism and hermeneutic phenomenology (Merleau-Ponty, Ricoeur) to medieval and early modern studies, while seeking to encourage serious attention to the social and economic histories of late medieval and early modern communities, much about the new forces was obviously welcome.[3] It seemed that they would necessitate the long-overdue interrogation of what Derrida calls the 'subtextual premisses', including the 'unspoken political interests' of past and present writing.[4] This is certainly happening and it is cause for celebration that widespread challenges to the unself-reflexive hegemony of positivism and idealist myths about the Middle Ages, so well analysed by Patterson, has facilitated the kind of work produced for *Literary Practice and Social Change in Britian, 1380–1530*, work which combines attention to modern critical theory with scrupulous respect for the history and politics of past culture.[5]

However, I have chosen to focus on a strand of modern theory that has generated a considerable quantity of work and has been extremely influential in early modern criticism since the late 1970s, especially among those described as New Historicists. I speak of deconstruction, its emergence in medieval studies visible since about 1986, when one finds a reading of the *Nun's Priest's Tale* in which quotations from *Of Grammatology* and 'White Mythology' far outweigh quotations from Chaucer while attention to Chaucer's own culture and social formation is conspicuously absent – Chaucer's poem demonstrates Derrida's theory of signification, *différance* and *supplementarity*, giving 'even as it suppresses, a sign of an epoch to come'.[6] Chaucer as a kind of John the Baptist to our own 'epoch' and its Master? But I have chosen to meet the limitations of space here by representing medievalists' deconstruction from an essay published in the following year by a gifted Chaucerian scholar whose work I respect, 'Oure Tonges *Différance*: Textuality and Deconstruction in

Chaucer'.[7] Before proceeding to consider this example, however, I wish to make it clear that nothing in the present essay puts in question the possibility that Chaucer's work includes within its great range of genres examples of the following: (a) critical exploration of the dominant institutions and practices of his own culture – or of emergent ones; (b) signs, in particular places, of incoherence or unresolved contradictions; (c) an unusually sustained concern with epistemological and hermeneutic complexities. Arguments that these possibilities are actualised in parts of Chaucer's work have been made by many distinguished commentators in the last three decades working in various traditions of inquiry quite *independent* of contemporary deconstruction and quite indifferent to its distinctive claims about meaning, interpretation and referentiality. Only sloth or chronic amnesia could persuade medievalists that it was not until the coming of deconstruction that we could identify what I have listed in the three points above, that it was not before Yale embraced Derrida that we had teachers who could show us how to identify contradictions between overt arguments and the implications of rhetorical forms, or between 'manifest' and 'latent', or between the putative controls of doctrinal abstractions and the play of metaphoric, metonymic or catachretic forces. Need one recall work by such diverse writers as Empson (less 'archaic' than perhaps the Yale disciples of Derrida assert[8]), Rossiter on Shakespeare and Wordsworth, Elizabeth Salter on Chaucer's *Clerk's Tale*, *Knight's Tale* and *Troilus and Criseyde*; by Volosinov/Bakhtin and the Russian Formalists; by Marcuse (especially in *One Dimensional Man*, *Counter-Revolution and Revolt* or *The Aesthetic Dimension*); by Marx and Freud, whose various critiques of ideology and common sense often involved the sharpest attention to language and contradition? The fact is that if medievalists deploy the distinctive terms of deconstruction they are deploying more than neutral 'tools' of rhetorical analysis – an observation to which I shall return.

The essay which provides my own *exemplum* makes the kind of move that is endlessly repeated in deconstructionist criticism in its very title: Chaucer's word 'difference' (*Troilus and Criseyde*, 1.395) is abstracted from its literary and cultural contexts and turned into *différance*, Derrida's neologism that has become one of the guiding concepts (or to defer to the jargon of the tradition, 'non-concepts') of deconstruction. The medievalist claims that Chaucer 'is an active deconstructionist', that Chaucer is 'like Derrida', that in *Troilus and*

Criseyde 'the issues central to deconstruction are made a central focus of the poem.[9] These are striking and unequivocal claims. Not only do they make Chaucer our contemporary, speaking the very language of postmodernism; but in doing so they make invisible the massive transformations in British society over the last 600 years. Chaucer becoming 'like Derrida' is Chaucer becoming the inhabitant of secularised, post-Enlightenment, liberal individualist culture in an advanced capitalist society. How can this be so? Let us see.

The essay is based on one of the familiar strategies of deconstructionist reading. First of all it is suggested that the writer may seem to, or even try to, subscribe to the set of 'logocentric illusions' which mark western philosophy from Plato up to Derrida. Then his text is shown to deconstruct the so-called 'ontological and logocentric pretensions' of his culture, here those mirrored in the first three books of *Troilus and Criseyde*. Chaucer's deconstructive activity displays the play of *différance*, the inescapable logic of the *supplement*. This task is carried out in Books IV and V of *Troilus and Criseyde*,[10] 'by calling attention more explicitly to the textuality of his own text' and its heterogeneity, destroying 'the illusion of connected narratives'. Here the critic notices often-discussed features concerning a shift in the narrator's stance and methods, but he re-describes them in deconstructionist terminology. He claims that 'like Derrida' Chaucer *mimes* logocentric discourse with the purpose of exposing it to deconstruction. The poet makes the final move in the deconstructive performance that is *Troilus and Criseyde* at what the critic calls 'the end of the poem'. Here he quotes these lines to show this: 'Go, litel bok, go litel myn tragedye. . . . That thow be understonde, God I biseche!' (v.1786, 1798).[11] By these lines Chaucer 'calls attention to the textual phenomenon of *absence*'.[12] It is certainly true that Chaucer takes note of the author's loss of control over scribes and audiences. But whether he is in fact making the specially deconstructionist point about '*absence*', and *how* this would be a possible intention in the purportedly 'logocentric' culture that begat him remains, at best, obscure. By describing the lines in the specialised language of post-structuralism the critic simply pre-empts discussion of such basic issues. Indeed, the very first paragraph of the article told us that Chaucer's poetry, in numerous passages, devotes itself to what the critic calls '*la chose Derridienne*, or simply Jacques Thing'.[13] Still, it may be worth recalling that 'the end of the poem' is actually a genre not much encountered in deconstructionist criticism: it is a prayer, addressed to the specifically Christian deity, and preceded by an invocation of the specifically Christian economy of salvation (V.1842–8, 1863–8). Even the lines the critic does quote include another prayer, once again to the addressee whose absence is also an inescapable though much mediated presence – in that tradition, in that culture.

Besides demonstrating the familiar reading strategies and terminology of deconstructionism, together with frequent referencing of *auctoritas* in the form of various texts authorized by Derrida,[14] the Chaucerian makes the familiar post-structuralist claims about *history* and *meaning*. *Troilus and Criseyde* is said to be 'a demonstration . . . of the impossibility of history, and . . . a general critique of all signifying systems, including social and religious institutions and language itself'. Not only *Troilus and Criseyde*, the scholar claims, but in fact all Chaucer's writing is a demonstration of the distinctively post-structuralist 'critique of logocentrism' – 'like Derrida' indeed.[15]

Let us take the 'impossibility of history' first. This is not explicated by the critic, perhaps because it follows from the system's theory of meaning, or rather non-meaning. Still, it is certainly a commonplace in criticism done under the authority of Derrida. For example, we find Jonathan Goldberg attacking Stephen Greenblatt's essay on *King Lear*, Harsnett and the Jesuit exorcists for referring to the 'historically embedded' nature of Shakespeare's text. Now Greenblatt has himself been heavily influenced by Derrida, but has not internalised what Goldberg takes to be the master's doctrines concerning referentiality, history and narrative sufficiently to gain an avowed disciple's approval. For Greenblatt begins his essay with this sentence: 'Between the spring of 1585 and the summer of 1586, a group of English Catholic priests led by the Jesuit William Weston, alias Father Edmunds, conducted a series of spectacular exorcism, principally in the house of a recusant gentleman, Sir George Peckham of Denham, Buckinghamshire.' Goldberg's objections are not the kind a 'new critic' might have offered – for example, that such extra-literary materials, like Harsnett's account of the events, one Shakespeare used in writing *King Lear*, are irrelevant to our understanding and appreciation of great literature. What the post-structuralist objects to is Greenblatt's evocation of 'the unquestioned reality of dates and facts, the local event that locates the Shakespearean text within a cultural economy'.[16] It is the acknowledgement of apparently verifiable, empirical dimensions within historiography, even within Greenblatt's Foucaultian version of history, that is unacceptable to

Goldberg. Because Greenblatt refers in a traditional historiographic mode to 'facts and dates' as empirical events which are not pure effects of textuality, he transgresses basic post-structuralist doctrine. Indeed, he compounds this transgression by maintaining what Goldberg calls 'the literary intentionality of the Shakespearean text',[17] something the Chaucerian post-structuralist also does. To Goldberg, deploying the histrionic political posturing so pervasive among post-structuralists of the late 1970s and early 1980s, this combination is a form of 'totalitarianism'.[18] (Why transgression of deconstructionist doctrines about the absolute 'impossibility of history' and about 'literary intentionality' are called 'totalitarianism' can be explained by the doctrines of *différance, dissemination* and active interpretation, to which I shall turn in a moment.) History, Goldberg insists, is nothing but textuality, a 'heterogeneous dispersal' in which 'texts and authors and events – can only be taken as tropes, speculations with counters that discourse fills . . . halls of mirrors in which resemblance does not halt'.[19] There is some irony that on the same page Goldberg refers to a book he himself has written and gives its date '1983', simultaneously laying claim to authorship, authorial intentionality, 'facts and dates' in a rather traditional way; as he does a few pages later when he relates *Macbeth* to James I, quoting *Basilikon Doron* and giving its date – '1616'. But such incoherences are common enough in this style of criticism. Indeed, the Chaucerian post-structuralist, having enunciated 'the impossibility of history', himself proceeds to offer us an extraordinarily simplified version of a very traditional grand historical narrative. This concerns what he calls the 'drift from a traditional, face-to-face' culture 'to a textual, disseminated modern culture . . . based in writing'.[20] However surprising to find it here, this is the grand linear narrative told by Marxists, Whigs, Eliotic or Yeatsian conservatives and by many who find consolation in imagining a pre-Reformation and pre-capitalist age of faith, intimately face-to-face communities, hierarchical, moral and social order. (True enough these stories do not associate the changes they identify with anything quite as vague as a 'drift from a traditional face-to-face' culture to one 'based in writing'; nor do they place the fourteenth century on the 'modern' side of the transitions they seek to address; nor do they make Chaucer and Derrida both inhabit 'modern' culture.)

As we read this story three responses seem appropriate. The first is to note the return of the repressed. The denial of the possibility of historical knowledge is followed by the most vapid writing of history.[21] The second response is to note a strange return of the long-since discredited base/super-structure model. This binary returns, with His Majesty the Economy, the real foundations in traditional Marxism, being replaced by textuality: in that modern culture which allegedly embraces Chaucer and Derrida, 'the modes of interpretation proper to reading, writing and textuality are the fundamental conditions of individual and social existence'.[22] Indeed, a new motor is discovered for world history: 'deconstruction produces a new world'. Such claims are the stuff of the most fantastical fetishisation of textuality.[23] The third response is just to recall Derrida's own words in *Of Grammatology*: 'there has never been anything but writing; there has never been anything but supplements, substitutive signification which could only come forth in a chain of differential relation'.[24] These views are often stated by Derrida and *no* historical narrative can be written around this 'there has never been anything but writing'.

I now move to one of the most distinctive features of post-structuralism. The Chaucerian scholar attributes it to Chaucer: 'a general critique of all signifying systems . . . and language itself'.[25] Indeed he has no doubts that there is 'Deconstruction in Chaucer'.[26] Now it is important that medievalists who are drawn to apply the terms and strategies of deconstruction should work out the implications and consequences of such terminology and its habitual interpretative strategies. This may seem a strangely obvious thing to say, but let me indicate why nevertheless it needs saying. In reading of recent early modern and medieval literary criticism I have encountered many examples of critics 'doing the magpie'; that is, plucking out terms and concepts from currently favoured systems and attaching them to essays whose overall intellectual commitments, epistemology and values are not congruent with the systems from which the terms are taken. I suspect the motives for 'doing the magpie' are the ones Chaucer ascribes to his Pardoner's use of Latin (Pardoner's Prologue, lines 344–6). Let us turn then to the 'deconstruction in Chaucer', the 'general critique' he allegedly undertakes hand-in-hand with Derrida.

It is helpful here to recall a couple of very characteristic statements about meaning, language and critical interpretation from the Master himself. From *Writing and Difference*:

> The meaning of meaning . . . is infinite implication, the indefinite referral of signifier to signifier . . . its force is a certain pure and

infinite equivocality which gives signified meaning no respite, no rest, but engages it in its own *economy* so that it always signifies again and differs.[27]

The essay on *'Différance'*, in *The Margins of Philosophy* provides one of the most careful theoretical statements of this position, as does the influential essay 'Structure, Sign and Play in the Human Science'. There we encounter the call that seems to have been a vital component of deconstruction's appeal to literary critics of the post-1968 period, a call for: 'Nietzschean *affirmation* – the joyous affirmation of the freeplay of the world and without truth, without origin, offered to an active interpretation'.[28] In these two quotations we encounter the hallmarks of the *distinctively* deconstructionist 'general critique of meaning' together with the implications of that 'critique' for interpretation. In cultivating Nietzsche's 'active foregetfulness', what Peter Dews encapsulates as 'a release from the longing for an impossible truth',[29] the critic is freed from the quest for truth – in interpretation or anywhere else. As Derrida himself so often observes, 'Every time a question of meaning is posed, it can only be within the closure of metaphysics.'[30] And the pride of deconstruction is, after all, to dissolve such 'closure' and return us to the indefinite referral of 'signifier to signifier', the endless play of *différance* without centre or origin or meaning, an infinite disseminative dispersal. We are all to become *active interpreters*, joyful seekers for power in the community of power-driven interpreters celebrated by Stanley Fish, the most eloquent apologist of American consumer capitalism the literary academy has so far produced. In this joyous will to power, this Nietzschean activity, we are already anticipated by Chaucer, for the medievalist tells us that the 'general message embodied in all the poems' is that 'texts do not *mean*, they are *used*'.[31] Chaucer's message, he reiterates, 'is consistently deconstructive'.[32] Chaucer, 'like Derrida'[33] has grasped that 'meaning' and 'truth' are terms belonging to the delusions of logocentric metaphysics, in a world 'without truth', one where interpretation and the attribution of determinate meaning can only be the *use* of a text in the arbitrary impositions of power. For deconstruction the commitment is 'to an endless free play, unconstrained by a sense of allegiance to anything beyond this freedom'.[34] It is important that medievalists observe how in the tradition adhering to the Master and his distinctive language there can be *no* place for the hierarchical binaries found in other western traditions, ones like true/false, accurate/inaccurate, reading/misreading, coerced/uncoerced, and so on. Before applying its distinctive terms and strategies a medievalist should appreciate how these substitute 'limitlessness' of free play, the 'absence of the transcendental signified' and the 'use' of texts for any remotely traditional attempts to discover determinate meaning of past works in their own traditions and social circumstances. In rejecting the binaries true/false, good/bad, deconstructionists necessarily renounce any search for the true and the good, for the *archai* we need to grasp if we are to know and practice the virtues, including the virtue (simultaneously individual and collective) of Justice. Deconstructionists necessarily reclassify traditional inquiries into the *telos* of human community and human beings as the illusions of logocentrism, a logocentrism 'always already' subverted by its own textuality, 'writing', whether Plato's or St Paul's, Aristotle's or Augustine's, Hitler's or Milton's . . . . It is hardly surprising that Derrida's own attitude towards the 'unspoken political interests' of his own output has been so evasive, his texts so comfortably assimilated to the American academy. As late as 1984 he was still ready to describe his 'political disposition' in as empty terms as 'responsible anarchy' – 'while stressing, of course, the interminable obligation to work out and to deconstruct these two terms – "responsible" and "anarchy"'.[35] Before seeking to follow this tradition and its terms, medievalists need to ponder these problems and the Master's own inability to give anything more than the most vague account of institutions and the historically specific relations between particular texts, institutions, social groups and classes.[36] It would certainly be a naïve error to treat deconstruction as a Lego kit from which the medievalist can pick a few useful and fashionable pieces or ornaments – as both Blake and the Frankfurt School taught us, the techniques, 'tools' and 'reasons' we use are not neutral instruments but value-loaded ones that inevitably effect our practices and our vision. Now is not the time for critics to collapse into some unselfconsciously instrumentalist positivism, complete with its splitting apart of fact and value.

If, however, certain medievalists decide that they will follow the path of deconstruction, claiming with the Chaucerian in question that 'texts do not mean' and can only be *'used'*, I think they should join in a meditation on Terry Eagleton's recent comments in *The Ideology of the Aesthetic*:

> One problem with the postmodernist or poststructuralist concern to place the skids under truth . . . is its uneasy, unwilling

complicity with certain of the less palatable political realities of late bourgeois society. For nobody who has read a government communiqué can be in the least surprised that truth is no longer in fashion. In such conditions, the true facts – concealed, suppressed, distorted – can be in themselves politically explosive; and those who have developed the nervous tic of placing such vulgar terms as 'truth' and 'fact' in fastidiously distancing scare quotes should be careful to avoid a certain collusion between their own high-toned theoretical gestures and the most banal, routine political strategies of the capitalist power-structure. . . . It is unwise to assume that ambiguity, indeterminacy, undecidability are always subversive strikes against an arrogantly monological certitude; on the contrary, they are the stock-in-trade of many a juridical enquiry and official investigation.[37]

In my view this is well said, although in a world abounding in dictatorial regimes where lying and arbitrary power are commonplace, there is no good reason for restricting the observations to 'late bourgeois society'. It is also far, far closer to the views of that most self-conscious of poets, Geoffrey Chaucer, than are any deconstructionist projects: we could recall the words of his *Balade de Bon Conseyl*:

> Flee fro the prees and dwelle with sothfastnesse;
> . . .
> And trouthe thee shal delivere, it is no drede.

Indeed, even in one of the very passages quoted to illustrate Chaucer's deconstructionist commitments, we find the poet praying to God that his poem *be understood* – not, be it noted, that it be *'used'* in the affirmation of a joyful freeplay without truth, without end.

But I wish to stress that whether or not we decide to follow the paths laid down by the Master of deconstruction and his numerous followers in Anglo-American literary criticism will depend on who 'we' are, how 'we' understand ourselves, and within what traditions we seek to understand the past and the present, within what traditions we seek to shape our lives and confront our deaths. For all its Nietzschean posturings about untrammelled freeplay and the 'impossibility of history' it is now perfectly clear that post-structuralism is a philosophical tradition. (Whether it is one within which anyone and any human community could live I doubt, but here is not the place to ponder this.) And we need to recognise with Alasdair MacIntyre that a tradition articulates 'concepts and theories already embodied in forms of practice and types of community'.[38] Given this, we need to discover the forms of community, justice and practical reason fostered by *that* tradition, deconstruction. My own view here accords with that of both 'left' and 'right' critics who have identified post-structuralism with the forms of life, institutions and modes of thought which it considers itself to have transcended: namely, the 'extreme subjectivism', the extreme individualism emerging within liberal post-Enlightenment forms of life and the forces of advanced consumer capitalism with their 'need to destroy all vestiges of tradition . . . all continuous and stable forms of reality in order to stimulate higher levels of consumption'.[39] If our real commitments are to such forms of thought and the forms of life in which they thrive, consciously and unconsciously, we may well find ourselves drawn to the tradition that elaborates them into a theory which promises a place of very superior judgement indeed to deconstructionist literary critics, a place of judgement above all it surveys from Plato onwards, offering, as the Chaucerian critic asserts, 'a general critique of all signifying systems, including social and religious institutions and language itself'.[40] St Thomas Aquinas and Rosa Luxemburg, St Augustine and John Milton, eat your logocentric hearts out! If, however, we do *not* adhere to the traditions fostered by post-Enlightenment liberal individualism, if our allegiance is to other traditions of enquiry and the forms of life they seek to foster, then we will be unable to take the paths followed by deconstructionists. Which does not, of course, mean we will not try to understand their language and arguments or to explore the relations between their theory and the practical reason we see them following in their lives. For whatever tradition we ourselves espouse must, contrary to Burke's version of tradition, be reflected upon, its rationality and claims elaborated in changing circumstances and in the face of competing traditions.[41]

But where does this leave Chaucer the deconstructionist? He is the product of an attempt to appropriate his writing for the projects of an alien tradition, one profoundly antagonistic to the forms of life and theory within which late fourteenth-century communities and individuals, whether orthodox, heterodox or heretical, sought to live and understand their lives and conflicts. Although our Chaucerian deconstructionist tells us of 'the impossibility of history' and tells us a fable in which Chaucer and Derrida both inhabit 'modern' culture, we need to recall again, alas, one or two facts. *Chaucer lived before Descartes*; he lived before the Enlightenment's attempt to develop a tradition-free, absolutely certain Reason with an autonomous absolutely self-present human subject; and he lived before the problems of this project were confronted by its heirs. He simply does not begin from the premisses of the traditions of post-Enlightenment liberalism, nor, unlike post-structuralism, is he haunted by the ghost of Descartes, by Enlightenment fantasies of certainty, total self-identity and self-present subjectivity. He confronted the massive dislocations of fourteenth-century institutions, their real enough political, theological, moral and logical problems, as well as opportunities for many, from within the traditions, communities and forms of life of a pre-capitalist, non-Cartesian, and non-Enlightenment culture. Nothing in the traditions he inherited precluded the most subtle enquiry into complexities of human claim to meaning, rationality, justice and truth. The traditions Chaucer worked with included the view that the 'transcendental signified', whether Truth ('"The tour uppon the tofte", quod she, "Truth is there-in"') or History, was complexly mediated, through a glass darkly, *'in enigmate'*, by human sign systems, themselves a product of the Fall, and after Babel, but also facilitated by God's grace and the inner Word (see, for example, Augustine's *On the Trinity*, Book IX; or *Piers Plowman*, B XV–XX). Embarrassingly banal as it may be, in this context we need to recall that Chaucer wrote, ironised and lived in traditions that included a vision of a God who was inescapably and necessarily *absent*, present through the mediation of the sacramental signs but a presence which is, in the jargon of an alien tradition, an absence, a deferral. (Certain possible links between traditions of negative theology and aspects of deconstruction have attracted attention, including the Master's.) These are Christian commonplaces around which, as I long ago argued in a study of *Piers Plowman*, Langland organised his own allegorical visions. But this deferral, this understanding of the limits, the inescapable mediations of human knowledge, be it knowledge of self, others, history or God, was not one that *in principle* committed people to a metaphysics in which textual *différance* is 'the absolute' (whether under erasure or not). Unlike deconstructionists, medieval Thomists, Ockhamists, Wycliffites and Augustinians maintained such hierarchical binaries as truth/false, good/evil, reason/unreason, justice/injustice. And, *unlike* post-structuralists they all subscribed to the traditional 'equation of contradiction and untruth'.[42] In neither Chaucer nor any of the traditions Chaucer knew and worked with was the connection between truth, rationality, the virtues and justice *in principle* severed, nor, in principle, turned into the arbitrary effects of a self-enclosed though endless textuality. So, I repeat, what we confront is an *appropriation* of Chaucer by an alien, homogenising and thoroughly imperialistic tradition, one 'with scant regard' for the discursive specificity of other traditions, cultures and texts.[43] My own view is that medievalists have a special responsibility to oppose such appropriations of medieval writing.

I think the vocation of medievalist should include the study of *just how* the paradigms and practices of modern culture emerged, *how* present versions of rationality, the good, the self, justice and community were formulated, *how and when* they became dominant. Our study gives us a special opportunity, I would say obligation, *to work against historical amnesia*, to resist the joyful forgetfulness preached by Nietzsche and deconstruction as well as the consolatory amnesia so common among conservative medievalists.[44] In doing this work we help those whom we teach to become aware that what we habitually take for granted, the way we know things are and must be, is the product of identifiable paradigms, paradigms with a specific history. This work will also facilitate the recognition of ways in which dominant cultural paradigms shape what may be presented as opposing, even antithetical theories.[45] In doing this work we shall be retrieving traditions of human enquiry that are rivals to those which won out. It is important that as far as possible we learn their language, that we do not simply re-describe their texts in the 'common sense' or 'radical' language of dominant paradigms.[46] It is within such a perspective as this that we can understand as imperialistic appropriation those many current projects which make Shakespeare, Herbert, Donne or Chaucer neo-deconstructionists doing work just 'like Derrida'.

Our task is to focus on the *rival* nature of the conceptions we encounter quite as much as it is, when appropriate, to show continuities with views favoured among the present cultural élites working in higher education. We need to show how rival traditions involve rival conceptions of the good and of the ends of writing. As Alasdair MacIntyre observes:

> what is or seems to be the same or a very similar argument occurring in two different philosophical epochs may have very

different import. Augustine's use of the *cogito* is not at all the same as Descartes' use. Augustine's account of the place of ostensive definition in language learning points towards the divine illumination of the mind; Wittgenstein's very similar account – that Wittgenstein erroneously took his account to be at odds with Augustine's reinforces my central thesis – points towards the concept of a form of life.[47]

And Chaucer's forms of self-reflexivity, his forms of critical interrogation of dominant institutions and their ideologies, these are not at all the same as contemporary forms of academic scepticism, not at all the same as deconstructionists' attempts to exorcise the ghost of Descartes, enlightenment rationalism and 1960s structuralism – an exorcism conducted within one of the most privileged areas of modern consumer capitalism. Without the nostalgic fantasies and consolatory amnesia of the conservative medievalism, analysed by Lee Patterson and others, medievalists today need to learn and teach the languages and contexts (social, economic, political, religious) of traditions that are *rivals* to those presiding over our own culture. They need to do so in an informed dialogue with the dominant and emerging traditions of modern culture. Nobody's interests are well-served by medievalists confining their attentions to their own separatist 'ghetto', to the 'marginal' position in literary studies from which the 'medieval' is allowed to be the fantasy object that is the 'other' of the modern.[48] In this dialogue they will show their students how there never was and never will be a tradition-free rationality, a tradition-free understanding of Justice and the Virtues – or a tradition-free 'deconstruction' of others' traditions. To do the critical magpie or to do a committed deconstruction belongs to quite identifiable traditions and quite identifiable élites in quite identifiable places in liberal capitalist states. We need to facilitate our own and our students understanding of competing traditions of justice and rationality, their histories, their communities, their various *archai* and their consequences. In doing so we shall necessarily be testing out the tradition to which we ourselves adhere in relation to its rivals; we shall be furthering our own and our students' abilities to reflect on current beliefs and current practices; we shall be encountering alternative forms of inquiry which may 'provide ourselves with one of the best means of preventing our current moral and political theories from degenerating into uncritically accepted ideologies'.[49] Where we choose to stand, the traditions to which we adhere, will both define who we are and shape what we shall become.

NOTES

1. L. Patterson, *Negotiating the Past* (Madison, Wis.: Wisconsin University Press, 1987); L. Patterson, 'On the Margin; Postmodernism, Ironic History and Medieval Studies', *Speculum*, vol. 65 (1990) pp. 87–108. See also D. A. Pearsall, 'Chaucer's Poetry and its Modern Commentators', in *Medieval Literature*, ed. D. Aers (Brighton, Sussex: Harvester, 1986) Ch. 7, esp. pp. 133–40; and D. Aers, 'Rewriting the Middle Ages', *JMRS*, vol. 18 (1988) pp. 221–40.
2. Patterson, *Negotiating the Past*, p. 38; see also his 'On the Margin'.
3. For examples of such attempts: Sheila Delany, *Chaucer's House of Fame* (Chicago, Ill.: Chicago University Press, 1972) and her 'Sexual Economics, Chaucer's Wife of Bath, and the Book of Margery Kempe', *Minnesota Review*, vol. 5 (1975), rept. in her *Writing Woman* (New York: Schocken, 1983); D. Aers, *Chaucer, Langland . . .* (London: Routledge & Kegan Paul, 1980), and with R. Hodge and G. Kress, *Literature, Language and Society . . . 1580–1680* (New York: Barnes & Noble, 1981); S. Knight, 'Chaucer and the Sociology of Literature', *SAC*, vol. 2 (1980) pp. 15–51; Judith Ferster's work of the 1970s culminating in *Chaucer on Interpretation* (Cambridge: Cambridge University Press, 1985).
4. J. Derrida, 'Deconstruction and the Other', in R. Kearney (ed.), *Dialogues with Contemporary Continental Thinkers* (Manchester: Manchester University Press, 1984) p. 115.
5. Lee Patterson (ed.), *Literary Practice and Social Change in Britain, 1380–1530* (Berkeley, Cal.: University of California Press, 1990); see also Paul Strohm, *Social Chaucer* (Cambridge, Mass.: Harvard, 1989); J. Ferster, *Chaucer on Interpretation* (Cambridge: Cambridge University Press, 1985); P. Knapp, *Chaucer and the Social Contest* (London: Routledge, 1990).
6. B. J. Harwood, 'Signs and/as origin: Chaucer's *Nun's Priest's Tale*', *Signs*, vol. 20 (1986) pp. 189–202.
7. M. Leicester, 'Oure Tonges *Différance*: Textuality and Deconstruction in Chaucer' in L. A. Finke and M. B. Schichtman (eds), *Medieval Texts and Contemporary Readers* (Ithaca, NY: Cornell University Press, 1987) pp. 15–26; in 1990 the author published *The Disenchanted Self* (Berkeley, Cal.: California University Press): this was advertised by the publisher (June 1990) as 'best understood as a post-structuralist activity' but on writing the present essay (July 1990) it had not yet reached British bookshops. For the same kind of claim in relation to Jean de Meun and his term 'differeance' in *Le Roman de la Rose*, II, 21543–52 (Lecoy edition), see R. A. Shoaf, 'Medieval Studies after Derrida after

Heidegger', in *Sign, Sentence, Discourse: Language in Medieval Thought and Literature* (New York: Syracuse University Press, 1989) ch. 1, esp. pp. 20–2. Shoaf notes 'a chasm that cannot be crossed' between the thirteenth-century Christian writer and Derrida but immediately decides it *can* be 'crossed out' by him in his identifying of Jean's 'differeance' and Derrida's *différance*. Both, he solemnly pronounced, 'accept "death as the concrete structure of the living present"' and both Shoaf and Heidegger, he informs us, 'read St. Augustine' (p. 22). See also J. Tambling, *Dante and Difference: Writing in the Commedia* (Cambridge: Cambridge University Press, 1988) esp. Introduction and pp. 100–1 and 134–7.
8. G. Hartman, 'Monsieur Texte: On Jacques Derrida, His *Glas*', *Georgia Review*, vol. 29 (1975) p. 782.
9. Leicester, 'Oure Tonges *Différance*', pp. 22, 17, 19.
10. Ibid., pp. 16–17, 19.
11. Ibid., p. 18.
12. Ibid.
13. Ibid., p. 16.
14. For example, ibid., notes 3–4, 7 and 13 on pp. 16–17, 18–19 and 22.
15. Ibid., p. 17.
16. J. Goldberg, 'Speculations: *Macbeth* and Source', in J. E. Howard and M. F. O'Connor (eds), *Shakespeare Reproduced* (London: Methuen, 1987) here p. 244; S. Greenblatt's essay, 'Shakespeare and the Exorcists', quoted here from *Shakespeare and the Question of Theory* (London: Methuen, 1985) ch. 9, esp. p. 163.
17. Ibid., p. 245.
18. Ibid., p. 247.
19. Ibid.
20. Leicester, 'Oure Tonges *Différance*', p. 21.
21. For some indication of the kind of information literary critics need, especially those wishing to make claims about change, see D. Aers, *Community, Gender and Individual Identity . . . 1360–1430* (London: Routledge, 1988) pp. 1–19, 179–85, and to the material there should be added R. J. Holton, *Capitalism and Civilization* (London: Allen & Unwin, 1986); R. J. Holton, *The Transition from Feudalism to Capitalism* (London: Macmillian, 1984); and J. E. Martin, *Feudalism to Capitalism* (London: Macmillian, 1983).
22. Leicester, 'Oure Tonges *Différance*', p. 24.
23. For a shrewd identification of the issues here and their sources, P. Anderson, *In the Tracks of Historical Materialism* (London: Verso, 1984) ch. 2; also F. Lentricchia, *After the New Criticism* (London: Methuen, 1980) pp. 156–88 and his *Criticism and Social Change* (Chicago, Ill.: Chicago University Press, 1984).
24. J. Derrida, *Of Grammatology* (Boston, Mass.: Johns Hopkins University Press, 1976) pp. 158–9.
25. Leicester, 'Oure Tonges *Différance*', p. 17.
26. Ibid., p. 15.
27. J. Derrida, *Writing and Différance* (London: Routledge & Kegan Paul, 1978) p. 25.

28. Ibid., p. 292.
29. P. Dews, *Logics of Disintegration* (London: Verso, 1988) p. 34; see also Derrida's characteristic line on hermeneutics in *Spurs: Nietzsche's Styles* (Chicago: Chicago University Press, 1979) pp. 123–31.
30. J. Derrida, *Margins of Philosophy* (Brighton, Sussex: Harvester, 1982) p. 51.
31. Leicester, 'Oure Tonges *Différance*', p. 26 (his italics).
32. Ibid., p. 26.
33. Ibid., p. 17.
34. Charles Taylor, *Sources of the Self* (Cambridge: Cambridge University Press, 1989) p. 488.
35. Derrida, 'Deconstruction', pp. 120–1.
36. Dews, *Logics*, p. 35.
37. T. Eagleton, *The Ideology of the Aesthetic* (Oxford: Basil Blackwell, 1990) pp. 379–80.
38. A. MacIntyre, *Whose Justice? Which Rationality?* (London: Duckworth, 1988) p. 290; my debts to this work and to his earlier works are immense, especially to *After Virtue*, 2nd edn. (London: Duckworth, 1982), and *A Short History of Ethics* (London: Macmillan, 1967).
39. Quoting Taylor, *Sources of the Self*, p. 590; and G. Graff, *Literature Against Itself* (Chicago, Ill.: Chicago University Press, 1978) p. 8; see also Eagleton's *Ideology of the Aesthetic*, ch. 14; MacIntyre, *Whose Justice?*, pp. 368–9, 385–7; and Q. Skinner, *Meaning and Context: Quentin Skinner and his Critics* (Cambridge: Polity Press, 1988) pp. 269–73 and 279–81.
40. Leicester, 'Oure Tonges *Différance*', p. 17.
41. See MacIntyre, *Whose Justice?*, chs 18 and 19.
42. Dews, *Logics*, p. 44.
43. Eagleton, *Ideology of the Aesthetic*, p. 406.
44. See Patterson, Pearsall and Aers cited in note 1.
45. The case of deconstruction as identified by those cited in note 39 is relevant here, its pretensions to being a dangerous revolutionary force and its 'deconstructive' strategies ones that are perfectly congruent with the place of well-rewarded élites in liberal capitalism: on the way that 'so-called conservatism and so-called radicalism . . . are in general mere stalking horses for liberalism', see MacIntyre, *Whose Justice?*, p. 392.
46. See ibid., chs 18 and 19.
47. A. MacIntyre, 'The Relationship of Philosophy to its Past', in R. Rorty, J. D. Schneewind and Q. Skinner (eds), *Philosophy in History* (Cambridge: Cambridge University Press, 1984) ch. 2, esp. p. 32.
48. See Patterson, 'On the Margin'.
49. Skinner, *Meaning and Context*, pp. 286–8.

Note
This essay was written in 1990.

4

Traces of Romance Textual Poetics in the Non-Romance Works Ascribed to the 'Gawain'-Poet

BARBARA KOWALIK

It is increasingly widely recognised nowadays that the study of medieval poetics should be firmly rooted in the context of the *trivium* – not only of rhetoric, but also of grammar and logic. Taken together, the disciplines of the *trivium* constitute a repository of a specifically medieval textual poetics. In the 'Introduction' to his recent book on medieval poetics – *From Topic to Tale: Logic and Narrativity in the Middle Ages*[1] – Eugene Vance gives a valuable survey of a variety of approaches to medieval textuality. He regards textuality as a pivotal factor that influenced medieval poetics from the twelfth century onwards and had an epistemic impact upon the whole of medieval culture. Under that impact, he claims, new and specifically textual models for understanding and expressing the reality developed. Romance is a genre the created world of which is modelled by such new, textual determinants, and Vance analyses Chrétien de Troyes's romances from the viewpoint of their relations to medieval logic.[2]

In the present chapter I wish to demonstrate that a sharp awareness of textuality underlies the 'Gawain'-poet's concept of romance as revealed in *Sir Gawain and the Green Knight* and constitutes a strong impulse of his poetics as manifest in his other works as well.

In the second stanza of *Sir Gawain* the narrator describes his story in a series of metaliterary designations, crowned with a compact description of the poem in the wheel. I believe that from this wheel much can be learnt about the poet's concept of romance and of the literary work in general:

> I schal telle hit astit, as I in toun herde,
>   With tonge.
>   As hit is stad and stoken
>   In stori stif and stronge,

> With lel letteres loken,
> In londe so hatz ben longe.
>
> (31–6)³

The speaker alludes here to his supposedly aural reception of the story – 'herde' – and creates an oral context for its transmission – 'telle', 'with tonge'. Yet these implications of the oral convention, reminiscent of minstrelsy, are inconsistent with the second half of the description, in which a visual image of the text is evoked.

The narrator perceives his story as 'with lel letteres loken'. The noun 'letteres', specifically, connects the concept of the poem revealed here with the discipline of *grammatica*, which was defined by John of Salisbury as a science of letters: *grama* means *littera*, that is, 'letter' or 'line'.⁴ 'Letters are figures (*figure*) which serve as visual indicators, first, of spoken words, and second, of things'⁵ Thus, the use of the word 'letteres' in the description of the romance evokes a visual picture of it as a written text and establishes its relationship to the art of *grammatica*.

The epithet 'lel' suggests a relationship of fidelity between the text of the poem and an order of material things which the poem imitates. John of Salisbury claims that *grammatica* 'imitates' nature,⁶ and poets, likewise, should faithfully represent nature as they write. The narrative 'I' of *Sir Gawain* seems to be fully aware of this basic requirement and assures us that it will be fulfilled in his story.⁷

However, he may also be referring here, at the simplest level, to the *mise en escrit* of his text, that is, to the linking of the letters of which it is composed. This conjecture is based upon the use of the verb 'loken', which may be translated as 'linked'.⁸ The phrase 'with lel letteres loken' would therefore depict a visual image of the written text as consisting of figures joined together. The word 'loken' is essential to the concept of the text revealed in these lines. In this concept the motif of ligature appears to be quite important. It brings to mind the literal sense of ligature as used in writing and printing as well as the notational device of ligature developed in medieval music. The idea of the text as a configuration of lines and strokes is supported by the description of the text written on the wall of Belshazzar's palace in *Cleanness* as 'Þe tyxte of Þe tede lettres' (1634),⁹ that is, 'the text of the letters joined together'.

The text, conceived of as a ligature of letters, constitutes a basis upon which the 'Gawain'-poet builds his poetics of ligature. The literal ligature of the written text becomes a model for a number of poetic ligatures such as alliteration, rhyme, concatenation, or the linking of beginning and end. The 'Gawain'-poet is particularly concerned with cementing his works into unified and well-knit wholes by means of various linking devices employed on all the levels of the poetic composition, beginning from the phonetic and metrical levels up to the thematic and narrative ones. In this sense his poems are indeed 'loken', and ligature on all the levels of the poetic work is, as illustrated by *Pearl*, an artistic ideal toward which he aspires. His works are modelled upon linear and visual designs; they invite comparisons with intricate configurations of lines joined together and forming geometrical patterns such as the circle or the pentangle. The question is where this keen awareness of the poem as a visual image comes from. My answer is that it may have been nourished, ultimately, by medieval textuality and the model of the book which underlies medieval culture.[10]

Another feature of the 'Gawain'-poet's concept of the literary work reveals itself in the same verb 'loken', which means not only 'linked', but also 'enclosed, enshrined'. This entails an idea of the literary work as something closed and self-contained, a concept which may again be seen as a result of the impact of textuality. The written text is closed in a double sense – materially, for it is usually bound and covered into a book, and semantically, for its meaning is closed to people unless they know how to read and interpret it. Reading and interpretation consist in opening and uncovering the text. This is evident from the poet's account of Daniel reading the inscription on the wall: he is portrayed as a wise man able to 'open vche a hide Þyng of aunteres vncouÞe' (1600), as a man who 'vnhyles vch hidde Þat Heuen-Kyng myntes' (1628) and can 'quere' it (1632). By implication, to write means to lock and cover up sense and to enshrine it in the container of the book.

When the Lord commands Jonah to preach His word to the Ninevites in *Patience*, he uses these words: 'Lo, My lore is in Þe loke, lauce hit Þerinne' (350).[11] The phrase 'in Þe loke' means 'locked, contained' and implies the enclosure of the Book of God's word, in which His wisdom is written down. The prophet is to open this enclosure, to undo the ligatures, and to proclaim the word to the people. The act of speaking and uttering the word is associated with unlocking and untying the enclosure and ligature of the written text. In the poet's mind the concept of the book entails the idea of enclosure. When he alludes to the *Roman de la rose* in *Cleanness*, for example, he uses the expression 'in Þe compas of [the] clene *Rose*'

(1057) which shows that he envisages the book as a closed, limited whole.

Again, this second feature of the written text becomes a basis for the 'Gawain'-poet's poetics of enclosure. It is his characteristic literary habit to enclose his poems in successive verbal, thematic and narrative frames. Each of his poems is framed in some way. Its beginning and end are heavily delineated so that we have a sense of its totality and self-containment. At the same time, each poem constitutes to a lesser or greater extent a puzzling, mysterious text the meaning of which must be unlocked and undone by the reader.

The 'metaliterary' wheel of the prologue of *Gawain* describes the romance not only as 'loken with lel letteres', but also as 'stad' and 'stoken', that is, 'fixed, set down, fastened, locked'. These verbs reinforce the implications of ligature and enclosure, and, apart from that, convey a sense of such fixity and permanence as are associated with writing. Vance argues that textuality brought about 'a shift from epic *mouvence* toward a culture of *grammatica* and monumentality'.[12] According to John of Salisbury, one of the main features of *grammatica* is its durability which may be compared to the permanence of monuments of stone: 'Triumphal arches add to the glory of illustrious men only when the writing upon them informs in whose honor they have been reared, and why. . . . Indeed no one has ever gained permanent fame except as the result of what he has written or of what others have written of him.'[13] The durability of writing, comparable to the durability of stone, is transferred in *Sir Gawain* on to the concept of the literary work. The romance is a story that is eternally fixed in writing; it is 'stad and stoken', 'stif and stronge', not passing, flexible and changing. The poet, in spite of his misleading guise of a minstrel, composes it as a written text, not an oral song unable to survive the flux of time.

The 'Gawain'-poet's textual poetics, with its features of enclosure, ligature and durability, determines also the world presented in the poems. The poet shows a preference for enclosed spaces – for example, the garden or the castle – as well as for complete cycles of time, such as a year or a day. The universe represented in his poems, just as the poems themselves, is 'loken' and 'stoken': these epithets are used, for example, in the description of Noah's Ark, which is a miniature world, of Jonah's bower, of the pentangle, the castle Hautdesert, and the green lace in *Gawain*, and of the city of New Jerusalem in *Pearl*. The dreamland in *Pearl* is infused with the qualities of permanence and artificiality which result from the abundant imagery of jerwellery and embroidery. The world is like a beautifully illuminated book. The poet explicitly compares the world to a book in *Cleanness* where the destruction of Sodom and Gomorrah is depicted as a violent unbinding of a book (966), and where, in the episode of the Writing upon the Wall, the narrator establishes equivalence between writing and ploughing (1547).

There is one more, perhaps the most important, area of the romance in which the impact of textuality is visible. This is the domain of the romance *aventure*. It should like to discuss it in greater detail.

Textuality influenced, as Vance claims, the semantic complexity of literature; it introduced equivocality and ambiguity into the romance world.[14] The 'Gawain'-poet's language reveals an interesting connection between writing and semantic obscurity. The verb 'merke', 'to write', has the same form as the noun 'merke' – 'darkness' – and the adjective 'merke' – 'dark, obscure'. Daniel is said to be able to explain the mysterious text on the wall even if it is dark and obscure: 'And Þaʒ þe mater be merk þat merked is ʒender, / He schal declar hit also cler as hit on clay stande' (1617–18). To be written, 'merked', means to be made dark and obscure – 'merk'. By contrast, to explain the meaning of the written text is to 'declar' it, that is, to make it 'cler'. Writing, therefore, is implicitly associated with mystery and darkness. The inscription on the wall remains dark in spite of the fact, paradoxically, that it is placed just opposite the candlestick: 'In contrary of þe candelstik, þer clerest hit schyned' (1532). The mystery of writing may have provided a model for the mysterious and equivocal world of the romance adventure.

Mystery and ambiguity are connected with the problem of interpretation. Vance points out that *grammatica*'s interest in interpretation was transferred in the epoch of textual poetics to the domain of fictional literature. Just as students of grammar occupied themselves with the explication of the classical *auctores*, so did vernacular writers begin to be concerned with reinterpreting their *matière*. Writing meant, in fact, rewriting the literary tradition; it arose out of the activity of interpretation which became a key preoccupation of both the romance writer and the romance hero. A hermeneutical attitude characterised the poet in relation to his inherited *matière* as well as the hero in relation to the equivocal world of his adventure. Vance observes that in Chrétien's romances there is a definite primacy of the activity of interpretation over heroic action.[15]

The 'Gawain'-poet's work shows close familiarity with these ideas. His writing is born out of interpretation either of biblical texts, as in the case of *Pearl*, *Cleanness* and *Patience*, or of romance tradition, as in the case of *Sir Gawain*. His hermeneutical attitude is clearly visible in the prologue of *Patience* where he carries out a neat piece of textual analysis. He treats the Beatitudes as 'Þe tyxte' (37) and pays close attention to the 'forme' of this 'tyxte'. He is aware of all the levels of the text's meaning, from the literal sense, through the *sensus*, to the *sententia*. The distinction between the levels of meaning is manifest in his account of Daniel who gives at first the literal meaning of the marks on the wall and then explains their significance (1726–40). The poet distinguishes between the reference of letters to words or to speech and their reference to ideas and things (for example, 1565–6).

As in Chrétien's romances so also in *Sir Gawain*, the protagonist's ability to interpret the world of his adventure is more important than his heroic action. Critics have observed that Gawain performs very few heroic deeds, and these are barely enumerated.[16] Instead, his heroic valour is measured by his success in dealing with the equivocal and enigmatic Green Knight and his world. Gawain's interpretation of the Green Knight in his double identity of the lord of the castle Hautdesert and the lord of the Green Chapel is paralleled by the reader's interpretation of the story. In a sense Gawain is forced to act as a 'literary critic'.[17] There is an identity between his adventure and the story which tells about it, an identity most succinctly expressed in the pun 'werkkez' (1515) – 'heroic deeds', but also '(literary) works'. Thus, Gawain's adventure is to a great extent literary and hermeneutical in nature; as such, it is shaped by the poetics of the text. Gawain's task is not unlike Daniel's, but unlike Daniel he fails to read and decode fully the complex text of the Green Knight.

The textuality of Gawain's adventure is latent, not explicit. 'Þe chaunce of Þe grene chapel' (2399) is written in the alphabet of the colours green, gold and red, in the grammar of binding and knotting motifs, and in the language of the signs of the pentangle and the green girdle. The hero and the reader have to discover the paradigms and syntagmas, the binary oppositions, of this text by themselves. *Sir Gawain* is the poet's most complex exercise in romance textual poetics. It is also a most complete translation of the language of grammatica into the idiom of romance fiction. Instead of letters and words, the hero and the reader face here the living pictographs of the poem's created world.

I wish to examine now two stories attributed to the 'Gawain'-poet in which the textuality of the marvellous is more transparent, though perhaps less interesting and complex, than in *Gawain*. At the same time, I shall be postulating the relation of these stories to romance textual poetics and illuminating, I hope, their generic indebtedness to the romance. The stories are: the episode of the writing on the wall in the narrative of Belshazzar's Feast in *Cleanness* and the discovery of the mysterious tomb in *St Erkenwald*.

The relation of Belshazzar's Feast to romance has already been observed by Davenport, who has classified the story as romance-chronicle and has commented on its romantic atmosphere.[18] It must be added that the sudden appearance of the writing on the wall has all the qualities of a romance adventure. It is quite similar to the intrusion of the Green Knight upon the castle of Camelot, even in the shared motif of dismemberment.[19] The narrator explicitly refers to the event as a 'ferly' (1529), repeating this important generic designation several times throughout his account (1563, 1629). Alternatively, he uses such other characteristic terms as 'chaunce' (1588), 'aunter(es) vncouþe' (1600), and 'þise syʒtes vncouþe' (1722).

What is distinct about this particular 'ferly' is its almost pure textuality. The narrator focuses our attention on the writing itself: the 'lettres' (1536, 1549, 1565, 1579, 1596, 1634), 'þe scrypture' (1546), 'þe wryt' (1552, 1567, 1630), 'þe draʒtes' (1557), 'þe tyxte' (1634), the 'wordes' (1725), the 'runisch sauez' (1545). In this way he underlines the textual nature of the marvel. The act of writing is amplified and extended in time through a long and detailed description full of repetition and variation. The picture of 'þe lettres' looming 'full large vpon plaster' (1549) is vivid and sensuous: we can visualise the horrible fingers holding a stylus ('poyntel', 1533), the rough, bare wall replacing parchment or paper ('þe roʒ wowe', 1545), the rough pen ('a scrof penne', 1546), 'þe wowe with þe roʒ penne', 1724); we can follow the movements of the pen upon the rough plaster as the figures are 'pared' (1536), 'purtrayed' (1536), 'grauen' (1544), 'scraped' (1546), 'merked' (1617, 1727), and 'rasped' (1724); we can hear the scratching of the stylus as it 'wrytes' (1534, 1725) and 'cerues' (1547) the text. It is the writing which terrifies Belshazzar and it is in the writing that the mystery of this marvel residess.

The textuality of the 'aunter' provides a hermeneutical rather than a chivalric challenge to Belshazzar and his court. It requires a hero skilled in reading and interpretation rather than one capable of performing mighty deeds of arms. Daniel turns out to be worthy of the task.

Daniel's heroic stature is emphasised through his delayed appearance on the stage of the adventure, at the point of utter helplessness of the king and his wise men. The poet elaborates this part of the story, as if preparing the way for the hero. The graphic presentation of a host of all kinds of 'scoleres' (1554) and 'warlaȝes' (1560), all of whom appear to be 'lewed' (1580) in the face of the mysterious inscription serves a double purpose: on the one hand, it lays stress on the unintelligibility of the enigmatic marks and, on the other, it magnifies Daniel's achievement. Neither those that 'were bok-lered' (1551) nor those 'þat war wyse of wychecrafte . . . þat con dele wyth demerlayk and deuine lettres' (1560–1) can manage to read even a single word, not to mention expound its significance. The long catalogue of all the 'clerkes out of Caldye þat kennest were knauen' (1575) accentuates the insufficiency of both human learning as well as of magic for the clarifying of this mystery. The 'clerkes' constitute a foil for Daniel's interpretative success.

Apart from the contrast with the 'clerkes', the poet precedes his direct introduction of the hero with the queen's speech praising his virtue. She describes Daniel as 'a haþel' (1597) who 'hatz þe gost of God þat gyes alle soþes' (1598) and whose 'sawle is ful of syence, saȝes to schawe' (1599). She eulogises Daniel's past achievements at Nebuchadnezzar's court. In contrast to the 'scoleres' and 'deuinores' (1578), Daniel is portrayed as a man in whom the profound knowledge of 'derne coninges' (1611), that is, all branches of learning, is aided by 'holy connyng' (1625) which resides not in the head but in the 'hert', as well as by 'Goddes gost . . . þat gyes alle þynges' (1627). He is a 'trwe . . . profete' (1623–4), capable of unlocking and uncovering all hidden and secret things.

Daniel is a new type of a romance hero. His heroism is defined not by physical strength and chivalric courage, but by his 'sapyence' (1626) and 'quayntyse' (1632) – wisdom. His heroic action expresses itself through wise and judicious words and through the courage of providing good sense to the world of mysterious and equivocal signs. A courageous act of interpretation, from deciphering 'vch fygure' (1726) and stringing the letters into words to expounding the *sententia* of the text, is the only proper response to the kind of adventure that takes place in the realm of semiosis. Moreover, in the 'Gawain'-poet's adaptation of romance textual poetics it is insufficient for the hero-interpreter to be a clever decoder of the grammar of the romance world. He can achieve a 'chaunce' in the universe of signs only if he possesses spiritual wisdom and is guided by the Holy Ghost.

Another example of the textuality of a romance *aventure* can be found in *St Erkenwald*.[20] The genre of this poem is commonly described as the saint's legend,[21] yet we may also find in it elements of romance-chronicle such as Belshazzar's Feast. The story is set in a vividly depicted historical context of seventh-century London, when christianisation of England was continued after St Augustine's mission. The poem's historical prologue, in which the history of Britian and London is traditionally linked with ancient history, and specifically with Troy, is not unlike the historical prologue of *Sir Gawain* and it may well have constituted an introduction to a romance.[22] But most importantly, the central even of this saint's legend resembles a romance 'ferly', while its protagonist, Erkenwald, has some attributes of a romance hero.

The incident which takes place during the renovation of part of St Paul's Cathedral is described by the narrator as a 'meruayle (43), and this term is a recurrent motif of his account (65, 114, 125, 158, 160). The marvel is also referred to as 'þe toumbe-wonder' (57), 'a quoyntyse strange' (74), 'a derfe wonder' (99), 'þe bolde wonder' (106), and the 'ferly' (145). The narrator repeatedly emphasises its mystery – 'þe mysterie of þis meruaile' (125) and the people's reaction of great wonder, perplexity and fear at its sight.

Erkenwald is introduced into the story somewhat in the manner of a romance hero. He is portrayed as an outstanding figure, rising above everyone else in the city. Like Daniel, he is the last one to come on the scene of the marvel, at the moment of utter helplessness and bewilderment of all the citizens. It seems that the poet deliberately delays his arrival, preceding it with an account of the discovery of the tomb and the unsuccessful attempts to explain it made by the scholars and governors of the town. As a result, Erkenwald arrives as a long-awaited hero into a seemingly impossible situation. His coming constitutes a climax of the steadily built-up tension. His composure contrasts with the general tumult and restlessness. He rides into the city like a heroic knight on a white steed: 'The bischop / . . . / buskyd þiderwarde by-tyme on his blonke after' (112).

The corpse enclosed in the tomb is 'loken' (147) there in a double sense: on the one hand, it is enclosed in the space of the grave, and on the other, its story is closed to its discoverers. The mystery of the marvel is intensified by the spatio-temporal dimension of the scene. The gradual disclosure of the marvel's meaning is paralleled by the downward movement in space as well as the backward movement in time. The marvel is uncovered in the most literal sense: the tomb is found deep underground, in the darkness of the earth, whereas the body itelf is enveloped within the successive layers of the ruins of the cathedral, the enclosure of the tomb, the coffin and the man's rich garments. The gradual penetration through these successive enclosures is like piercing the darkness surrounding the discovered body. Spatial movement downwards, into the very centre of this structure of Chinese boxes, is paralleled by temporal movement backwards, though the dark recesses of the libraries, where human memory is stored.[23] This organisation of space and time serves to increase the mystery and create the atmosphere of darkness around the marvel. Spatial darkness of the inside of the earth as well as temporal darkness of the remote past intensify the semantic darkness of the marvellous puzzle. Significantly, Erkenwald's prayer for the solution of the mystery takes place in the darkness of the night, and when the answer finally comes, it is exactly at the break of day: 'and afterwarde hit dawid' (127). The corpse is like a nucleus of an unknown story; it is only when the corpse itself begins to speak that the story becomes manifest and is crowned with sense. Up to that moment, it remains 'loken' within the gold figures carved in the marble, the meaning of which is unattainable to the observers.

The marvel in *Erkenwald* is shaped by a poetics of the text. The marble sacrophagus found deep in the earth resembles a closed book both literally and metaphorically. The durability of the Cyclopean stones of which the tomb is made is comparable to the durability of *grammatica* as described by John of Salisbury. The bright, gold letters with which the tomb is embellished (51) are the most tangible manifestation of its textuality. Yet although they stand clean-cut upon the marble, their meaning remains closed to those who gaze upon them (52–6). To a considerable extent, the mystery of this 'ferly' resides in the 'roynyshe' (52) writing, in the rune-like figures and arcane sentences. Their significance is closed even to the wisest scholars of the metropolis, who find themselves unable to string the letters into words and pronounce, at least, their *sensus*. When they decide to take off the lid – to 'vnlouke þe lidde' (67) – this is like the act of opening a book.

With the unlocking of the tomb the mystery, instead of being clarified, increases. The marvel of the body untouched by decay comes into view, but the narrator introduces it gradually, building up suspense. He leads us through the successive layers of the enclosure, beginning with the glittering, gold interior of the coffin, describing, next, the corpse's clothing and accessories – the royal, gold-hemmed gown embroidered with many precious pearls, the gold girdle around the waist, the fur-trimmed mantle, the coif, the crown and the sceptre – and ending with the description of the body (75–92). Like the *Gawain* narrator in the portrayal of the Green Knight, he leaves the most important detail – the freshness of the body – till the end of the description.

Like the gold characters carved in the marble, the body constitutes a puzzle for those who are gazing upon it. It increases the sense of the marvellous. Although it is no longer a text in the literal sense, the Londoners try to read it as a text; they search the books for the explanation of the mystery (97–100), but all their attempts are unsuccessful:

> Bot þat ilke note wos noght, for nourne none couthe,
> Noþer by title, ne token, ne by tale noþer,
> Þat wos breuyt in b[rut], ne in bok[e] notyde,
> Þat euer mynnyd suche a mo[n], more ne lasse.
>
> (101–4)

The textual model of interpretation is extended here from the first stage of the marvel – the inscription upon the tomb – over its second and main stage – the inside of the coffin. The Londoners treat the strange body as a book or a text which they try to place within the realm of writing. The body, which like the marble tomb is unsusceptible to the flux of time, invites such a placement within the universe of *grammatica*, where meaning is stored forever within the permanence of the written word.

However, a hermeneutical approach based upon pure textuality turns out to be unsuccessful. Through his hero, Erkenwald, the poet indicates the limitations of such an attitude. Erkenwald transcends the enclosure of textuality, which may be envisaged as the enclosure of the book. He is first introduced as a teacher of the law who 'At loue London ton . . . the laghe teches' (34) and 'Syttes semely in þe sege of Saynt Paule mynster' (135). The words 'the laghe teches' evoke an image of Erkenwald as a man buried in books. The verb 'syttes' suggests a static and stabilised way of life within the enclosure of the 'mynster'. However, this initial picture of the hero is undermined when we learn that at the time of the discovery of the marvel he 'was partyd fro home' (107) and when we are allowed to envisage him riding swiftly on his white horse. Clearly, Erkenwald's life is not confined to the enclosure of books of the law and the temple.

Erkenwald's response to the marvel, likewise, thwarts our expectations. He does not resort, as all the others did, to books. Instead, he kneels down in prayer, beseeching the Holy Spirit's counsel. Supposedly, he values divine grace, which is unbound like the wind, over the learning contained in the bound codices of the law. Erkenwald chooses not to listen to the sensational accounts of those who have seen the marvel and he does not hasten, as all the world did, to see the tomb and the corpse himself (113–16). Instead, he shuts himself away from people, staying alone with God. Instead of taking a rest after what must have been a tiring journey, he stays up all the night, alert to the promptings of the Holy Ghost. He is aware that only God is able to 'vnlouke' (162) this marvel. Erkenwald manages to explain the mystery not by the pride of his own learning and wisdom but by the grace of God which he humbly receives. It is divine grace and mercy that move through him when, after hearing the ancient judge's story, he sheds a compassionate tear upon his body. The baptismal water from his eyes softens the body's frozen, stony enclosure. The flow of the water parallels the flux of time. Within a fraction of a second the body decays, whereas the spirit is liberated to go to the heavenly banquet.

The examples of Daniel and Erkenwald demonstrate both the textuality of the marvellous as well as the limitations and transcendance of pure textuality in dealing with the marvellous. I have tried here to trace the impact of textuality upon the poetics of the 'Gawain'-poet. It may be even more interesting to examine his ways of departure from the model of the world and the literary work determined by a poetics of the text as nourished within the context of medieval *grammatica*. But the limits of this chapter do not allow me to pursue this path further.

NOTES

1. Eugene Vance, *From Topic to Tale: Logic and Narrativity in the Middle Ages*, Theory and History of Literature, vol. 47 (Minneapolis: University of Minnesota Press, 1987) pp. xxvi–xxxii.
2. He explores the impact of dialectics upon the concept of fictive truth, illustrating it by examples from *Erec* and *Yvain* (ibid., pp. 14–27); the development of the self in literature in the light of the logical distinction between substances and accidents (ibid., pp. 28–40); and the influence of the topical theory in logic upon narrative art (ibid., pp. 41–52).

3. All quotations from *Gawain* and from: *Sir Gawain and the Green Knight*, ed. J. R. R. Tolkien and E. V. Gordon, 2nd edn, rev. Norman Davis (Oxford: Clarendon Press, 1967), henceforth referred to as *TGD*.
4. John of Salisbury, *Metalogicon*, 1.13, ed. by Clement C. J. Webb (Oxford: Clarendon Press, 1929).
5. Quoted by Vance, *From Topic to Tale*, p. 3.
6. John of Salisbury, *Metalogicon*, 1.14.
7. See P. J. Frankis, '*Sir Gawain and the Green Knight*, 1.35: "With lel letteres loken"', *Notes and Queries*, vol. 206 (1961) pp. 329–30.
8. *TGD* prefer to read 'loken' as 'fastened' rather than 'linked' (op. cit., p. 72, nn. 35 and 36), yet other editors admit that deliberate ambiguity is possible here: cf. *The Poems of the Pearl Manuscript*, York Medieval Texts, 2nd series, ed. Malcolm Andrew and Ronald Waldron (London: Edward Arnold, 1978) p. 208, nn. 31–6, henceforth referred to as *AW*.
9. All quotations from *Cleanness* are from *AW*, ibid.
10. A view of medieval culture as determined by the model of the book has been proposed and developed by Jesse M. Gellrich, *The Idea of the Book in the Middle Ages: Language Theory, Mythology, and Fiction* (London: Cornell University Press, 1985) esp. pp. 29–50.
11. All quotations from *Patience* are from *AW*, op. cit.
12. Vance, *From Topic to Tale*, p. xxii.
13. John of Salisbury, *Policraticus*, ed. Clement C. J. Webb (Oxford: Clarendon Press, 1929). Quoted by Vance, ibid., p. 4.
14. Vance, *From Topic to Tale*, p. xxi.
15. Ibid., pp. 7–8.
16. For example, J. A. W. Bennett, *Middle English Literature*, ed. and completed by Douglas Gray; Oxford History of English Literature, vol. 1, part 2 (Oxford: Clarendon Press, 1986) p. 210.
17. SunHee Kim Gertz, 'Translatio studii et imperii: Sir Gawain as Literary Critic', *Semiotica*, vol. 63, nos 1/2 (1987) pp. 185–203, esp. p. 185.
18. W. A. Davenport, *The Art of the Gawain-Poet* (London: Athlone Press, 1978) pp. 66–76.
19. Cf. ibid., p. 71.
20. The poem is preserved in one manuscript: Brit. Mus. Harl. 2250, ff.72b–75a. I have used the following edition: *St Erkenwald: Select Early English Poems*, ed. Sir Israel Gollancz (London: Oxford University Press, 1932).
21. See, for example, *The Pearl-Poet: His Complete Works*, trans. and introd. by Margaret Williams (New York: Vintage Books, 1970) pp. 84–91; *The Owl and the Nightingale, Cleanness, St. Erkenwald*, trans. and introd. Brian Stone (Harmondsworth: Penguin, 1971) pp. 13–27. This generic designation has been questioned by Paul F. Reichardt, 'The Art and Meaning in the Middle English *St Erkenwald*', unpublished doctoral dissertation, Rice University, Abst.: *DAI*, 32/1971/, 2101–02A.
22. For a detailed discussion of the prologue of *Erkenwald* see Gollancz (ed.), *St Erkenwald*, pp. xii–xxv.
23. See S. L. Clark and Julian N. Wasserman, 'St Erkenwald's Spiritual Itinerary', *American Benedictine Review*, vol. 33 (Sept. 1982) pp. 257–69.

5

Structure and Meaning in *Guy of Warwick*

MALDWYN MILLS

Guy of Warwick (*GW*)[1] could fairly be described as the romance that has everything, with Guy himself embodying almost every important characteristic of a romance hero, and undergoing almost every kind of experience that a romance hero has a right to expect.[2] Beginning as a text-book case of the self-abasing and inexperienced courtly lover, he is soon obliged to move away from home to the proving grounds of tournaments and battles – it is not always easy to distinguish one from the other – where he forms new (essentially masculine) relationships, both supportive and hostile, and adopts new ideals of conduct. This part of the story goes on for so long, and generates such momentum of its own, that it is easy to lose sight of Felice as the ultimate motive force behind Guy's endeavours, but in the end he does come back to her, now so unmatchable in renown that he can no longer be refused. But only a fortnight after marriage, his whole life is changed by the realisation that his long service of Felice has caused both the neglect of his God and the slaying of his fellow men, and he sets off on a pilgrimage of atonement, in the course of which he champions the cause of more than one victim of oppression. On his final return to England, he achieves one last great combat of this kind (which frees the country from the threat of Danish rule), and then undergoes a final metamorphosis into a hermit. Finally, at the point of death (and only then), he is reunited with Felice, who does not long survive him. This already considerable range of romance themes and incidents is further extended by the incorporation into the romance of the story of Guy's son Reinbrun; in this the most notable addition to the stock of romance themes and incidents is an encounter with the Fairy Otherworld.[3]

In the past, *GW* has been classified both as a romance of the 'Matter of England' and as one of 'Exile and Return', and both labels

Structure and Meaning in 'Guy of Warwick' 55

are justified, the first by some of the locations, the second by the larger patterns of its story. But the same comprehensiveness that makes it so useful a guide to the preoccupations of romance in general makes it more difficult for the reader to detect in it the detailed symmetries of plan that distinguish the exile-and-return narrative structure. For a clear demonstration of these we must turn to the story of Horn as represented in its two earliest versions, the Anglo-Norman *Romance of Horn* (*RH*) and the early Middle English *King Horn* (*KH*),[4] which, for all their differences of nomenclature and scale, are both free from the kind of subordinate adventures that characterise *GW* and *Beves of Hamtoun* (*BH*). A summary account of the story which they tell is given below, with the distinctive enclosing of one pair of linked (that is, exile-and-return) components by another thrown into relief by the alphabetical symbols used.

A[1] After the death of his father, Horn is forced to leave his native land.

B[1] He arrives at a land whose king at first both protects and honours him, and to whom he gives military help in return. The king's daughter offers him her love, which he (finally) accepts; the king is informed that he has seduced her, and sends him into exile for a second time.

C   He comes to Ireland and again finds a protector in the king of the land, as well as a princess who offers him her love (which he rejects), and the opportunity of distinguishing himself in battle (which he takes). He leaves the country when he discovers that his real love is to be married to another.

B[2] He arrives in her father's land and wins her back by force of arms, then returns to his own country.

A[2] There he overthrows the usurper who had slain his father, but is warned in a dream that his wife has been forcibly married to the man who had earlier betrayed him to her father.

B[3] Once again he breaks up a wedding feast and this time kills the traitor.

Here the only complication of what would otherwise be a wholly symmetrical pattern relates to B[2] and B[3], the second of which is at once the doublet and the necessary complement of the first, in that it not only again sets right an injustice perpetrated in B[1], but does so in an absolutely conclusive way.[5] Even in the most tightly structured of romance narratives, it seems, the urge to give a second airing to the exciting business of securing the love and person of the heroine might prevail over strict economy of narrative. In the less tightly structured romances of Beves of Hamtoun and of Guy, such duplication involves not a single episode, but a complete sequence of such.

Such elaborate duplication is not, of course, confined to Old French and Middle English romances of English heroes. Within the medieval period a particularly striking example is found in the Middle High German *König Rother*, whose eponymous hero has twice to undertake the abduction of the lady chosen as his wife from her father, the king of Constantinople.[6] More recently, a number of examples of such fresh narrative beginnings are found in Russian fairy-tales,[7] of which Vladimir Propp noted that

> A tale may have another misfortune in store for the hero: a villain may appear once again, may seize whatever Ivan has obtained. ... In a word, an initial villainy is repeated, sometimes in the same forms as in the beginning, and sometimes in other forms which are new for a given tale. With this a new story commences.[8]

He called extended doublets of this kind 'moves', and the label is a handy one, even though – as he himself recognised – it is not always easy to decide whether we have before us two moves within a single 'stretched' tale, or two distinct tales that have been yoked together as one. He also noted that each of the moves of a fully developed 'two-move' tale, will contain some elements ('functions of dramatis personae') that will not be found in the other,[9] and that the same character may fulfil quite different roles in each. These points are also quite clearly exemplified in *BH* – the one 'Matter of England' romance to enjoy a shelf-life equal to that of *GW*, and which – to judge from the number of surviving copies – actually surpassed it in popularity, within both the medieval and the early modern period.[10]

In marked contrast to *Horn*, the names of most of the characters are identical in the Anglo-Norman and Middle English texts of *BH*, and the summary which follows (based upon the first of these) is thus more specific than that given for *RH/KH*. But this time the application of the same alphabetical symbol to diverse narrative components may signify only the presence of the same dominant character(s) in these, and not of the same geographical locations as well.

First move (*BH* I)

A^1 Beves is sold into slavery after the murder of his father by his wife's lover, the emperor of Germany.

B^1 At the Armenian court he accepts the love of the princess Josian and defeats her father's enemy Brademond, but is sent to the latter to be killed after he has been accused to the king of seducing Josian.

C^1 In Damascus, Brademond has him thrown into a dungeon. Josian is told that Beves has married the king of England's daughter.

B^2 She herself is married to Yvor of Mombraunt but with the help of magic preserves her virginity.

C^2 After seven years' imprisonment, Beves kills his gaolers and escapes. After various adventures he comes to Jerusalem, where the patriarch exhorts him to marry only a virgin.

B^3 Disguished as a palmer he comes to Mombraunt, where he is given alms by Josian. He escapes with her, and later defeats – and takes into his service – the giant Ascopart. They come to Cologne, where Josian is baptised by the bishop (Beves's uncle), and then left in Ascopart's keeping.

A^2 Beves returns to Southampton to lay claim to his heritage.

B^4 In his absence, Josian is trapped into marriage with earl Miles, but strangles him on their wedding night. Sentenced to be burnt, she is rescued by Beves and Ascopart.

A^3 Beves defeats the emperor, and has him executed (his mother is killed at the same time). He is married to Josian, and succeeds to his father's earldom.

Second move (*BH* II)

A^1 After his horse has accidentally killed the king's son, Beves goes into exile with Josian, Terri (the son of his one-time tutor, Saber) and Ascopart.

B^1 Ascopart changes sides once again, and carries off Josian after she has given birth to Guy and Miles; Beves and Terri find foster parents for these.

C Beves wins the hand of a princess in tournament, but is allowed seven years' grace before consummating the marriage.

B^2 Saber finds and kills Ascopart, and wanders with Josian for seven years, at the end of which they are reunited with Beves. The princess then marries Terri.

A[2] After various adventures, Beves returns to England. He then returns to Armenia with Josian, where in due time they die together.

A comparison of these moves with each other (and with those of *RH/KH*) shows how the initial displacement of the hero in each may be promoted by very different kinds of incident and detail. The first exile of Beves, like that of Horn, is provoked by the deliberate slaying of the hero's father and usurpation of his land; the second, by the accidental killing of the king's son. On the other hand, the same character may stand in a quite different relationship to the hero and heroine in each;[11] Ascopart, their well-meaning if incompetent helper for much of the first, becomes the agent of their principal enemy in the second. Finally we may note, as a feature which sets both moves apart from anything in *RH/KH* and *GW*, the much more obvious and dynamic involvement of the heroine in the action. In the first move, indeed, she is foregrounded to such an extent that the encounter between the hero and an amorous Other Woman found at the heart of the major action-sequences of both *RH/KH* and *GW* is deferred to the second move, being replaced in *BH* I by the actual imprisonment of the hero, and the fictitious claim, on the part of Josian's father, that Beves has got involved with somebody else.

When, finally, we turn to *GW*, we find that the constituent moves of the story have been increased to three,[12] and that the patterns of all but the first of these are even less obviously symmetrical than that of *BH* I. The third move is particularly difficult to relate to the exile-and-return structure, and the initial impetus to the action is significantly different from in the first two: where they, like their counterparts in *König Rother*, were set in motion by the hero's desire for a woman, this is dominated by Guy's wish to be reconciled with God. What is more, this, the concluding part of Guy's story is interrupted by an account of the birth and abduction of his son Reinbrun, and of Heralt's search for him.[13]

The most substantial move in Guy's own story is the second, where, to an even greater extent than in *BH* I, the underlying symmetry can be perceived only in the recurrence of certain major characters: of Otes of Pavia, the implacable and treacherous enemy of Guy, and of Terri of Worms, who appears first as the hero's worthy opponent but later becomes his sworn brother. By contrast, the geographical locations in which these characters flourish are wholly diverse, with B[1] set principally in Louvain, and B[2] in Lorraine. And as in *BH* I the number of disparate geographical settings is further increased by the inclusion of other episodes of a self-contained or transitional kind, some of which have motifs or themes in common with *BH*.[14]

First move (*GW* I: E 209–1054; A 235–1130; c 177–792)

A[1] Guy, the son of duke Roalt's steward, falls helplessly in love with the duke's daughter Felice; after long entreaty she concedes that she will grant him her love once he has proved himself as a knight.

C He leaves for France with his tutor Heralt and two other companions, and distinguishes himself in a tournament at Rouen called by the daughter of the German emperor Reiner, Blancheflor, whose love constitutes one of the prizes offered the victor.

A[2] He returns to England to claim the love of Felice.

Second move (*GW* II: E 1055–7562; A 1131–7306, stanzas 3–19; c 793–7116)

A[1] Felice tells him that she will grant him her love only when he has proved himself the best of all knights.

B[1] Again he crosses the sea; again he distinguishes himself in a series of tournaments. After one held near Benevento he is ambushed on the orders of duke Otes (whom he had earlier wounded in Rouen) and only he and Heralt survive the attack. On Heralt's advice he later goes to help Seguin, the duke of Louvain against the emperor Reiner; the most powerful champion of the latter is Terri, but Otes is also fighting on his side, and violently opposes the reconciliation that Guy finally effects between the two former enemies.

C Guy next goes to the help of Hernis the emperor of Constantinople who offers him his daughter in marriage if he frees his land from the forces of the sultan. Guy does this but is hated by the emperor's steward Morgadur, who slanders him and kills his pet lion. Guy kills him in his turn, refuses to marry the daughter, and leaves.

B[2] In Lorraine he rescues Terri and his mistress Osille from malefactors; he and Terri become sworn companions, and help Albri (Terri's father) against Loher (Osille's father), and Otes (now her intended husband). Heralt and Terri are taken prisoner by treachery; Guy rescues the latter and at last kills

Otes; he and Terri return to Lorraine. While hunting a boar in Brabant, Guy kills a young knight, and has to fight with the vassals of Florentin, the knight's father.

A² Despite Terri's entreaties, he returns to England where he kills a dragon that is devastating Northumberland. After visiting Wallingford (where he learns that his father is dead) he returns to Warwick, where he is at long last married to Felice, and begets a child on her.

Third move (*GW* III: E 7563–8974, 9393–11412; A stanzas 20–281; c 7117–8396, 8745–10520)

A¹ Only a fortnight after the marriage, Guy repents that he has so long neglected God through his excessive devotion to Felice, and after telling her to entrust to Heralt the child that she has conceived, sets out on a pilgrimage of atonement.

B¹ After visiting Jerusalem and Bethlehem, he successfully fights for king Triamour against the sultan's gigantic champion, and by his victory secures the release of the Christian prisoners of the king, and access to the Holy Places for all pilgrims.

C While travelling through Germany on his way back to England, Guy meets with Terri and defends his cause against the steward Berard. Despite Terri's entreaties, Guy refuses to stay with him but returns to England.

B² There he meets king Athelstan at Winchester, and averts the threat of Danish rule by defeating their gigantic champion, Colebrant.

A³ He then goes to Warwick where he receives food and drink from the hands of Felice without being recognised.

Epilogue (E 11413–11656; A stanzas 282–99; c 10521–786)
Still incognito, he takes up residence in a hermitage to the north of the city, where he serves God assiduously. When death is imminent he sends a messenger to Felice with the ring that she had given him when he had left her for the Holy Land; she reaches him when he is on the point of death, and dies soon afterwards. Hearing of Guy's death, Terri asks for and obtains his body, and has it buried in Lorraine.

For all their diversity in scale and range of detailed content, the first two moves are clearly variants of a common sequence, each of which has at its centre an encounter between the hero and a woman who, to a greater or lesser degree, constitutes a threat to his relationship with Felice. In contrast to Josian, the latter remains fixed in one place throughout, and can invade this central part of the story only by being called to mind by the narrator, by the hero himself or by some other character. *GW* III, however, is so different in its inception that – even after we have excluded from consideration the beginnings of the Reinbrun story – we can find very little trace of the characteristic 'exile-and-return' pattern here, although it has its own kind of symmetry in having as the first and third of its major episodes two combats with giants which have larger implications than the freeing of an estimable character from the threat of death. On the whole, however, the motivic and thematic links with *GW* II are more persuasive than the structural, as when both the Alexandrian king and his Saracen champion in B^1 recall the damage that Guy had done in the Constantinople scenes of *GW* II (E 8285–96, 8606–10; A stanzas 82–3, 111–12; c 7803–812, 8090–4), or when, in C, Terri recalls the feud between Guy and Otes (E 9487–94; A stanza 147; c 8835–40).

But where *GW* is most crucially innovative, in both its first and second moves, is in the way it presents the outer (A-)components of the Matter of England pattern. On his first appearance in the story, Guy – in marked contrast to both Horn and Beves – is dominated not by any male aggressor, but by the lady with whom he falls hopelessly in love (the much less dominating equivalents of this character do not, of course, appear in *RH/KH* and *BH* until B^1, after the first exile of the hero). Equally novel are the haughty and demanding character of this lady and the corresponding meekness and subservience of the hero. But, as we shall see, these differences co-exist with some equally impressive similarities, some on the surface of the narrative, some a little below it.

At the beginning of the romance, the hero's father, Sequard, is certainly spared the harassment and final violent death that his counterparts in the other romances endure; for want of any information to the contrary, we assume that his death, when it did come, was a natural one. But Guy, in addition to his sufferings for love, is at this same point in the story not without his own fears of meeting a violent end from a powerful antagonist, although the danger is more hypothetical than real, comes not from any foreign usurper but from count Roalt, the heroine's father, and is directly bound up with his presumptuously misdirected affection:

> *Si jo l'amasse e il le seust,*
> *Et il puis ateindre me peust,*
> *Arder me freit u decoler,*
> *Pendre en halt u en mer noier.*
>   (E 259–62)

[If I were to love her and he found out about it, and if he were then able to lay hands on me, he would have me burnt or beheaded; hung on high, or drowned in the sea.]

Much the same view is expressed by Felice, once Guy has confessed his love to her:

> *Se jol vois dire a mun pere,*
> *Des menbres te freit desfaire,*
> *E a chevals trestuit detraire,*
> *Par quei serreient chastiez*
> *De la folie plusurs assez*
> *De faire itel deshonur*
> *A la fille lur seignur.*[15]
>   (E 364–70)

[If I were to tell my father of this, he would have you torn limb from limb; drawn to pieces by horses, so that many others would be warned against the madness of behaving so dishonourably to the daughter of their lord.]

In fact, the real counterpart to Roalt in *RH* and *BH* are the fathers who further on in the story (in B¹) are angered with the hero through the false report that he has seduced (and not, like Guy, only prospectively 'disparaged') their daughters, even though they still do not proceed against Horn or Beves with anything like the violence that Guy imagines Roalt will use against him.[16] In any case, the baleful hypotheses of Guy and Felice are never put to the test; Roalt has so little idea of Guy's state of mind at this point that he unwittingly furthers his cause by making him a knight, and by the time he really is aware of Guy's feelings for his daughter, the hero has become the most eligible bachelor imaginable, who has refused offers of marriage from ladies greatly superior in rank to Felice (E 7481–5; A stanza 10; c 7039–42). And even at the beginning of the romance, his general behaviour is of a kind that makes it difficult to imagine so violent a reaction to Guy's pleadings;[17] although it is easy to see how a character as inexperienced and confused as the young Guy might have thought such a reaction likely. That Felice should have had the same idea, however, could reflect (at the very least) some less than courtly tendencies in her own nature, that are evidenced by the heroines of the two other romances, though not in so extreme a form.

This brings us to her behaviour as a whole during the two interviews with Guy in *GW* I, and the third – even more crucial – in *GW* II. As in their counterparts in *BH*, the attitudes of both hero and heroine are progressively modified in the course of these, with the initial hostility of one of the parties (Beves, Felice) gradually overcome by the insistence of the other. But the roles have been reversed, with Guy now the one who initiates the courtship, Felice the one who holds back. The version of *GW* stands much closer, in fact, to some of the encounters of ill-matched lovers that are set out in the dialogues of Andreas Capellanus,[18] and closest of all to the opening sections of the romance of *Amadas et Ydoine*, already noted as particularly akin to *GW* in its opening scenes. And all these distinctive features in her characterisation are of course reinforced by the fact that her first (and most impressive) appearance in the story is now in A[1] (and not B[1] as with Rimenild and Josian), so that (theoretically, at least) she dominates the hero's thoughts and actions from the beginning of his story.

Altogether, it is a situation of intriguing complexity, with Felice exercising over Guy both of the forms of power (active and passive) that could be denoted by the Anglo-Norman and Middle English word *da(u)ngier*. Her disdain and refusal to give any kind of encouragement at all to Guy bring to mind the conventionally 'feminine' senses of the word that are listed under OED 2 and MED 4(a): retreating behind an established position of superiority; holding back; discouraging. But like the personification of the lady's 'Danger' in the *Romance of the Rose*,[19] her discouragement of the hero has also its positive and aggressive side, which is of course reinforced by her evocation of the physical violence that her father might use against Guy. But more interesting still as an effect peculiar to *GW* is the way in which all the features defined above serve to link Felice with those male tyrants of *RH* and *BH* who are a real threat to the hero's life, and against whom he must finally be avenged.

One of her principal functions within the narrative is precisely equivalent to theirs: like the Saracen king of *RH* or the German emperor of *BH* it is she and no one else who is the direct cause of his exile. Indeed, by surviving the first move of the romance unscathed, she is in a position to bring about his exile in the second move as well; there is no need for a new antagonist to be created, as in *BH* II – all she has to do is to restate in a more extreme form the terms she had imposed upon the hero in *GW* I.[20] In consequence she is, in both these moves, at once the hero's (as yet unattainable) 'Good' and the 'Evil' that forces him away from all that had previously been dear to him. Or, if we prefer to use Propp's terms for the alternative ways of setting in motion the action of a tale, she is at once a 'Lack' as far as the hero is concerned (which must later be made good), and an agent of 'Villainy' (which he may later avenge). In relation to these two aspects of Felice, Guy becomes at once a 'Seeker Hero' and a 'Victimized Hero'.[21] But *GW* differs radically from such Russian Tales and Middle High German romances as are set in motion by the hero's 'Lack' of a necessary bride in the fact that its hero journeys to foreign parts not in order to find and abduct the lady he desires – Felice is on the premises already, and would prove highly resistant to carrying off – but to achieve a degree of prowess that will satisfy even her exacting nature. Any other lady whom he may encounter during his long apprenticeship in tournament and war (Blancheflor in *GW* I, Laurette/Clarice in *GW* II), while superficially a reward for prowess, is really only a stumbling block in the way of his achieving the supreme prize (of Felice's love).

Complex too is the role of Felice at the other end of the principal move of the romance. At the same point in *RH* and *BH* the hero's revenge on the usurper and recovery of his heritage cancel out the act of 'Villainy' that had first pushed him into exile; here his marriage to the heroine makes good the 'Lack' that had earlier dominated his life.[22] Felice now whole-heartedly accepts Guy as her equal (E 7439–46; A stanza 6; c 6997–7004), but memories of her older self have not been entirely erased for Guy and, under pressure, they come back and play their part in motivating his third period of exile.

It has long been recognised that the framing structure and pietistic tone of *GW* III owe much to the popular life of Saint Alexis[23] whose hero, after marrying in deference to the wishes of his father, tells his wife on their first night together that his whole mind is turned to God, and leaves her for the Holy Land where he serves God in total poverty for seventeen years. Guy is not quite as abrupt – he and Felice enjoy a fortnight as man and wife before he experiences the spiritual illumination that changes his life – but, unlike Alexis, he has a past which must be atoned for, as well as a future

Structure and Meaning in 'Guy of Warwick'

that is to be wholly devoted to the service of God. And Felice is deeply implicated in it:

> Puis que primes vus amai,
> Tant malz pur vus sufferz ai,
> Ne qui que home fust unc né
> Qui tantes dolurs ait enduré
> Pur une femme cum jo ai pur tei.
> Pur vu ai fait maint grant desrei,
> Homes ocis, destruites citez,
> Arses abbeies de plusurs regnez.
> (E 7603–10)

[Since first I came to love you I have suffered so many evils on your account, that I do not believe that the man was ever born who has endured such hardships for a woman as I have for you. I have caused havoc for your sake: with men killed, cities destroyed, and abbeys burnt in various kingdoms.]

All of which makes the beginning of *GW* III distinctly more complex than at first appears. In addition to being very obviously dominated by a new sense of 'Lack' (this time, of God's forgiveness), that leads to another long period of exile and of striving, it also involves a reaction to the 'Villainy' inherent in or provoked by the past behaviour of the lady to Guy. The reproaches that are most explicitly laid at her door – the death and destruction that Guy had brought about in her search for renown – are actually the ones that seem most off the mark. The fighting in *GW* II in which the really heavy loss of life took place was neither immediately nor explicitly undertaken for the sake of Felice;[24] here the advice or approval of Heralt, Guy's companion was much more to the fore (E 1747–58; A 1907–12; c 1543–54, and E 2937–8; A 2855–6; c 2767–8). And the same fighting was in any case viewed at the time as being both 'just' on its own terms, and laudable in its final results: there were undeniably fewer Lombards or Saracens around by the time it was over.

What was more obviously reprehensible in the earlier conduct of Felice was what she made Guy himself suffer, both at the beginning of his story (in terms of mental and psychosomatic anguish) and further on in it (in terms of physical hardship). Both of these consequences of loving her could be implied by E 7604–6, quoted above, and her imperious treatment of Guy's early pleas for mercy is now strikingly balanced by his own inflexibility when she laments and swoons before him for a second time (E 7687–93; much softened in the ME versions); this time it is Guy who imposes the conditions, and Felice who must submit to them. Both these scenes are followed by a long absence of the hero in foreign parts, with the heroine firmly fixed at home. But this time there will be no later reunion of the kind found at the end of *GW* II (even though one is vaguely suggested in E 7685–6), and Felice becomes more sedentary than ever through being pregnant with Guy's child.[25] For all his new-found penitential anguish, Guy is once again physically free to wander at large, meet up again with old friends and enemies (or their kinsfolk), and keep the story going for longer than one might earlier have supposed possible.

NOTES

1. Reference will be made throughout to the Anglo-Norman version of British Library MS Additional 38662 (= E), which forms the basis of A. Ewert's edition, *Gui de Warewic*, Les Classiques français du Moyen Age, 74, 75 (Paris, 1932-3), and to the two most substantial Middle English versions (which go back to a revised version of E). These last are contained in the Auchinleck MS (= A), and in Cambridge University Library MS Ff.ii.38 (= c), and are set out, respectively, in *The Romance of Guy of Warwick*, ed. J. Zupitza, Early English Text Society, Extra Series, 42, 49, 59 (1883–91), and *The Romance of Guy of Warwick: The Second or 15th-Century Version*, ed. J. Zupitza, Early English Text Society, Extra Series, 25, 26 (1875–6).
2. Appropriately, the final chapter in V. B. Richmond's *The Popularity of Middle English Romance* (Bowling Green's Ohio: Bowling Green University Popular Press, 1975) is devoted to *GW*.
3. In E and in C (but not A, where the material has been radically rearranged) Reinbrun's story is told in two instalments of which the second alone is concerned with his adventures as a knight; see note 13 below.
4. For *RH* see *The Romance of Horn by Thomas*, ed. M. K. Pope, Anglo-Norman Text Society, 9–10 (1955); revised and completed T. B. W. Reid, 12–13 (1964); for *KH*, *King Horn*, ed. R. Allen (New York: Garland, 1984). A third medieval text is *Horn Childe and Maiden Rimnild*, ed. M. Mills, Middle English Texts (Heidelberg: Carl Winter, 1988); here the locations are very specifically English in the first part of the narrative, but the overall symmetry of plan is less clear-cut.
5. This duplication is examined in detail by Susan Wittig, in her *Stylistic and Narrative Structures in the Middle English Romances* (Austin: University of Texas Press, 1978) pp. 141–3.

Structure and Meaning in 'Guy of Warwick'   67

6. C. Gellinek indeed has tried (unconvincingly) to present *RH* as a whole as parallel in its structure to *König Rother*, by taking A^1 and B^1 as the first move of *RH*, and components C to B^3 as the second one (*König Rother* (Bern, 1968) pp. 49–52).
7. Notably those tales collected by A. Afanasev. The most accessible selection of these in English is in the translation of Norbert Guterman, *Russian Fairy Tales* (New York: Pantheon, 1973).
8. Vladimir Propp, *Morphology of the Folktale*, trans. Laurence Scott, 2nd edn (Austin: University of Texas Press, 1968) p. 58. While it would be inappropriate to apply Propp's scheme as a whole to the Matter of England romances, individual points of his terminology or detailed analysis are very useful in attempting to analyse them.
9. Ibid., pp. 94–6; 101–3.
10. *BH* was the only ME romance to be repeatedly printed in something like its original form after 1575: see R. S. Crane, *The Vogue of Medieval Chivalric Romance During the English Renaissance* (Menasha, Wisconsin: University of Wisconsin Press, 1919) p. 7. It also survived in substantially more printed copies than *GW*, even if we count among these last a number of late rewritings of the story (of which the most notable and influental was the 1608 stanzaic poem by Samuel Rowlands). For the ME versions of *BH*, see E. Kölbing, *The Romance of Sir Beues of Hamtoun*, Early English Text Society, Extra Series, 46, 48, 65 (1885, 1886, 1894). For the Anglo-Norman version, see A. Stimming, *Der Anglonormannische Boeve de Haumtone* (Halle, 1899).
11. 'One and the same person can play one role in the first move and quite another role in the second (a devil as helper in the first move, but as villain in the second, etc.)' (Propp, *Morphology of the Folktale*, p. 86).
12. In the past a bipartite division of the part of *GW* relating to Guy himself has been usual: see, for example, Dieter Mehl, *The Middle English Romances of the Thirteenth and Fourteenth Centuries* (London: Routledge & Kegan Paul, 1968) pp. 224f.
13. These take up E 8975–9392 and c 8397–744, and (after Guy's death) E 11657–12926 and c 10787–11976. In the Auchinleck MS Reinbrun's story does not interrupt that of Guy, but is set out as a separate and homogeneous tail-rhyme romance that immediately follows *GW* III on f. 167rb. This story is, very broadly, again one of exile-and-return, but without any love-interest at all.
14. Two of the most striking similarities involve the first move of *BH* and the third of *GW*. In these the disguised hero meets with his companion (named Terri in both romances) and with his lady (who charitably gives him food). In both he preserves his incognito.
15. Further gloomy fears are expressed by Guy in E 557–60; A 587–90, c 309–11, and by Felice in E 586–92; A 631–6; c 327–9. The alleged coincidence of the views of father and daughter on the matter recalls Propp's claim that in the Russian fairy-tales, the sphere of action of a princess ('a sought-for person') and of her father are the same; he goes on to note that between them they may, among other functions, assign difficult tasks to the hero (with the father rather more likely to do this because of his innate hostility towards the suitor) (Propp, *Morphology of the Folktale*, pp. 79–80).

16. In *Amis and Amiloun*, however, the duke very nearly kills the first of the eponymous heroes after learning that he has slept with his daughter (ed. McE. Leach, Early English Text Society, Original Series 203 (1937) lines 805–16).
17. The lady's father is never evoked as a source of danger in the very closely related opening scenes of the Anglo-Norman and Continental French romance of *Amadas et Ydoine*, ed. J. R. Reinhard, Les Classiques français du Moyen Age, 51 (Paris, 1974).
18. Although none of the eight specimen dialogues given by Andreas involves characters of the same relative status as Guy and Felice; the closest we get is in the second and third, where the male suppliant is of the middle class, and the lady of the (higher) nobility: Andreas Capellanus, *The Art of Courtly Love*, trans. J. J. Parry (New York: Columbia University Press, 1941) pp. 44–62.
19. See particularly lines 3130–8 (*The Riverside Chaucer*, gen. ed. L. D. Benson (Oxford: Oxford University Press, 1988) p. 720).
20. Her principal reason is that if she granted him her love immediately he would become uxorious and slothful (E 1061–6; A 1137–42; c 799–804); such consequences of marriage are real enough in such romances as Chrétien's *Erec*, and her reaction is sensible enough in itself. But in the context of *GW* it is hard not to feel that the lady is moving the goalposts.
21. Propp, *Morphology of the Folktale*, pp. 36-7.
22. As in the other two romance stories, this follows the hero's acquisition of lands previously held by his father. In *RH* and *BH* such lands had fallen into the hands of the usurper, and so constitute another major 'Lack' that has to be made good by the hero; here the motif is much more lightly stressed, as the domain comes effortlessly to Guy as his father's heir, and he at once bestows it upon Heralt (E 7411–22; A stanzas 3–4; c 6967–82).
23. *La Vie de Saint Alexis*, ed. G. Paris, Les Classiques français du Moyen Age, 4 (Paris, 1917).
24. More directly related to Felice and her demands is an anti-feminist passage that forms part of Guy's lament for companions slain in an ambush mounted to avenge his success in a tournament at Benevento (A 1557–66; c 1155–68). But while this passage is found in all the surviving English versions, and about half the French ones, it was not present in the original Anglo-Norman text: see Ewert (ed.), *Gui de Warewic* I.xvi and II.193.
25. Her condition has the narrative function of preventing her from committing suicide: in a violent piece of prophetic imagination that recalls A 405–12, she images that such an act will be construed as murder on her husband's part (E 7753–70; A stanza 35; c 7289–306).

6

Women and Chaucer's Providence: *The Clerk's Tale* and *The Knight's Tale*

CATHERINE LA FARGE

Emelye and Griselde have long been experienced as problems by the modern reader. Emelye is felt to be too perfunctory a heroine to motivate *The Knight's Tale*; Griselde's perfection often seems more of a trial than her husband's cruelty. Students are advised that a proper understanding of medieval narrative and of Chaucer's Boethianism will dispel these initial impressions.[1] Allowing fourteenth-century writers little of the latitude we readily grant those of the twentieth, we are in danger of eradicating from our sight Chaucer's most penetrating investigations of contemporary social and religious beliefs in the name of correct historical understanding. This chapter will argue for a less dutiful approach.

In both *The Knight's Tale* and *The Clerk's Tale*, what happens to a woman can be read as an example – in both cases a rather extreme example – of the destiny of humankind. This destiny is, for much of each tale, apparently disastrous but in the end apparently favourably resolved. A powerful ruler is the immediate, visible instigator of what happens, a leader who, it is suggested, is the surrogate for the superhuman force of destiny. At the same time, great emphasis is placed upon salient qualities of this man which are precisely counter to such a role. Each ending then asks that the immediate suffering and the seeming injustice with which suffering is meted out be interpreted as belonging to the flawless purposes of Providence rather than to the ulterior, mundane or irrational needs of the human lord. Neither woman is made attractive or explicable to the reader, whereas the man who wields the power is comparatively understandable and viewed at close quarters. These tales, I shall argue, merge the uses of power in such ways that traditional analogies and expectations of justice – familial, political and divine – are seen as strained and dubious.

Central to Chaucer's methods is his employment of disparate fictive modes. The insistence that medieval stories are not peopled by characters of a modern sort should not prevent us from noticing the heterogeneity of modes within a single tale and the dynamics such differences set in motion. Theseus's healthy-minded sampling of the service of the gods in turn and his tolerant amusement at the lovers well befits a type of Middle Age,[2] but his comparatively complex construction also places him in a special relation both to the reader and to the other figures in the tale. His being moved to pity for the Theban widows, his keen sense of pleasure, his 'busy cure' to the building of the theatre and burying of Arcite, and his frequent revising of his own decisions provide readers with ample material, of a kind not on offer for others in the tale, for arguing his possible virtues and limitations (A 953, 1673ff, 1881ff, 2853)[3].

A notable aspect of Theseus's behaviour is his indulgence in his own freedom to do as he pleases. The form which this freedom characteristically takes is that 'he wol his firste purpos modifye' (2542) or, put less pompously, he keeps changing his mind. When Theseus has killed Creon and taken Thebes, the narrator says that he slept on the battlefield 'and dide with al the contree as hym leste' (1004). One of the things that it pleases him to do is to pick up two handsome young Thebans off the field, deciding to keep them caged like a couple of rare birds, 'perpetuelly – he nolde no raunsoun' (1024). As it happens, Arcite – but not Palamon – is let out 'on pull'; he has an old friend who moves in the right circles. Later, having sworn by Mars that both must die, Theseus then somewhat repetitively announces instead that 'ye shul noon oother ende with me maken, / That *oon* of yow ne shal be deed or taken. / . . . This is youre ende and youre conclusioun' (1865–6, 1869; cf. 1857–59). But at the last minute he has a herald announce from a scaffold that he has changed his mind yet again and that *neither* is to die:

> The lord hath of his heigh discrecioun
> Considered that it were destruccioun
> To gentil blood to fighten in the gyse
> Of mortal bataille now in this emprise.
> (A 2537–40)

A question mark hangs over much of what it pleases Theseus to do. If his 'heigh discrecioun' partakes of the wisdom and mercy of Providence, how is it that Arcite's blood, once again chosen without desert, is mortally shed anyway? There is something playfully useless about Theseus's projects and inspirations: they can be read as the decadent exercise of power and expenditure of wealth simply because they are there and at his disposal. A glimpse of the accounts – the explicit detailing of payment in food and wages and the apparently vulgar statement that the shrine of Mars cost a 'fother' (a cartload) of gold – calls attention to the responsibilities of the rich to make their schemes work (1881–1908).

Suspicions are augmented rather than allayed by a narratorial sleight of hand which makes it sound as if Theseus is Providence itself. Palamon and Arcite ankle-deep in blood, the narrator says:

> And in this wise I lete hem fightynge dwelle,
> And *forth I wole of Theseus yow telle.*

Immediately, as if he is doing as he said, he continues:

> The destinee, ministre general,
> That executeth in the world over al
> The purveiaunce that God hath seyn biforn,
> So strong it is that, though the world had sworn
> The contrarie of a thyng by ye or nay,
> Yet somtyme it shal fallen on a day
> That falleth nat eft withinne a thousand yeer.
> For certeinly, oure appetites heer,
> Be it of werre, or pees, or hate, or love,
> Al is this reuled by the sighte above.

He then goes on in the next line:

> *This mene I now by myghty Theseus,*
> That for to hunten is so desirus,
> And namely at the grete hert in May,
> That in his bed ther daweth hym no day
> That he nys clad, and redy for to ryde
> With hunte and horn and houndes hym bisyde.
>   (1663–78)

Modern editions and some of the surviving manuscripts, including Ellesmere and Hengwrt, reinforce the digressive aspect of the destiny passage by bracketing it off in a separate verse paragraph.[4] But

'This mene I', a phrase common in explications of figurative and allegorical passages as well as in simple narrative,[5] has a Janus quality here, its backward glance strengthened by synonymy ('strong' destiny, 'myghty' Theseus) and by the possibility of reading 'so' (1674) and 'that' (1676) as correlatives.

The same blur of Theseus and destiny occurs when the duke says that he will give Emelye to whichever lover wins, 'to whom that *Fortune* yeveth *so fair a grace*'; thirteen lines later the narrative remarks on the general rejoicing 'Whan *Theseus* hath doon *so fair a grace*' (1861, 1974). Theseus devises the theatre like God creating the world (a project to which he himself will refer somewhat later when discoursing upon the consequences of his own): 'Whan it was doon, hym lyked wonder weel', and on the great day itself 'Duc Theseus was at a wyndow set, / Arrayed right as he were a god in trone' (2092, 2528–9).

But the final merging of Theseus and the forces of Providence is the most discomforting because it hinges precisely upon the problem of Providence's inscrutable, or Theseus's not so inscrutable, purposes. Palamon is sent for; it was *'unwiste of hym* what was the cause and *why'*, but he does as he is told and comes along in haste, still wearing the mourning occasioned by Theseus's last idea (2976). Theseus, who does know why (and we have been informed of his ulterior political motives), then launches into his celebrated speech, saying that the First Mover way of lofty purpose – 'heigh was his entente' – when he first made the world: *'wel wiste he why*, and what thereof he mente' (2990). In between these two linked statements comes a characteristic description of Theseus playing things just as he pleases. Everyone is gathered, and the duke allows a hush to fall over the proceedings. Then 'his eyen sette he ther *as was his lest'* (2989, 2984). The familiar phrasing, the theatricality of gesture, the very triviality of this display of power not only dramatise the gap between the helplessness of the political subject and the freedom of the lord but also call into question the god-like qualities upon which it is supposedly based.

The stumbling block to a Boethian defence of Theseus is that the recurrent figure of the duke as God is accompanied so indefatigably by the figure of the ruler who does as he likes and changes his mind. If there is one thing which for Boethius sums up the difference between Providence and humankind it is that Providence never changes. The distinction made is one between the infinite motion of temporal beings and the simplicity and never-ending present of God's purposes.[6]

An examination of Boethius's metaphorical language reveals how precisely Theseus lays claim to these incompatible attributes. *The Consolation of Philosophy* employs that incalculably influential Platonic metaphor which equates seeing with knowing; the divine intelligence differs from the temporal as sight from touch. The latter, 'in coming close to and grasping [e.g. a sphere], perceives its roundness part by part', its imperfection, therefore, the result of intimacy, whereas divine knowledge is comprehensive and stable because it 'remains at a distance' 'as though *looking down from above*' (v.iv, pp. 157, 159). Theseus straddles this metaphorical divide: the tale goes out of its way to bestow upon him both the height from which he indeed looks down and an intimacy of characterisation which mitigates his figural aspects. The hallmarks of this intimacy are recognition and recognisability: with a mixture of emotions he sees his former self in Palamon and Arcite; he is easily moved, tolerant, jovial in the ordinary as well as the etymological sense, one who is in touch with and savours the variety of life and whose mode of fictional existence makes a bid for readerly recognition. This specificity creates a tension: we are to perceive him as distant and godly, yet familiar and fluid in mood.

It will be argued that Theseus is after all human, and pagan to boot. He modifies justice with mercy, a god-like aspiration, but unlike God, being unable to see and control all eventualities, he can only fail. If the tale gives an oddly high profile to his failure, the defence runs, this is because of Chaucer's strong sense of anachronism and his interest in the case of the virtuous pagan who, given his situation in history, sees through a particularly dark glass.[7]

The problem with such pleading is that the tale gratuitously characterises Theseus as enjoying change as if for its own sake. Alongside the lovers' cries of pain, this relish – for instance, his 'appetit' for hunting and for the springtime weather, serving Diana after Mars – seems pointless and self-indulgent rather than the sad limitation of being human. Such exercisings of pleasurable liberty, and the moments where 'heigh entente' is particularly invisible to the reader, provide an unfavourable context for the moments when common profit is indeed at stake. Peace between Athens and Thebes is a good idea, but by that stage the ground has been prepared for a wary reception of Theseus's inspirations. His failure to mention his political motives amid the pious Boethian formulae do nothing to avert such worries. Even his profound grief at Arcite's death fails to erase the sense that his power and zest for the management of human lives outstrips the reliability of his judgement. The reader is inclined to feel that if this is Theseus's best, his best is not good enough, even for a pagan.

Emelye, meanwhile, seems to be jerked through the tale like the last in a child's string of mechanical quacking ducks; she is tacked on to the end of sentences as an afterthought, doing whatever is expected of the ladies at the moment. She is syntactically expendable: Ypolita is brought to Athens – *'and eek hir yonge suster Emelye'* (871). Theseus goes hunting 'with his Ypolita, the faire queene, / And Emelye, clothed al in grene' (1685–6). When Theseus condemns Palamon and Arcite to death, 'The queene anon, for verray wommanhede, / Gan for to wepe, *and so dide Emely*' (1748–9). While 'observaunce' of nature might suggest decorum and even virtue, Emelye is hooked up to the ineluctable events of life to a comic degree; on the morning of the tournament, for instance, 'Up roos the sonne, *and up roos Emelye*' (2273), and most anticlimactically, when Arcite dies, the story reads: '"Why woldestow be deed," thise wommen crye, / "And haddest gold ynough, *and Emelye*?"' (2835–6). The exception to this automatic demeanour is Emelye's plea to Diana that she be allowed to remain single, but this prayer operates in such a vacuum that John Burrow is able to read her desire merely, 'as modern parents would say, a "phase"'.[8]

Dismissive readings of Emelye's blankness – as only a reflection of her lovers' desire, or a sign of the anti-romance elements of the tale, or, conversely, an unremarkable example of romance depiction – are made problematic by the narrator going just that little bit too far. The ordered division of gods and humans according to the Three Ages of Man, each with its own proper point of view, and the narrator's inclination toward the middle one, render his treatment partial and interpretative. He speaks from such a distance of 'thise wommen' as to make us hesitate to fall in line. Women weep continually and, if they lose their husbands, he bluntly observes, eventually die (1771, 2822–26). They 'folwen alle the favour of Fortune' which 'chaunge[s] both up and doun' (2682, 2840). They are simply more puppetlike versions of 'thise loveres' who go 'now up, now doun, as boket in a welle' (1531–3). The state of lover encapsulates the helplessness of being human; the state of womanhood mimics the state of lover, nudging the figuring of what it is to be human over the edge into absurdity. Palamon and Arcite get what they ask for by way of equivocation, the small print being written in later by amphibologie-uttering gods, but there is no pretence that Emelye's prayer has been granted, nor is her consent sought as in the case of the *Parliament*'s formel eagle. It is one of the strategies of the tale that Emelye is so resistant to imaginative sympathy, that she, even more than the other representatives of the age of Youth, seems to be viewed through the wrong end of a telescope. While her suitors figure the incapacity of the unempowered political subject, 'she for whom they han this jolitee' (1807) is a caricature of their incapacity, a satirical sketch in which the forces of the satire rebound upon that less impenetrable figure, Theseus.[9]

Nor is it clear that its scope ends there. One of the features of these two studies in power is that to the end they leave in play the variables apparently occasioned by analogy. Theseus is like a god and like God. The tale lets us read this the other way around: God is like Theseus. Chaucer's Providence has too long been granted amnesty on the grounds of its Boethian affinities. Analysis is stymied by a familiar heads-I-win, tails-you-lose approach whereby a Boethian resolution is assumed to be hovering over the text, either present by being articulated or present by being absent due to paganism. The poem does not attempt to demonstrate that Providence in fact differs crucially from Theseus, and that its reasons are always sound. In so far as Providence may be responsible for the apparent arbitrariness of the plot, its methods are more than odd: the death of Arcite is a circuitous route to the happy marriage of Palamon and Emelye.

Walter, lord of *The Clerk's Tale*, would appear to be an even less suitable candidate for divine surrogacy than Theseus. He is subject to his own whims which, being the lord, he is capable of fulfilling. His thought is 'on his lust present' (E 80) whether this be to 'hauke and hunte' as a carefree bachelor, or to make a somewhat eccentric choice of wife, or to abandon her to extraordinary pain, or to take her back again. His intentions and demeanour are repeatedly characterised by words such as 'lust', 'liberte', 'free wil', 'as hym leste', 'plesaunce' (for example, 80, 145, 171, 150, 183, 193, 964). The only time he speaks of constraint, of doing 'nat as I wolde, but as my peple leste' he is lying (490). His manipulations of the plot are disturbingly accessible to psychological readings; he seems to be taken by sudden, implacable obsessions resembling a sickness 'that he ne myghte out of his herte throwe', a 'lest' which is 'caughte' like a virus (453, 619). A narrative rhetoric of compulsion and struggle divests him of any godliness his freedom might suggest, leaving in its place a human dissembling, achieved with difficulty, which is the very opposite of divine simplicity. We are invited to recognise his desires, however, 'merveillous', as far from unique: 'ther fil, as it bifalleth tymes mo' (449). There is a whole constituency of people, we are informed, of 'swich condicion' that they cannot let go of their purpose, 'right as they were bounden to that stake' (701, 704).

Griselde, meanwhile, is the one who is characterised, to the virtual exclusion of any other features, by lack of change (the word most frequently used): she is 'stidfast', 'stable', 'constaunt' (for example, 564, 931, 1047); it is she who displays the imperviousness to time and circumstance which is the definition of Boethian Providence. Walter is all feverish movement: he 'gooth . . . ful faste ymaginyng' while she 'noght ameved'; 'evere in oon so pacient' she bears no trace of the doubleness which has held such sway among accounts of woman's nature (598, 498, 677).[10] She is afforded this oneness despite a lack of foreknowledge which she regrets in the very terms used for God's claim to it: 'if I hadde prescience / *Youre wyl to knowe*' (659–60); God 'preves' us '*Nat for to knowe oure wyl*, for certes he / Er we were born, knew al' (1159–60). Again and again Walter tries to find her 'chaunged' and, failing to do so, announces that he will change her for another woman, that the Pope has said he may, 'if hym leste' (742). Griselde's lack of change is offset by his restless, infectious variation of the world around him: he counterfeits the Pope's bull, he toys with the loyalties of his people until the weaker among them fall victim to a cluster of stock figures for women: 'unsad', 'ful of clappyng', 'chaungynge as a fane', waxing and waning 'lyk the moone' (995–9). Walter and the people whose faith he exploits are as women are said to be; the woman, comparatively speaking, is as God and his male surrogates in political office are supposed to be.

'I may nat doon as every plowman may', says Walter as he evicts his wife, advising her to see his action as that of 'Fortune' (799, 811–12). The ironies of this disdain for the poor and powerless are not lost in a poem which, diverging from other estates literature, makes the plowman the paragon of 'pees and parfit charitee' (A 532).[11] The pretence of *noblesse oblige* and the projection of antifeminist rhetoric upon manipulated political subjects mockingly preserves the traditional parallelism: seen as analogous in defences of hierarchy, the two structures, marital and political, remain yoked in Chaucer's critical analysis.

As in *The Knight's Tale*, but to a greater degree, *The Clerk's Tale* exploits the disparity between two modes: while Walter is interiorised out of line with what one expects in fourteenth-century narrative, Griselde is typical and emblematic. This combination sets up a peculiar dynamic whereby Walter's efforts are made to resemble, given the narratorial insistence upon making familiar, the mixed pleasure and frustration of a man finding himself married to saint. Griselde's patience is not traceably achieved in the manner of Walter's 'lust'. References to the ox-stall and intimations of the Annunciation form a halo around her exemplary steadfastness: in the way of *exempla*, they have no interest in showing us where it came from psychologically (398, 319–20, 335–64).

The assignment of the two modes is remarkable if not perverse. After all, it is Griselde rather than Walter whom the reader is asked to learn from. If the tale can be availed of in the allegorical manner recommended by the Clerk, it is by way of assuming that what looks cruel on the part of Providence is due to its very opaque purposes which we have no hope of grasping, and yet it is the surrogate for Providence – Walter – who is made comparatively accessible, and the human exemplar who is given a smooth and inscrutable surface. A figure 'ay sad and constant as a wal' does not give one much of a way in (1047).[12]

It will be protested that Ricardian poetry does not seek to make the ways of heaven cosily like those of earth: witness the rather unpleasant austerity of the Pearl maiden and her choice of a particularly disagreeable parable, or even the maddeningly tolerant, Theseus-like laughter of the Green Knight as he leans upon his axe. But these are a far cry from a figure whose testing of his subordinate is depicted not as the impatience of the perfect or the games of an ambiguous shape-changer but rather as the fulfilment of a pathological desire. Even if we take as unreliable the narrator's exclamations of horror at what he sees as needless cruelty, we find ourselves confronting a largely explained and familiar kind of emotional tyrant rather than an unknown and unknowable Prime Mover.

Alternatively, it is argued that God is exonerated because Walter is *not* like God. The narrating Clerk himself, having dismissed the possibility of reading the story as a model contemporary marriage, gestures toward the inappropriateness of Walter as a stand-in for the heavenly Lord. The word 'tempte' is used repeatedly for Walter's strivings to 'know' Griselde's constancy;

> sith a womman was so pacient
> Unto a mortal man, *wel moore* us oughte
> Receyven al in gree that God us sent . . .

'*but*', the Clerk adds – and the implications for the *exemplum* of this adversative are not spelt out – 'he ne tempteth no man' (1149–53).

One is led to ask how much difference in practice the proffered distinction between 'preeving' and 'tempting' can make. The passage seems determined to do as bad a job as possible of justifying the ways of God to man. There is no mention of grace or any other accompaniment to God's 'sharpe scourges of adversitee' which might lend substance to what seems to amount to little more than a quibble. The syntax of 'he . . . suffreth us, as for oure excercise . . . ful ofte to be bete . . . *nat for* to knowe our wyl' (1155–9) expects a balancing '*but for*' which never comes. Instead we are served up the bland, paratactic '*And for* oure beste is al his governaunce' (1161). The promise of 'excercise', defined as 'training, ?chastising' in *A Chaucer Glossary*,[13] does little to solve the problem; training for what, other than more scourges? If 'greet skile is he preeve that he wroghte' (1152), it is not at all clear why; the easy anthropomorphism the phrase assumes is out of place in a passage otherwise bent upon theological distinctions. Unlike a blacksmith or a shoemaker, God, as the text says itself eight lines later, is automatically apprised of the 'freletee' of his handiwork. He is constitutionally incapable of curiosity. The point about tempting is likewise purely definitional; being God, God cannot tempt because he cannot be said to have any tendency toward evil.

If God already knows everything then there is even less excuse for him to test us than there was for Walter to keep prodding his wife to see what she would do. Far from stabilising the structure of the tale, the tempte/prove passage and the Clerk's further playing with interpretation provide a cue for the reader to query the traditional analogy upon which the exemplum is based, or, alternatively, the comfort it piously offers. If God isn't much like Walter, then what is the point of the story? If he is rather like Walter, we are in for a bad time of it.[14] The tale comes equipped with a built-in safety device for defusing interpretation: if you read Walter as a husband, you are told that he's God; if you say he's an unprepossessing God, you are told he's only a man. It seems important not to be foxed by these very Chaucerian ploys, which would appear to comment upon the inevitable obstacles to figuration and to mimic the excuses which any figurative endeavour can muster.

As in the case of *The Knight's Tale*, to ask whether *The Clerk's* is a questioning of the familial power of men, the political power of rulers or the providential power of God is to offer a false choice. While each of the three is employed as a way of talking about the others, none can be exempted from scrutiny on the basis that it has only been introduced analogically. These comparisons were perhaps the most widespread ways of explaining the marital, social and religious practices of the Middle Ages and recommending appropriate behaviour. What Chaucer has done is to formulate the analogies in such a way that their explanatory forces are redeployed as discomforting enquiries into successively higher levels of government.

In Chaucer's work, women and language about women are crucial levers for exploring power and freedom. What people are shown to be able to do varies according to genre; in some cases, notably *The Merchant's Tale*, genre appears to vary according to what people are able to do. *The Knight's Tale* intensifies in an intricate form the vertical motivation characteristic of romance,[15] minimising the extent to which human beings, and particularly Emelye, can lay their hands upon the controls of their destinies. Women 'folwen alle the favour of Fortune', but given the structure of the tale, it is hard to see how they, or anyone else with the notable exception of Theseus, could do otherwise. In stressing the occluded human view of Providence, romance has an affinity with saints' lives and allegorical exempla. None of Walter's subjects is in a position to understand or affect the marquis's plans, and while Griselde is said to be constant, stable, all that (so the tradition runs) a woman should be but by nature is not, she paradoxically acquires these attributes by clinging unswervingly to her lord's erratic changes, ignorant of their rationale: by having no stability, no will of her own (E 655–6). Her reaction, after all, to her husband's apparent intention to abandon her for another woman is only a more unhesitating version of the reaction of the 'stormy peple' (981–1005). Both follow Fortune's favour; once again, they have little choice except in the degree of enthusiasm they express. The employment of language for the people which is commonly used for the feminine exposes the social basis both of the behaviour assessed and of the assessments themselves, positive and negative.

Weathervanes change because they are pushed; not inherently 'stormy', they make visible, by way of effect, overwhelming but unseen forces and to these forces they can only be true.

It is illuminating to turn for comparison to another of Chaucer's genres. Fabliau is, among other things, about being able to get what one wants. This is the case with 'hende' Nicholas but even more so with Alisoun who alone finishes up unscathed. *The Merchant's Tale* and *Troilus* combine the features of romance and fabliau. May and Criseyde, in the manner of romance, are given an 'aventure' but both, in the manner of fabliau, have a considerable degree of choice about what they do with it. One might more accurately say that their adventure creates them, and does so in an enabling way unsuspected by romance. May herself is formed by Januarie's own rhetoric which outstrips what he, blind as he is, would have been able to envisage; she is indeed malleable wax, not a given but an effect of speech and experience. Similarly, it is the externally motivated 'chaungynge of Criseyde' which makes her, in order to survive, 'slydynge of corage' (*Tr.* IV 231, V 825).

Emelye's and Griselde's own tales are not about the appropriation of circumstances, but rather about the severe delimitation of power which circumstances enforce. *Pace* the Host and the Merchant himself (E 1212b–d, 1213 ff), it is the task, in this regard a happier one, of the fabliauesque sequels to *The Knight's Tale* and *The Clerk's Tale* to illustrate the possibilities which would have been available to them in a different kind of story.

NOTES

1. The classic defence of these difficulties as conventional is C. Muscatine's *Chaucer and the French Tradition* (Berkeley and Los Angeles, Ca.: University of California Press, 1957) pp. 175–97. For Chaucer's Boethianism, see B. L. Jefferson, *Chaucer and 'The Consolation of Philosophy' of Boethius* (Princeton, NJ, Princeton University Press, 1917; rpt. 1968); R. M. Lumiansky, 'Chaucer's Philosophical Knight', *Tulane Studies in English*, vol. 3 (1952) pp. 47–68.
2. See J. A. Burrow, 'Chaucer's *Knight's Tale* and the Three Ages of Man', in his *Essays on Medieval Literature* (Oxford: Clarendon Press, 1984) pp. 27–48.
3. All references to Chaucer's work are to L. D. Benson (ed.), *The Riverside Chaucer*, 3rd edn (Oxford: Oxford University Press, 1988).
4. It should be noted in passing that capitals and paragraphing in the

manuscripts involve a wider repertoire of forms and a somewhat different rhetorical range of expression than modern indentation, and are often applied to passages whose style rather than focus marks them off from the surrounding narratives; cf. Ellesmere 1459, 1491 (see *The Ellesmere Chaucer Reproduced in Facsimile*, vol. I (Manchester, 1911).

5. See 'menen', 1a, 1b, 3a, and examples cited in S. M. Kuhn (ed.), *Middle English Dictionary*, Part M.1 (Ann Arbor, Mich.: University of Michigan Press, 1975).
6. Boethius, *De Consolatione Philosophiae*, ed. H. F. Stewart, E. K. Rand and S. J. Tester (Cambridge, Mass.: Harvard University Press, 1973) esp. bks IV, V. Translations below are from *The Consolation of Philosophy*, trans. V. E. Watts (London: Penguin, 1969; rept 1988).
7. For Theseus as 'the most perfect of Chaucer's good pagans', see A. J. Minnis's excellent *Chaucer and Pagan Antiquity* (Cambridge: D. S. Brewer, 1982) pp. 109–30. I agree, however, with H. Cooper's opinion that the pagan setting does not resolve the problems of the tale (*The Structure of the Canterbury Tales* (London: Duckworth, 1983) p. 210). See also E. Salter, 'Chaucer and Boccaccio: *The Knight's Tale*', in his *Fourteenth-Century English Poetry, Contexts and Readings* (Oxford: Clarendon Press, 1983) pp. 141–81; S. Knight, *Chaucer* (Oxford: Basil Blackwell, 1986) pp. 83–90.
8. Burrow, 'Chaucer's *Knight's Tale*', p. 35.
9. For different explanations of Emelye's slightness, see Minnis, *Chaucer and Pagan Antiquity*, pp. 131–3; Cooper, *Structures of the Canterbury Tales*, pp. 95, 111.
10. See J. Swan, 'Difference and Silence: John Milton and the Question of Gender', in S. N. Garner, C. Kahane and M. Sprengnether (eds), *The (M)Other Tongue: Essays in Feminist Psychoanalytic Interpretation* (Ithaca, NY: Cornell University Press, 1986) pp. 142–68.
11. See J. Mann, *Chaucer and Medieval Estates Satire: The Literature of Social Classes and the General Prologue to 'The Canterbury Tales'* (Cambridge: Cambridge University Press, 1973) pp. 67–74.
12. For two studies which stress Walter's faults, see C. F. Heffernan, 'Tyranny and *Commune Profit* in the *Clerk's Tale*', *Chaucer Review*, vol. 17, no. 4 (1983) pp. 333–40; and J. Mann, 'Satisfaction and Payment in Middle English Literature', *Studies in the Ages of Chaucer*, vol. 85 (1983) pp. 31–45. Both argue that Walter is transformed by Griselde's virtue and by mutual love.
13. N. Davis *et al.* (eds), *A Chaucer Glossary* (Oxford: Clarendon Press, 1979).
14. For the view that God is exonerated by the distinction, see D. C. Steinmetz, 'Late Medieval Nominalism and the *Clerk's Tale*', *Chaucer Review*, vol. 12, no. 1 (1977) pp. 38–54. For an admirable description of the difficulties of 'Fortune, Providence and Suffering' here and in Chaucer generally, see Cooper, *Structure of the Canterbury Tales*, pp. 209–21.
15. See M. Bloomfield, 'Episodic Motivation and Marvels in Epic and Romance', in his *Essays and Explorations* (Cambridge, Mass.: Harvard University Press, 1970) pp. 111–12.

7

Popular Reading Tastes in Middle English Religious and Didactic Literature

JOHN J. THOMPSON

> Man yhernes rimes for to here
> And romans red on maneres sere
> . . .
> Storis als o ferekin thinges
> O princes, prelates and o kynges;
> Sanges sere of selcuth rime,
> Inglis, frankys, and latine,
> To rede and here Ilkon is prest,
> Þe thynges Þat Þam likes best.
> (*Cursor Mundi*, lines 1–26)[1]

> Dytees and letters them can I make my selfe
> Of suche ynowe ben dayly to me brought
> Olde morall bokes stonde styll vpon the shelfe
> I am in fere they wyll neuer be bought
> Tryfles and toyes they ben the thynges so sought
> Theyr wyttes tryndle lyke these flemyshe boules
> Yet gentyll clerkes folowe hym ye ought
> That dyd endyte the parlyament of foules.
> (Robert Copland, preface to the 1530 de Worde print of Chaucer's *Assembly* or *Parliament of Foules*)[2]

This chapter will offer a survey of the interpretative difficulties faced by modern literary scholars who search for evidence of English popular reading tastes in the later Middle Ages. My title itself reflects some of these difficulties. Anyone who uses the term 'popular' when describing an aspect of life and culture in this period (or, indeed, in any other) must also be prepared to gloss it. And other major related issues that must be faced are not just the paucity of surviving evidence from the period – a situation that most medievalists know well and will recognise as an occupational hazard – but also the realisation that we can now only imperfectly understand so much of the extant textual evidence which might initially seem relevant to my chosen topic.

The extracts quoted above illustrate well several aspects of these general problems. Both the early fourteenth-century *Cursor Mundi* poet and the sixteenth-century printer-poet Robert Copland reveal their rather jaundiced perceptions of contemporary literary interests and tastes as they describe the types of literature with which they feel that their own writings have to compete. But these two views of 'contemporary' literary tastes are also separated from each other by 200 years and a number of important technological developments and social changes. So they cannot easily be said to reflect different facets of the 'same' late medieval world picture or, indeed, to signal a move from 'medieval' to 'medievalism'. And just how 'popular' are the listening and reading tastes that both poets are attempting to describe, since writers obviously also make fictions when they attempt to locate their sense of a particular work's potential audience within the imaginative compass of the work itself?[3] Because of these complicating factors, late twentieth-century students of late medieval cultural history must recognise their obligation to test the sense of a contemporary audience that emerges from reading some of the literature that was written in this period against other extant physical and textual evidence. All too often, the latter consists of little more than scattered shards and fragments.

MANUSCRIPTS AND TEXTS

A vernacular author's 'sense of an audience' obviously became an important literary preoccupation for some late fourteenth-century English poets, most notably, perhaps, for Chaucer in the *Canterbury Tales* or *Troilus and Criseyde*.[4] While Chaucer offered more highly developed insights into this theme's fictional potential than most of his contemporaries, many other vernacular writers also enjoyed the challenge of envisaging the tastes and expectations of their intended listeners and readers, and defining more clearly the relationships they perceived between author, text and public.[5] Their handling of a topic which usually required demonstrable fact to be blended with speculative fiction naturally varied according to their particular interests and situation. English writers as diverse as Richard Rolle, John Gower, Thomas Hoccleve, William Caxton and John Skelton chose to give their writings a strong sense of authenticity by making direct allusions to what modern scholars now accept were the circumstances in which some of their works were first commissioned or written. Our efforts to guess at their earliest intended audiences are frequently aided by sympathetic late medieval copyists and early readers who leave further clues about contemporary literary interests and readership in the surviving manuscript copies of Middle English works. Fifteenth-century copyists and collectors like the Londoner, John Shirley, to take a notable example, sometimes also recorded scraps of potentially valuable information about the ways in which texts had earlier been produced, circulated and read in the period before printing.[6] Other copyists with less-developed interests and tastes, or with fewer resources, have simply left correspondingly fainter traces.

Throughout the later medieval period there is ample literary evidence that many Middle English authors of religious and didactic writings were anxious to engage their listeners and readers by entertaining as well as instructing them. A great many anonymous writers, about whom we possess virtually no background information, take care to locate their religious and didactic poetry within more or less believable narrative settings, in town or country, at court, or in and around church and cloister. Many of these writers also enthusiastically adapt the conventions of dream vision, *chanson d'adventure*, dialogue, debate or epistolary forms, to provide 'some storial thing' for the edification and delight of their intended audiences.[7] Still other anonymous Middle English writers, notably romance writers, seem to have been purposefully nostalgic as they conjured up a role for themselves as minstrel narrators or singers and a performance setting for their works in hall or tavern.[8]

These narrative guises (fictional or non-fictional) may well have had some practical effects on the ways in which certain types of Middle English literature were received by copyists and presented by fifteenth-century readers to their own listening audiences. But it is difficult to know how to comment on this when we know virtually nothing about the performance aspects of reading aloud Middle English literature in this period. We should note, however, that many fifteenth-century book producers recorded copies of Middle

English romances alongside lyrics and other religious and instructional writings, including many of an oral-didactic cast, in their own literary miscellanies. Some of these homemade collections are 'holster books' which, because of their long narrow shape, were once thought to have started life as the portable property of travelling minstrels.[9] This view is now widely discredited, but it could equally well be argued that the slightly unusual shape of these 'holster book' literary collections and the allusions to minstrel performance some of their texts contain reflect the extent to which later medieval book producers, listeners and readers were prepared to enter into a fictional world celebrating a popular oral literary culture when they used such books.[10]

The extent to which it is possible to talk about 'popular' reading tastes for the literature I have just described, therefore, rests on the uncertain evidence of surviving manuscripts and texts.[11] I would maintain, however, that the idea of 'popular reading tastes' in the period is useful and appropriate, first, because the term 'popular' goes some way towards acknowledging the existence of a thriving literary culture for English religious and didactic writings outside court circles (even if we accept a fairly generous definition of the idea of the late medieval 'court' and its literature); and, secondly, because ideas of 'popular' and 'reading' tastes together issue a direct challenge to those with preconceived and limiting notions about the likely nature and extent of late medieval 'pragmatic' literacy.[12]

It has to be admitted, however, that for the *Cursor Mundi* poet the idea of 'popular reading tastes' would probably have seemed a contradiction in terms. He was writing his episodic biblical narrative and accompanying instructional materials in English, he tells us, for the common folk ('Inglis lede of Ingland, / For the commun at understand', lines 235–6), and, particularly, for those who do not understand French (line 240). But, perhaps paradoxically, in the opening lines of his lengthy poem, quoted in abbreviated form above, the poet seems to be looking to earlier literature, written in French and Latin, rather more than to contemporary English literature, for evidence of the current 'English' vogue in romance-style writings.[13] For this poet, the literary tastes of the 'common' reader that his own Middle English narrative will attempt to either satisfy, or perhaps even rival in popularity, are also those of the sophisticated listener. He assumes, furthermore, in the lines quoted above, that his listening and reading audience will be made up of those whose tastes were fixed precisely because they were prepared to read and hear their favourite fictional writings in any one of the three languages used for business, education and entertainment in late thirteenth- and early fourteenth-century England.[14] This audience for the poem is not only fictionally conceived by the poet, therefore, but can also be shown, from evidence derived from other medieval contexts, to be clearly not a fiction.[15] This poet's sense of an audience broadly resembles, for example, the readers and listeners who were intended to enjoy the trilingual manuscript anthology, now British Library MS Harley 2253, containing among other items the Middle English 'Harley Lyrics'.[16] It is this very real but also, arguably, quite 'uncommon', readership that the *Cursor Mundi* poet seems to have had in mind when he attempted to characterise the forces that dictated current literary fashions in his world.[17]

If the evidence of the numbers of surviving manuscripts and texts is to be given any weight, the arbiters of popular reading tastes in religious and didactic literature throughout the later middle ages were not 'the people', to any significant extent, but remained rather the many different clergy who made up an important part of that amorphous institution which William Langland and other English writers characterise as 'Holy Church'. Langland's fiction often sets in conflict the learned world of Holy Church and the common religious experience of ordinary humanity. But the seeds from which such conflicts grew were not sown for that reason. From at least 1215 (the date of the Fourth Lateran Council), Holy Church had been given a directive which many of its English members rightly interpreted as a mission to educate and direct both clerical and lay listeners and readers, using the vernacular as the preferred medium for religious instruction.[18] The teaching programmes, set out by Archbishops Pecham in Lambeth (1281) and Thoresby in York (1357), were attempts both to initiate training for their local clergy and to regulate the manner in which such vernacular written materials were used by both the teachers and the taught. Many fourteenth-century Middle English compilations (often appropriately classified as vernacular pastoral manuals) were assembled to inform their audiences of the fundamental tenets of the Christian faith and to deal with related religious topics.[19] Like *Cursor Mundi*, these often envisaged serving lay listeners, and perhaps even readers, but their earliest surviving written copies seem to have been directed, in the first instance at least, towards the local clergy themselves. And it was the parish clergy or other local spiritual directors, confessors and educators (the 'lered') who probably acted as intermediaries through which devout layfolk ('the lewed') usually gained their initial experiences of Middle English verse and prose writings such as *Cursor Mundi*, the *Prick of Conscience*, Robert of Brunne's *Handlyng Synne*, William Nassyngton's *Speculum Vitae*, *Jacob's Well*, *Speculum Christiani*, *St Edmund's Mirror* or *John Gaytryge's Sermon* (the so-called *Lay Folk's Catechism*). Throughout the period, as Langland was also only too aware, the means whereby ordinary men, women and children were introduced to the fundamental tenets of their Christian faith by these English religious compilations must have varied immensely.[20]

Because of its complexity as an institution, we can assume that the late medieval English Church's propaganda efforts were often successful in reaching a popular audience for a number of different, sometimes contradictory, reasons. Direct interventions in the religious experiences of ordinary layfolk by both conservative and radical thinkers and writers obviously had some effect on the nature of public worship, variously promoting, for example, increasing lay interest and involvement in (or, alternatively, perhaps even scepticism about) Church sacraments such as Penance and the Eucharist. On specific occasions, such interventions must have had an effect on the private lives of those devout and literate English readers who found time, and had the inclination, to engage in their own devotional activities, usually perhaps supervised by a confessor or other spiritual director.[21] The so-called 'paramystical' practices of small clusters of late medievel English gentry and certain groups of female religious provide the most spectacular examples of such activities.[22] But while some fascinating evidence has recently been uncovered, much more still needs to be found out about the day-to-day religious experiences of ordinary devout layfolk before extrapolating further about the interests and tastes in such writings of the majority of late medieval listeners and readers. Modern scholarship has, however, highlighted the direct involvement of members of religious orders, particularly the Carthusians, in promoting and circulating appropriate forms of Middle English religious writings by the mystics and others among a wider readership (particularly members of the English gentry) in the later Middle Ages.[23] That readership would have included, presumably, both religious and lay enthusiasts for the works of Rolle and Hilton.

Middle English verse texts like Nicholas Love's prose *Mirror of the Blessed Life of Jesus Christ* (perhaps the most widely read Middle English life of Christ in the fifteenth century) and related English versions of the pseudo-Bonaventuran *Meditationes Vitae Christi*, or the *Abbey of the Holy Ghost*, pose similar modern scholarly challenges.[24] These items seem genuine attempts to promote private meditative practices or to popularise the 'mixed' life among a wide reading audience and advertise themselves as such. If the evidence of the surviving manuscripts is to be trusted, however, copies or versions of these texts rarely found their way between the same book covers as Middle English romances in the miscellanies of the period. Their absence may signal some unforeseen problems of supply or limitation of choice about which we are unlikely to be able to discover anything further. Or perhaps it indicates an understandable disinclination to combine such very different types of English writings on the parts of the compilers of certain types of miscellaneous collections. I should add here that the main exceptions to the general rule just outlined are, first, the massive and encyclopaedic Vernon and Simeon anthologies, produced in the late fourteenth century by small teams of copyists, working in a well-supplied North Worcestershire religious house to compile vernacular materials that would assist their intended readers achieve 'sowlehele';[25] and also the two-volume 'Thornton' collection, now Lincoln Cathedral MS 91 and BL MS Additional 31042.[26]

The development of fifteenth-century reading tastes for religious and didactic literature took place against a background of increasing lay literacy. But this was also a period of official anxiety about the types of religious material, especially biblical translations and paraphrases, being made available to English listeners and readers.[27] William Nassyngton's *Speculum Vitae*, written by a proctor of the York ecclesiastical court, and intended, its author says, to be read aloud to illiterate folk who have no knowledge of French or Latin, was carefully examined by the Chancellor and Council of the University of Cambridge in 1384.[28] In 1410 Nicholas Love's *Mirror* was also searched and officially approved for devout reading under Arundel's Constitutions (1407). Legislation such as this was being set in place, moreover, just as pragmatically literate readers were developing their own voracious appetites for reading matter which would not only ensure their spiritual and moral well-being but also assist and confirm their education and social advancement. Consequently, by way of contrast to our suspicions of a possible lack of engagement with some English religious writings by certain members of the fifteenth-century reading public, there seems to have been an explosion of interest in others which catered for these tastes.[29]

Throughout the fifteenth century, English writers like John Lydgate – the best known, most prolific, and, possibly, most frequently copied and recopied fifteenth-century author of such religio-didactic works – were busily engaged writing poetry on a multitude of informational, practical, moral and religious topics.[30] These range from verses which describe appropriate behaviour during mass or at table to lines which extol the merits of regulating one's diet. Lydgate greatly admired Chaucer, but some time after the great poet had cast his wry glance at the domestic living habits of his age, the Bury monk could still quite unselfconsciously offer his readers practical tips in his verse for keeping clothes, as well as souls, free from stains.[31]

Many other fifteenth-century English writers whose poetry seems to have circulated less widely than Lydgate's (in both social and geographic terms) worked or reworked similarly varied 'Lydgatian' themes, and even borrowed extracts from him, or from earlier English versifiers, for their own writings.[32] Much of the other inspiration for religious and didactic Middle English 'songs' came from the hymns, psalms and liturgical commonplaces of the medieval Church. The main development in the tastes for such verse seems to have been a move away from the octosyllabic and septenary couplet forms which had been favoured for *Cursor Mundi* and in other didactic writings such as the *Prick of Conscience* (in short couplets) and the *South English Legendary* (in septenaries), towards instructional poetry written in more decorative stanza forms, often employing refrains or burdens.[33] An interest in such verse accounts for the known English poetic output of writers such as William of Shoreham, Richard Maidstone, Thomas Brampton, John Audelay and many other anonymous poets, including, of course, the *Pearl* poet.[34] If the evidence of these Middle English texts is considered, fifteenth-century readers obviously wanted to be imaginatively engaged by material which detailed proper social attitudes and behaviour as they prepared for mass and confession; they enjoyed being taught the moral and Christian lessons to be learned from the carefully graded ups and downs of their everyday lives, or those of the rich and famous; and some of them even appreciated uncontroversial literature of 'protest' and 'complaint'.[35] In short, the fifteenth-century English reading public were encouraged to read the literature that the *Cursor Mundi* poet had earlier suspected an English audience always enjoyed, namely 'storis . . . O princes, prelates and o kynges' and 'sanges sere of selcuth rime'.[36]

PRINTED TEXTS AND PUBLISHING

The coming of printed books to England, and the advent of English printing, add important new dimensions to our understanding of the burgeoning interests in certain types of English religious and moral writings among many late fifteenth-century readers. We should remember, however, that William Caxton's career as printer and publisher started on the Continent, and even when he moved to England, in 1476, his earliest trade seems to have been in imported French texts for English customers and supporters who obviously had already been exposed to continental influences.[37] Throughout the period also, the English demand for Church service books and *Horae*, another potentially lucrative market for printed books, was being met largely by foreign imports. And until the early years of the sixteenth century, as one modern scholar has recently put it, 'there were fewer printers in the whole of England than might have been found in any reasonably prosperous year in Paris or Venice'.[38] None of this makes the task of determining popular reading tastes for the English printed word any easier. By exercising their own speculative judgements and literary preferences, however, the earliest English printers and publishers (and, through them, their patrons) did at least help direct or 'shape' the reading tastes of their customers. Interestingly, the stance of literary arbiter is precisely the one adopted by Robert Copland in the verse quoted at the beginning of this essay. This is taken from his introductory preface to de Worde's 1530 edition of Chaucer's *Parlement of Foules*, first printed by Caxon in 1477–8.[39]

Copland is here 'introducing' the *Parlement of Foules* to new sixteenth-century readers. He obviously wishes to share in the genuine admiration for Chaucer's poetry that was also directly expressed in similarly enthusiastic and equally conventional terms by many other contemporary and near-contemporary English writers. Our sense of the respectable textual pedigree of the de Worde print also belies the impression given by Copland's discreet but witty allusion to neglected 'olde morall bokes' that de Worde is taking a risk of some kind in publishing a new text of the *Parlement* for a fickle literary public. We can, in fact, assume from the length of time that they stayed in business that printers like Caxton and de Worde minimised such risks by trying to identify the likely demand for and current levels of interest in the manuscript writings or new translations they wished to print. Caxton takes great pains to tell his readers as much in his own writings, and also to describe how his opinions as to the worth of the texts he prints is often formed by talking to his social betters and equals. He counts among his acquaintances the Duchess Margaret (wife of Charles the Bold of Burgundy and sister of Edward IV), Earl Rivers and members of the Woodville faction, Alderman Hugh Bryce and other notables from good London families. These sometimes act, he tells us in his prologues and epilogues, as patrons and supporters.[40] If his words ring true, some of these metropolitan acquaintances may also have been his underwriters when he started printing and publishing in London. England's first printer presumably needed some such business contacts to assist him financially on those occasions when he worried that he had failed to gauge correctly the real level of public interest in the chivalric romances and moral tracts upon which his reputation is now so firmly based.[41]

De Worde's case is rather more interesting for the student of popular literary culture. As Copland himself probably already knew, Caxton's prolific successor had not only consolidated his older colleague's achievements in developing an English audience for the printed word, but he also seems to have cornered the English market for semi-ephemeral printed texts.[42] This was a market for which Caxton seems to have had little or no interest. A surprising number of slight religious, moral and topical pieces printed cheaply by de Worde survive to the present day. These seem to represent attempts to capitalise on long-established reading tastes for written materials in English which offered homely advice, or gathered together a few lyrics and carols, riddles and puzzles, or brought together other light topical reading matter, or made entertaining, usually brief, written efforts at basic religious and moral instruction.[43] Sixteenth-century London mercers like John Colyns and Richard Hill, and the tailor, copyist and collector of manuscripts, John Stow, seem to have had a voracious appetite for such delights.[44] And cheaply produced quartos which contained similar light reading, and retailed at a penny or less, seem to have sold well for John Dorne in Oxford and other provincial sellers.[45]

As far as Copland's own career can be reconstructed from the surviving evidence, he also seems to have secured his future by tying himself to the fortunes of de Worde during the years 1508–35.[46] His career as writer and translator, printer and publisher, embraced both 'Olde morall bokes', such as his translation of *St Edmund's Mirror* (printed for de Worde in 1521 and reissued in 1527; STC 965,

966); and 'Tryfles and toyes' such as 'the Complaynte of them that ben to late maryed' (de Worde, 1505?, reprinted 1518?; *STC* 5728, 5728.5) and, inevitably, a 'Complaynte of them that be to soone maryed' (de Worde, 1535; *STC* 5729). Seen from this perspective, Copland's grudging acknowledgement of the popularity of his own literary ephemera also now reads like a reluctant tribute to the business acumen of his busy printer-colleague who was still able to find time to publish a 'new' text of Chaucer's *Parlement*.

De Worde's sense of the ready market for certain English texts may have been far more firmly based than Caxton's on observation of the popular reading interests of those around him and the manuscript books they used. Some recently gleaned testamentary evidence suggests, moreover, that de Worde was also a member of a metropolitan parish fraternity and contacts made there may have shaped his thinking on such matters.[47] Parish fraternities met and seem to have flourished in London during the period 1352–1550 and can sometimes be shown to have included English stationers among their members.[48] Chaucer may even have fictionally conceived of one such gathering in his description of 'a solempne and a greet fraternitee', to which his haberdasher, carpenter, dyer and weaver belong ('General Prologue', lines 361–78). These voluntary associations also existed outside the organisational structures of either guilds or religious confraternities and were made up of both men and women, usually from the middle ranks of society, who were encouraged to link together for the 'common profit'. This may make such gatherings sound a little like the parliament of birds in Chaucer's poem of that name, but, in the case of the parish fraternities, the term 'common profit' means that members met together regularly to provide mutual charitable help and to offer communal prayers for both the living and the dead. Much remains to be discovered about fraternity members' other interests and activities, including, of course, their contacts with local secular and religious clergy and their private reading.[49] The presumed network of informal social contacts built up by the activities of such a grouping is, nevertheless, one likely way in which de Worde and some of his Fleet Street neighbours may have experienced the listening and reading tastes of 'common devout folk' from the merchant class in their London.

The great technological advance brought about by printing suddenly meant that texts which had once circulated as individual handwritten copies in manuscript forms could now be rapidly produced in multiple copies. But even if a printer used small print runs to test the potential market for his work, or, in the absence of copyright laws, produced 'pirate' copies to capitalise on someone else's earlier successes, he still had to distribute these printed copies to his own sellers at competitive wholesale rates or else attempt to retail them himself.[50] Few sixteenth-century printers could have often afforded to speculate on books for which they felt that there was not a secure market. And there may have been many early publishing disasters about which we can now know very little. Copland, therefore, also conjures up for his readers every publisher's nightmare when he talks of old and unsold printed book stock. In Copland's fiction, and in real life, this situation was presumably even worse than having to face the prospect of throwing away unwanted broadsheets or unbound pamphlets containing 'dytees and letters' by the hundreds.

One means of identifying a likely safe market for printed texts in the sixteenth century was not to ignore clerical interests and tastes, and also, of course, not to fall foul of the ecclesiastical authorities. It seems no accident, therefore, that Nicholas Love's *Mirror* which was officially approved by Church authorities was printed early, by Çaxton, in 1484 (*STC* 3260) and enjoyed no fewer than eight further printings before 1530. It was reprinted by Caxton in 1490, with editions by both de Worde and Pynson in 1494 (*STC* 3261, 3262), with another Pynson edition in 1506 (*STC* 3263), and four more by de Worde in 1507?, 1517, 1525 and 1530 (*STC* 3263.5, 3264, 3266, 3267).[51] If the evidence of surviving prints is any guide, there also seems to have been a ready market for some other English devotional books, especially those intended for clerical instruction or to assist priests in their parochial duties. This was again serviced early by Caxton and his contemporaries.[52] Caxton even seems to have known and plundered the *Cursor Mundi* account of Old Testament history for his *Golden Legend*, but, perhaps because of its extraordinary length rather than its content, he chose not to print it entire.[53] And the similarly lengthy *Prick of Conscience*, which was the most popular Middle English poem in the Middle Ages to judge by the number of its surviving manuscripts, had to wait until *c*.1534, when R. Wyer printed Book 4 only, in octavo, as *A Little Book of Purgatory* (*STC* 3360).[54] This was followed, *c*.1542, by Wyer's edition of Books 1–3 of the poem, in quarto, as *A New Treatise divided in Three Parts* (*STC* 24228).

De Worde was perhaps responding initially to the pressures of Carthusian reading interests and tastes in the London Charterhouse, or perhaps even to those of the nuns at Syon, when he published a print of Walter Hilton's *Scale* in 1494 (*STC* 14042).[55] His venture must have met with some success since it was followed by Julian Notary's edition of the *Scale* in 1507 (*STC* 14043) and by three other de Worde editions, in 1519, 1525 and 1533 (*STC* 14043.5, 14044, 14045). In 1530(?), Wyer also attempted to capitalise on Hilton's assumed popularity by issuing his print of Hilton's *Mixed Life* (*STC* 14041). And in 1501, again possibly influenced by Carthusian enthusiasm and assistance, de Worde had produced a rendition of the *Book of Margery Kempe* (*STC* 14924). This now reads like a radically shortened, but also less controversial, version of this English mystic's earlier autobiography.[56] But lack of similar caution with material in *The Image of Love* by John Ryckes, now surviving in two de Worde editions, one printed in 1525, the other in 1532(?) (*STC* 21471.5, 21472), led to de Worde's being summoned for printing at least 60 copies of a heretical text which he had then issued to the nuns at Syon.[57] It was not only unsold stock, therefore, that might sometimes have been returned to sixteenth-century printers as unsuitable retail merchandise.

Literary historians cannot faithfully reconstruct the past. We must continue to work with the many tiny parts of that infinitely complex late medieval world-picture that have survived, none the less always seeking to establish patterns and make connections which might allow some further piecing together of aspects of our scattered English literary inheritance. Throughout this essay I have also tried to emphasise that there were a number of fairly obvious artificial constraints imposed upon ordinary late medieval English readers by the practical circumstances in which Middle English literature was written, produced and disseminated in the period. Factors like the accidental survival of one type of literature alongside another, in one type of manuscript miscellany but not another, or the even more fortunate survival of some written texts, but presumably not others, from a vernacular literature which has such deep roots in a predominantly oral-didactic vernacular culture, surely warrant as much modern critical attention as we are able to give them. But it has to be admitted that most such details will always remain uncertain guides to truly popular reading tastes. All that we can do is to keep examining the range of available evidence and watch as it continues to produce further puzzles. It seems appropriate, therefore, to end this essay with a final unresolved query concerning the earliest reading audiences for a great Middle English religious writer who is still causing his modern readers and critics enormous interpretative difficulties. Why was it, we might ask, that the earliest English printers seem to have followed the example of so many mid-fifteenth-century and later copyists and either ignored, or else avoided, the alliterative poem called *Piers Plowman*?[58]

Langland's poem received its first known printing as late as 1550, one year after the *Book of Common Prayer* had been printed and introduced.[59] This was presumably when the poem's first English printer, Robert Crowley, had become aware of a growing enthusiasm for proto-Protestant narrative adventures and speculative theology and attempted to satisfy some of this demand by his London print. The first printing was rapidly followed by Crowley's further efforts in the same year, in one of which was added helpful 'notes in the mergyne' for his intended readers (*STC* 19907, 19907a). And a new imprint was undertaken by O. Rogers in 1561, shortly after Elizabeth had replaced Mary on the English throne (*STC* 19908). But, from the earliest period in its long history, *Piers Plowman* seems to have been a poem that is capable of being all things to all people.[60] Langland's own eccentric narratives of the poem survive in over 50 early manuscript copies, variously belonging to both clerical and lay readers from all over England. And his texts not only attracted the attentions of conservatives and radicals, but also seem to have enjoyed good circulation and, one must suspect, an established reputation among copyists from areas outside London.[61] Was it simply that a liking for *Piers Plowman* was an acquired taste that printers like Caxton and de Worde did not acquire? Or is it possible that, some time before their change of religion, late fifteenth-century Londoners and their printers really did regard Langland's exasperating poem as another 'old moral book' that had had its day and was now perhaps best left unread on the printer's bookshelf?

NOTES

1. Richard Morris (ed.), *Cursor Mundi*, vol. 1 (of 7), Early English Text Society, Original Series 57 (London: Kegan Paul, Trench, Trübner, 1874). I follow the line-numbering of this parallel-text edition and quote from the Cotton Vespasian A.3 test. Lines 3–20, which list specific examples of romance writings known to the poet, are omitted here solely for reasons of space.

2. Fourth and final stanza of prefactory poem described as 'Roberte Coplande boke prynter to new fanglers' edited in 'Musa Typographica', Appendix II in Percy Simpson, *Proof-Reading in the Sixteenth, Seventeenth and Eighteenth Centuries* (London: Oxford University Press, 1935) pp. 221–2.
3. See, for example, Walter J. Ong, SJ, 'The Writer's Audience is Always a Fiction', *PMLA*, vol. 90 (1975) pp. 9–21.
4. Such preoccupations are often most readily associated with the English 'Ricardian' poets, for which see John Burrow, *Ricardian Poetry* (London: Routledge & Kegan Paul, 1971).
5. This potent theme was also an important inspiration for many visual artists in the period; see Elizabeth Salter and Derek Pearsall, 'Pictorial Illustration of Late Medieval Poetic Texts: the Role of the Frontispiece or Prefatory Picture', in F. G. Andersen *et al.* (eds), *Medieval Iconography and Narrative* (Odense: University of Odense Press, 1980) pp. 100–23.
6. For bibliographical details and recent discussion of a multitude of English copyists in the fifteenth-century English book trade, see the essays in Jeremy Griffiths and Derek Pearsall (eds), *Book Production and Publishing in Britain, 1375–1475* (Cambridge: Cambridge University Press, 1989). Shirley is discussed, pp. 284–8 and *passim*.
7. Some sense of the range of surviving texts on these themes can be gleaned from consulting the indexes of two standard modern bibliographical works: Carleton Brown and Rossell Hope Robbins (eds), *The Index of Middle English Verse* (New York: Columbia University Press, 1943) and its *Supplement*, ed. Robbins and John L. Cutler (Lexington, Ky: University of Kentucky Press, 1965); and J. Burke Severs and Albert E. Hartung (gen. eds), *A Manual of the Writings in Middle English, 1050–1500, based on 'A Manual . . . ' by John Edwin Wells, New Haven, 1916 and Supplements*, 8 vols, in progress (New Haven and Hamden, Conn.: Connecticut Academy of Arts and Sciences and Archon Books, 1967–). Specific references to the *Manual* are cited where they have seemed useful in the discussion below.
8. Brave modern attempts both to identify the Middle English romance 'canon' and characterise the reading or listening interests of its audiences on the basis of something more than just modern literary preconceptions, include those in *Manual*, 1 (1967); also Gisela Guddat-Figge, *Catalogue of Manuscripts Containing Middle English Romances* (Munich: Wilhelm Fink Verlag, 1976).
9. Sensibly discussed in Guddat-Figge, *Catalogue*, pp. 30–6.
10. Other examples of household reading are discussed in Julia Boffey and John Thompson, 'Anthologies and Miscellanies: Production and Choice of Text', in Griffiths and Pearsall (eds), *Book Production and Publishing*, pp. 279–315.
11. For a recent book-length survey which demonstrates well the difficulties of doing justice to surviving examples of popular Middle English literary forms, see Thomas J. Heffernan (ed.), *The Popular Literature of Medieval England* (Knoxville: University of Tennessee Press, 1985).
12. I borrow the term from Malcolm B. Parkes, 'The Literacy of the Laity',

in D. Daiches and A. Thorlby, *The Medieval World* (London: Aldus Books, 1973) pp. 555–77. See also H. J. Chaytor, *From Script to Print* (Cambridge: W. Heffer, 1945) and the recent account in M. T. Clanchy, *From Memory to Written Record* (London: Edward Arnold, 1979) esp pp. 175–201.

13. For summary details, see Sarah M. Horrall (ed.), *The Southern Version of Cursor Mundi*, vol. 1 (Ottawa: University of Ottawa Press, 1978) Explanatory Notes, pp. 341–2.

14. Clanchy, *From Memory* covers the period 1066–1307 in England and supersedes all previous surveys.

15. See Elizabeth Salter's sadly interrupted but exciting work on the status of English among the Latin and vernacular literatures of this early period, in Derek Pearsall and Nicolette Zeeman (eds), *English and International* (Cambridge: Cambridge University Press, 1988) esp. pp. 29–74.

16. Dating from c.1330–1340; useful summary description of the manuscript in Guddat-Figge, *Catalogue*, pp. 195–201.

17. See the excellent and continuing work on the scribe, patronage and milieu of Harley 2253 by Carter Revard in *Notes and Queries*, vol. 224 (1979) pp. 199–202; also vol. 227 (1982) pp. 62–3, continued in an unpublished lecture at the 5th York manuscripts conference, University of York, July 1989.

18. Useful survey diagram charting this development in Leonard E. Boyle, OP, 'The Fourth Lateran Council and Manuals of Popular Theology', in Heffernan (ed.), *Popular Literature*, pp. 30–43, at p. 38.

19. Further commentary and bibliographical details for all the Middle English items referred to in this paragraph in *Manual*, vol. 7 (1986) XX, pp. 2255–2378, 2467–2582 (contributed by Robert R. Raymo).

20. See also, for example, Vincent Gillespie, '*Doctrina* and *Predicacio*: The Design and Function of some Pastoral Manuals', *Leeds Studies in English*, NS, vol. 11 (1980 for 1979) pp. 36–50.

21. For an interesting Latin example of the type of spiritual direction on offer in the period (translated into modern English), see W. A. Pantin, 'Instructions for a Devout and Literate Layman', in J. J. G. Alexander and M. T. Gibson (eds), *Medieval Literature and Learning* (Oxford: Clarendon Press, 1976) pp. 398–422.

22. Term borrowed from John C. Hirsh, *The Revelations of Margery Kempe: Paramystical Practices in Late Medieval England* (Leiden: E. J. Brill, 1989).

23. Michael Sargent, 'The Transmission by the English Carthusians of some Late Medieval Spiritual Writings', *Journal of Ecclesiastical History*, vol. 27 (1976) pp. 225–40. For a comprehensive annotated bibliography of modern scholarship, see Valerie Marie Lagorio and Ritamary Bradley, *The 14th-Century English Mystics* (New York and London: Garland, 1981).

24. For Love's *Mirror* and related texts see Elizabeth Salter, 'The Manuscripts of Nicholas Love's *Myrrour of the Blessed Lyf of Jesu Chirst* and Related Texts', in A. S. G. Edwards and Derek Pearsall (eds), *Middle English Prose: Essays on Bibliographical Problems* (New York and

London: Garland, 1981) pp. 115–27. For the *Abbey*, see *Manual*, vol. 7, pp. 2340–1, 2545–7.
25. A. I. Doyle (introd.), *The Vernon Manuscript: A Facsimile of Bodleian Library, Oxford, MS Eng. poet.a.1* (Cambridge: D. S. Brewer, 1987).
26. Further discussion and references in my *Robert Thornton and the London Thornton Manuscript* (Cambridge: D. S. Brewer, 1987).
27. Much, not all, of this agitation was no doubt prompted by Lollardy, and fear of suspected Lollard influence, on the many different forms of Middle English religious writings being made available. For a reasoned summary of Lollard interests in producing the written word, see Anne Hudson, 'Lollard Book Production', in Griffiths and Pearsall (eds), *Book Production and Publishing*, pp. 125–42.
28. Perhaps, on this occasion, the anxiety was due to Nassyngton's use of Rolle's *Form of Living* as part of his translation and rearrangement into Middle English couplets of *Somme le Roi* materials. See commentary and summary in *Manual*, vol. 7, pp. 2261–2, 2479–80.
29. The best general survey is offered by Derek Pearsall, *Old English and Middle English Poetry* (London: Routledge & Kegan Paul, 1977).
30. For commentary on the Lydgate canon and bibliography see *Manual*, vol. 6 (1980) pp. 1809–1920, 2071–5 (contributed by Alain Renoir and C. David Benson).
31. John Lydgate, *A Tretise for Lavandres*, in rhyme royal stanzas; for one of its extant versions, see Henry N. MacCracken (ed.), *The Minor Poems of John Lydgate*, vol. II, *Secular Poems*, Early English Text Society, Original Series 192 (London: Oxford University Press, 1934) p. 723.
32. For example, *Peter Idley's Instructions to His Son*, written in rhyme royal (*Manual*, vol. 7, pp. 2257–8, 2474–5).
33. Early Middle English examples of short instructional couplet verse include items on the *Pater Noster*, the Fiftieth Vulgate Psalm and the Seven Deadly Sins, now found in the famous Auchinleck manuscript (National Library of Scotland, MS Advocs' 19.2.1; *c*.1340). See summary description in Guddat-Figge, *Catalogue*, pp. 121–6 (items 14, 15 and 36 in her list of contents); also discussion of these and other literary treatments in my 'Literary Associations of an Anonymous Middle English Paraphrase of Vulgate Psalm L', *Medium Aevum*, vol. 57 (1988) pp. 38–55.
34. For example, the authors of the Vernon lyrics, for which see my 'The Textual Background and Reputation of the Vernon Lyrics', in Derek Pearsall (ed.), *Studies in the Vernon Manuscript* (Cambridge: D. S. Brewer, 1990) pp. 201–24.
35. On the latter, see the challenge recently thrown down by George Kane, 'Some Fourteenth-Century "Political" Poems', in Gregory Kratzmann and James Simpson (eds), *Medieval English Religious and Ethical Literature* (Cambridge: D. S. Brewer, 1986) pp. 82–91.
36. The clusters of short Middle English poems in the late fourteenth-century Vernon manuscript, particularly in parts II, III and V, now offer a modern 'reader's guide' to the types of religio-didactic English writings that might have been on offer to certain members of the reading public in Chaucer's day; see summary bibliographical description in Doyle (introd.), *Vernon Manuscript Facsimile*, unnumbered

foldout at the back (see n. 25 above). In common with many other surviving manuscripts containing copies of these writings, neither Vernon nor its sister contain any works by Chaucer.

37. N. Kerling, 'Caxton and the Trade in Printed Books', *Book Collector*, vol. 4 (1955) pp. 190–9; other bibliographical details in G. Painter, *William Caxton, a Quincentenary Biography of England's First Printer* (London: Chatto & Windus, 1976).

38. Martin Lowry, 'The Arrival and Use of Continental Printed Books in Yorkist England', in Pierre Aquilon and H.-J. Martin (eds), *Le Livre en Europe dans la Renaissance* (Paris: Promodis, 1988) pp. 449–59, at p. 449.

39. The indispensable bibliographical guide to early printed books is W. A. Jackson, F. S. Ferguson and Katharine F. Pantzer (eds), *A Short-Title Catalogue of Books Printed in England, Scotland, and Ireland, 1475–1640*, first compiled by A. W. Pollard and G. R. Redgrave, 2 vols (London: Bibliographical Society, 1976 and 1986); hereafter *STC*. The Caxton text is *STC* 5091; de Worde's is *STC* 5092. Note also the print by Rastell (*STC* 5091.5; *c*.1525?), published about five years *before* Copland probably wrote the prefatory verse under discussion.

40. N. F. Blake (ed.), *Caxton's Own Prose* (London: André Deutsch, 1973).

41. For further commentary and bibliography on Caxton's English writings see *Manual*, vol. 3 (1972), IX, pp. 771–807, 924–51 (contributed by Robert H. Wilson).

42. I am grateful to Dr Julia Boffey for allowing me to read a copy of her forthcoming essay on de Worde's interest in 'Popular Entertainment and Practical Instruction' in advance of its publication.

43. For a sampling of these 'Nifles, Trifles, and Merry Jests', see Douglas Gray (ed.), *The Oxford Book of Late Medieval Verse and Prose* (Oxford: Clarendon Press, 1985) pp. 368–81.

44. One possibly direct point of contact between Colyns and de Worde is described in Carol Meale, 'Wynkyn de Worde's Setting-Copy for *Ipomydon*', *Studies in Bibliography*, vol. 35 (1982) pp. 156–71. I discuss the likely nature of some of Hill's lyric exemplars in my essay on the Vernon Lyrics (n. 34 above) pp. 212–3.

45. See F. Madan, 'The Day-Book of John Dorne, Bookseller in Oxford, A. D. 1520', in *Collectanea*, first and second series, Oxford Historical Society (1885, 1890) pp. 73–177 (first series), 454–78 (second series); also text and bibliographical references in D. M. Palliser and D. G. Selwyn, 'The Stock of a York Stationer, 1538', *Library*, 5th series, vol. 27 (1972) pp. 207–19.

46. F. C. Francis, *Robert Copland: Sixteenth-Century Printer and Translator* (Glasgow: Jackson and Son, 1961) esp. pp. 25–30.

47. Mary C. Erler, 'Wynkyn de Worde's Will: Legatee and Bequests', *Library*, 6th series, vol. 10 (1988) pp. 107–21. For parish fraternities, see Caroline M. Barron, 'The Parish Fraternities of Medieval London', in Caroline M. Barron and Christopher Harper-Bill (eds), *The Church in Pre-Reformation Society* (Woodbridge, Suffolk: Boydell Press, 1985) pp. 13–37.

48. See, for example, the will of William Breton, publisher of liturgical and other works that were printed in Paris for the London market

1506–10. Details in Wayne H. Phelps, 'Some Sixteenth-Century Stationers' Wills', *Studies in Bibliography*, vol. 32 (1979) pp. 48–59, at pp. 49–50.

49. For books which were written for the 'common profit' with the encouragement of London religious, but usually from the funds of the lay deceased, see Parkes, 'Literacy of the Laity', p. 568.

50. The point was well made by Graham Polland in the 1959 Sandars lectures; see now his 'The English Market for Printed Books', *Publishing History*, vol. 4 (1978) pp. 7–48, esp. p. 12.

51. Elizabeth Salter, *Nicholas Love's 'Myrrour of the Blessed Lyf of Jesu Christ'*, Analecta Cartusiana, vol. 10 (Salzburg: University of Salzburg, 1974) pp. 18–20.

52. F. A. Gasquet, 'The Bibliography of Some Devotional Books Printed by the Earliest English Printers', *Transactions of the Bibliographical Society*, vol. 7 (1904) pp. 163–89.

53. Sarah M. Horrall, 'William Caxton's Biblical Translation', *Medium Aevum*, vol. 53 (1985) pp. 91–8.

54. Also *Manual*, vol. 7, pp. 2268–70, 2486–92.

55. Pace George R. Keiser, 'The Mystics and the Early English Printers: the Economics of Devotionalism', in Marion Glasscoe (ed.), *The Medieval Mystical Tradition in England*, Exeter Symposium 4 (Cambridge: D. S. Brewer, 1987) pp. 9–26; also the interesting discussion of lay readership in Martha Driver, 'Pictures in Print: Late Fifteenth- and early Sixteenth-Century English Religious Books for Lay Readers', in Michael G. Sargent (ed.), *De Cella in Seculum: Religious and Secular Life and Devotion* (Cambridge: D. S. Brewer, 1989) pp. 229–244.

56. Sue Ellen Holbrook, 'Margery Kempe and Wynkyn de Worde', in Glasscoe (ed.), *The Medieval Mystical Tradition*, pp. 27–46.

57. This unfortunate, and small, de Worde print run in aptly described in Driver, 'Pictures in Print', pp. 230–1. H. S. Bennett estimated much larger print runs than this for some other early editions of religious works; see his *English Books and Readers, 1475–1557*, 2nd edn (Cambridge: Cambridge University Press, 1969) pp. 224–9.

58. My question is prompted by Dr A. I. Doyle's recent 'Remarks on Surviving Manuscripts of *Piers Plowman*', in Kratzmann and Simpson (eds), *Medieval English Religious and Ethical Literature*, pp. 35–48.

59. STC 19906; interestingly misdated as 1505 in this print, but subsequently overprinted to make the correction.

60. See also Anne Middleton, 'The Audience and Public of *Piers Plowman*', in David Lawton (ed.), *Middle English Alliterative Poetry and its Literary Background* (Cambridge: D. S. Brewer, 1982) pp.101–23.

61. Doyle compares *Piers Plowman* manuscripts to others containing the *South English Legendary*, the *Prick of Conscience*, and the *Speculum Vitae*: he characterises these as 'lengthy religious poems of apparently wide circulation in more than one region, well established by the end of the fourteenth century outside the metropolis, and probably not much handled in later trade there' ('Remarks on Surviving Manuscripts', p. 47).

8

The Double-Armed Man: Images of the Medieval in Early Modern Military Idealism

SIMON BARKER

The hero of this essay is the extraordinary figure who first appeared as an illustration at the beginning of William Neade's 1625 book of military theory and tactics, *The Double-Armed Man*.[1] I shall return to him later, along with his rather less heroic mounted counterpart, leaving him for the moment as the accompanying caption describes, standing 'couch and charged for the horse with his Sword drawne'. Neade's text is one example from a wide-ranging canon of early modern documents arguing the case for an enhanced awareness of the military requirements of the developing late-Tudor and early-Stuart state, and the frontispiece illustration is a perfect image of this canon's relentless idealism. My particular concern is with the way in which this idealism is guaranteed for the reader by means of a not altogether untroubled marshalling of representations of medieval militarism and chivalry.

The military writing of the late sixteenth and early seventeenth centuries is an extensive genre which has held the attention of military historians for a number of years, especially since the publication of M. J. D. Cockle's seminal work, *A Bibliography of English Military Books up to 1642*.[2] Cockle discovered some 150 late fifteenth- to early seventeenth-century English language books devoted to issues of warfare. He extended his list to include what he described as 'contemporary foreign works', thereby embracing such influential European texts as Machiavelli's *The Arte of Warre* which first circulated in translation in Peter Whitehorne's edition of 1560.[3] There are other familiar names, such as De Pisan, whose *The Boke of the Fayt of Armes and of Chyvalreye* was printed in London in 1498 (and much quoted by subsequent military writers) and Barnaby Rich, whose polemical style is fairly typical of Elizabethan militarists, demanding urgent attention to both the *idea* of an English standing army and its *ideal* composition and tactical approach.[4]

101

The issues at stake in this writing are wide-ranging. Many writers were concerned with what might be called the *practical detail* of warfare, the detail of weapons and equipment, soldiers' clothing and rations, or of the best method of digging tunnels in order to undermine a fortress. Yet Henry Webb's summary of these issues hints at the links between such detail and the wider *ideological* concerns – of organisation, responsibility and discipline, of training and expertise – issues which are the material of *militarism*, especially so far as relations between the individual and the state are concerned. For Webb, the Elizabethan military writers were concerned with matters such as

> what moral and physical qualities were requisite in officers and private soldiers, what training was necessary to achieve expertness in battle, what sorts of organizations could be formed and were best suited for different kinds of exploits, and what kinds of tactics might be most serviceable on the battlefield.[5]

It proved impossible for early modern militarism to analyse these issues of strategy, tactics and organisation, or even to address such matters as, say, the importance of keeping weapons in good order, without first engaging in ethical and ideological debate.

From the earliest fifteenth-century accounts of chivalry to the late Caroline propaganda, there is a preoccupation with setting the contemporary and accelerating *decay* in military structures, and therefore the ill-preparedness of the state, against an idealised history. The common concern is with the value and necessity for the state to maintain a powerful and efficient body of prepared and well-equipped men in order to deter invaders or to pursue just wars abroad on behalf of the monarchy. The writers discuss moral and religious justifications for warfare, the importance of classical models, foreign armies, model military leaders and contemporary attitudes to militarism. But all the sixteenth- and early seventeenth-century writers lament the decay of the medieval *fief* system and call for the immediate establishment of a standing army, or at least some action to prevent the seemingly terminal decline of the militia system which had evolved from the *fief*.

It is worth noting how some modern historians have responded to Tudor and Stuart military writing. For the last hundred years or so the view has been expressed in some quarters that it is evidence of an 'enlightenment' – substantiated by the recognition in the early writing that militarism was a 'science'. Contradictions and hesitation in the canon of writing as a whole have been smoothed over in order to represent it as a homogeneous genre synchronically and one which is situated diachronically in a military continuum essentially unaffected by political change, one which therefore embraces everything from Falvius Vegetius to the Falklands.[6] Writing in 1926, Eric Shepperd was able to compensate for the fact that the Tudor and Stuart years saw little military activity by the English, and some decline in standards of military preparedness by noting that 'individual Englishmen were gaining experience in the armies of foreign powers and proving in Holland, France and Germany that the war-like virtues of the race had not been lost.'[7] An example of early seventeenth-century medievalism in William Barriffe's *Military Disciple* was ignored, in the terms I wish to advance in this essay, by a particularly influential historian called Robert Higham who in 1939 could only note a slight anachronism, since 'it must be confessed that at one point Barriffe provides for "the beneficial use of bow and pike" and it may therefore be argued that his line, although modern and scientific, is less enlightened than it might be'.[8]

These are extreme and distant examples, but in fact the sense of *contrast* between the medieval and the early modern which is so central to the exhortations of the military writers is disregarded by some postwar historians as well. The clear sense of *crisis* which underpins the early writing is obscured by an optimistic comparison between the Tudor period and modern times by important military historians as such Correlli Barnett. For Barnett, the Elizabethan militia system, based on levying men from the shires, proves by its very continuation during a time of 'social flux' that the Elizabethan period was one of unusual homogeneity.

> Elizabethan England was in social flux, some men (and families) rising and some falling. Perhaps for this reason stress was laid on the distinction of rank, yet this was a distinction of degree, rather than the absolute barrier of a distinction of kind. The society of an English shire was therefore homogeneous despite its differing social levels.[9]

The state of the Elizabethan militia system is considered not in comparison with the medieval but with modern engagements. Noting that, although during five months in 1591 3500 men sent to France to participate in the Protestant cause were reduced to 800 by neglect and disease, the Elizabethan resistance to foreign service simply compares unfavourably with the more decisive national response of recent times so that 'the ordinary people of Elizabethan England did not therefore spring to volunteer like their descendants of 1914'.[10] The military climate of Elizabethan England was poor, but the social cohesion of this early period was to mature into a twentieth-century society enhanced by military awareness and responsibility.

For other late twentieth-century commentators, the call-to-arms of the early-modern military writers is uncritically explained as out of line with contemporary policy. John Hale has written that 'whilst almost constant wars were absorbing the other European powers, England, from the security of her island position, was relatively unaffected'.[11]

These responses to Tudor and Stuart militarism do not acknowledge the clear sense of historical difference which is evident in the canon of military writing. Such 'medievalism' sought to evaluate the decay in contemporary military consciousness (and to qualify the resultant decline in standards) by reference to an earlier epoch – often unspecified temporally, unless particular battles were invoked – but one defined as a history by three principal contingencies. It was the national history of 'the English' despite the involvement of the Welsh as historically instrumental to the victories which shaped the ideal, not to mention the eclecticism of its writers who folded narratives of European medieval militarism into their texts, giving them as suitable examples from an almost forgotten past. Secondly, it was a history which spoke of the homogeneity of the society which had forged it – an important aspect of a 'medievalism' which further revealed an anxiety over matters of social order in the present. Thirdly, it was a history which was *regainable* by attention to both the details and the philosophy of the new militarism.

The substance and imperative form of this writing, and especially its preoccupation with 'medievalist' revivals of the symbolic order and chivalric codes of the past, is partly explained by the absolutist project advanced during the late Tudor and early Stuart years. Such an explanation would also acknowledge a fear of popular unrest which is never far from the business of military order. Seen in this context, the historiography which chooses to regard the military texts as expressive of some form of military 'enlightenment' is reductive and reactionary, especially when a rhetorical link is made with the present through the notion of a transhistorical militarism.

Evidence of popular disturbances in the late sixteenth and early seventeenth centuries has proved a contentious area of investigation among scholars. For some, these events have been exaggerated in order to represent them as determining an early class conciousness which is not justified by examination of their sporadic form and the fact that they were both disorganised and lacking objective. Others have resisted this marginalisation and emphasised the widespread nature of the disturbances, regarding them as preconditioning later combinations and popular political movements.

Whatever the case it seems clear that the persistent pattern of disturbances which resulted in the use of the 1411 Riot Act and Tudor Statutes can be seen in the context of the quasi-absolutism finally achieved by the Tudor and early Stuart governments. Certainly the Privy Council saw fit to record the instances and significance of these events. In the county of Essex alone, anti-enclosure violence was recorded in various areas before 1563, and there were disturbances from 1567 to 1570 in Walthamstow.[12] Note was made of 'certain lewd persons' who thought 'to move some rebellion' in 1576, and there were riots in 1577 at South Weald and Brentwood, between 1582 and 1588 at Rivenhall, at Burnham in 1584, Finchingfield in 1585, Halstead in 1585, 1586 and 1587, at Burnham (again) in 1589, at Waltham Abbey in 1592 and so on until the failure of the harvests in 1595–7 led to more extensive rioting in London and the seizure of food along the grain roads of Somerset, Wiltshire and Kent in 1596.[13] The so-called Midlands Rising of 1607 involved co-ordinated unrest throughout Warwickshire, Leicestershire and Nottinghamshire and the Western Rising of 1626–32 spread from the Forest of Dean across the counties of south-west England following extensive food rioting in Somerset, Wiltshire, Hampshire, Berkshire, Sussex, Hertfordshire and Suffolk over the previous two years.[14] The leading participants in the Western Riots were accused in Star Chamber of having 'in Contempt of all Authority combined together and resolved to pull down all the present and ancient Inclosures'.[15]

Records of rioting in the late Tudor and early Stuart years seem to suggest three principal but related areas of grievance: shortage of food, land enclosure (and the draining of the fens) and the imposition of military training. It is the last reason which provides the link with the militarism of the period, written on behalf of the state, but also as a critique of the state's absolutist experiments. As the record of the Privy Council show, the state was considerably occupied by these continuing riots. Buchanan Sharp's survey of the evidence concludes that 'fear of riot, and of riot's accompanying potential for overturning the established order, is a constant theme in Tudor and Stuart political pronouncements'.[16] And where military training combined with other grievances, as was the case in the Forest of Dean disturbances, a major irony appeared in the relationship between public order and militarism. Not only did the late Tudor and early Stuart state retain insufficient means by which to suppress popular unrest, but it also discovered that attempts to reconstitute the medieval *fief* system in order to raise men for foreign expeditions and to institute a disciplined internal police force (including the 'trained bands' of the larger towns) led in itself to further discontent. Thus K. Wrightson's account of the potentially more violent of these events concludes that the armed rioters were 'simply employing the methods learned (and the equipment employed) at musters of the militia'.[17]

In whatever fashion history interprets these disturbances, and Wrightson is of the opinion that this riot was 'more in the nature of a controlled and remarkably disciplined demonstration than abandonment of restraint on the part of the people', it is clear that the system of raising and training men for domestic and foreign military duty had decayed at the opening of the seventeenth century to the point where it was not only a cause of rioting, but also a system too ineffectual to police the troubled state in the first place. Sharp continues:

> the tenacious resistance of such people to the Crown's will made it imperative that all the police and judicial authority of the state be brought to bear for the punishment of the rioters and the prevention of further outbreaks; otherwise, politically dangerous and socially destabilizing consequences were feared. But it became obvious in the course of this work that in the court of Star Chamber, commissions of the oyer and terminer, the *posse*, and the militia, the Stuart state lacked efficient or effectual means of repression.[18]

As far as overseas service was concerned, mutinies had not been uncommon during the last years of Elizabeth's reign. Edward Cheyney reports that in 1595 'there had been a serious mutiny of the drafted men of Norfolk, Suffolk and Essex at Ipswich . . . the men "utterley refusinge to goe beyond the seas", disembarking after they had been put aboard, threatening to march on London, and stirring up the discontented masses of that old rebellious district'.[19] The pressing of soldiers, 17,800 for duty in Europe and 2293 for duty in Ireland between 1589 and 1596, had resulted in the dual problems of potential mutiny and local resentment at the pressure of concentrated groups of ill-disciplined soldiers going to and from the wars.[20]

Furthermore, pragmatic attempts to introduce some order into the procedure of raising armies met resistance from members of the gentry forced to fund and organise musters and supplies, who questioned the legality of such impositions, just as Parliament itself was to do in the Petition of Right in 1628 over billeting, and over forced taxation (Ship Money) in 1634.

Popular unrest in the early modern period never proved a material threat to the monarchy until it became allied to the more coherent causes of the mid-seventeenth century. Yet its continued re-emergence during the years during which these causes gathered momentum troubled an increasingly centralised state that was experimenting with a form of absolute government which, in marked contrast to similar endeavours in Europe, lacked the vital ingredient of a trained and disciplined standing army. Without the ability to *impose* its will by force, English quasi-absolutism relied upon an expensive *display* of power in order to flood any channels through which discontent might flow towards the heart of the state. The limitation placed on the project of absolutism in England by an absence of the very military apparatus and medieval ideal espoused by the military writers had effects well beyond an inability to suppress the continual acts of unrest that plagued successive administrations. The crucial display of sovereign power was an expensive spectacle that required a concerted and coherent foreign policy (including a commitment to the Reformation) which would be seen to be effective.

This, unfortunately, necessitated the raising of an army and therefore consultation with a series of Stuart Parliaments as increasingly unwilling to finance what proved to be a series of mismanaged adventures as they were to finance domestic extravagance. The English attempt to conjure a sense of absolutism led to the contradictory situation in which, lacking a repressive apparatus for internal policing (and thus the *enforcing* of consent), it none the less attempted a foreign policy which required parliamentary approval. This highlights the importance of the relationship between domestic stability and foreign policy – a point focused in the contemporary military writing.

In terms of both technique and deployment, the armies of England and the leading European states underwent considerable transformation during the sixteenth and seventeenth centuries when various forms of absolutism were being consolidated. Spain and France, with their large populations and constant military engagements, developed massive and sophisticated armies. England, meanwhile, could no longer participate in such extensive operations from across the Channel. The smaller (and lighter) medieval cross-Channel expeditions, which had characterised English rule and influence in Northern France and beyond, could no longer be realised, and Henry VIII's calamitous adventures utilising levied armies in France in 1512–14, 1522–5 and 1543–6 were the last series attempts at major intervention on a scale to match the European rivals. These experiments both drained the exchequer and *limited* the prestige of the Tudors, so that when the late Tudor militarists sought to correct the mistakes of the recent past, to speculate on the qualities of an ideal military state (and therefore a mature and authentic *absolutist* state), it was no surprise that they had to create it from a number of sources, including images of the medieval, which presented a picture that was in sharp contrast to the reality of the recent past. The raising of mass armies had produced foreign policies which had produced no gain and still less acclaim, and even if naval power assured insular security, that security in itself had led to the atrophy of the military body so essential to the absolutist project and the policing of the state. As to the remnants of the noble class whose ancestry was to be recruited to the contemporary image of previous centuries, Perry Anderson has noted that:

> in the isolationist context of the island kingdom there was an exceptionally early demilitarization of the noble class itself. In 1500 every English peer bore arms; by Elizabeth's time, it has been calculated, only half the aristocracy had any fighting experience. On the eve of the Civil War in the 17th century, very few nobles had any military background.[21]

This demilitarisation of the aristocracy fuelled the polemic of the early modern militarists; but it has to be reckoned against the inability or refusal of the Tudor and Stuart state to keep up with the technical revolution in weaponry which occurred in Europe from the mid-fourteenth century onwards. Whilst there was a considerable decline in the use of heavy cavalry, this was not compensated for by a development in the use of gunpowder as a propellant. There is evidence of early enthusiasm, such as the English use of 'crakys of war' in action against the Scots in 1327, and 'gonnes' at Berwick in 1333, and Henry V had depended on artillery at the seige of Harfleur, yet the rapid adoption of the cannon as a standard battlefield weapon of fifteenth-century Europe seems to have been ignored by the English military strategists. Added to this, R. C. Smail notes that 'in the use of firearms by the infantry the English were even more hesitant. Their victories in France had made the archer and the longbow into objects of national pride, and they reluctant to adandon them.'[22] At the same time, English (and perhaps more damagingly, Welsh) proficiency with the longbow declined to the point where it could no longer be relied upon as it had at Crécy, Poitiers and Agincourt where bows had been as instrumental in victory as had the vanguard of knights.

It was against this background of military decline that the early modern militarists formulated a discourse which might be described as one of 'medievalism' – a nostalgia for an idealised chivalric order. In the climate of popular disorder, itself partly a result of the chaotic military structures which so poorly imitated those of the idealised past, these writers were impelled to construct a militarism which could combine the values of that past with a contemporary and innovative sense of what would constitute the relationship between the individual and the military institution, and between that institution and the state.

I want to discuss three issues in the early modern military writing which exemplify this concern for the medieval. First, there is a re-assertion of the Christian justification for warfare which echoes arguments from earlier centuries. In addition to this are discussions of the relationship between the ideal re-militarised subject and the state, and in particular a preoccupation with the discipline and knowledge which the soldier should have in order to conform to the demands of the early modern military ideal. Thirdly, there is the crucial concern for a retention of that weaponry which had come to symbolise the achievements of the past which themselves informed the emerging sense of a 'military heritage'.

Early modern militarism included a concern for the reinforcement of the idea that warfare could be justified in the name of Christianity. In the pursuit of this, the military writers depended upon the presentation of a 'history' of warfare derived from biblical sources, carefully blended with accounts of warfare from earlier centuries.[23] Little account is made of the kinds of uncertainties about warfare which modern scholars have discovered in medieval literature and particularly that of the fourteenth century, such as *The Alliterative Morte Arthure* or *Wynnere and Wastoure* of Edward III's reign.[24]

Indeed, the heroic figure of the earlier crusading knight becomes for the early modern militarists the epitome of the Church Militant, renewed for service on behalf of the Reformation, whether in the Low Countries, which were:

> (a patterne for all Christendome) whose valor the Lord hath exceedingly blessed, in delivering them by force of Armes, from the tyrannie of the cruell Spaniards, to the great comfort of all true-hearted Protestants[25]

or during the English Civil War, when the ideal of the Christian soldier is linked to that of divine determination of the outcome:

> If Christianity should blame, or tax all warrs, then when the souldiers asked Christ what they should do for the salvation of their soules, he would undoubtably have bidden them to cast away their weapons, and to give over war, which he dothe not.
>
> . . .
>
> Civil war makes that King who undertakes unjust wars against his subjects to repent him of his victory, when he truely sees what he hath done . . . for victory in war is neither got by multitude, nor strength, but by the ayd, assistance, and power of God. And therefore these military means must now be used.[26]

If the early modern writers did not acknowledge positions in earlier literature which arguably destroyed 'commonplaces of chivalry and knightly warfare through inversion, irony and black humour', there is instead a studied and forceful repudiation of the kind of quasi-pacificism of some early Tudor theologians, and especially the writing of Erasmus and Thomas More, whose work, it seems, was read widely during the sixteenth and seventeenth centuries.[27]

Erasmus's position in *Moriae Encomium, Quera Pacis, Institutio Principis Christiani, Militaria* and other texts was perfectly clear:

war is so monstrous a thing that it befits beasts and not men, so violently insane that poets represent it as an evil visitation of the Furies, so pestilential that it causes a general corruption of character, so criminal that it is best waged by the worst men, and so impious that it has no relation with Christ.[28]

The early modern militarists contested this kind of writing on all counts. Piecing together a selected representation of classical and medieval warfare they constructed a counter-thesis which insisted that war was manly, praised by most poets, dependent upon character (and a dependable enhancer of character), waged by the best of men and blessed by God. That this representation was favoured by absolutism is best exemplified by the anecdote Erasmus records for Good Friday 1513 when John Colet preached an anti-war sermon in the presence of Henry VIII and a congregation of troops set to embark for the wars in France. Urging that princes should follow the example of Christ rather than of Caesar or Alexander, Erasmus reports that Colet concluded by stressing that:

> they who through hatred or ambition were fighting one another by turns, were warring under the banner, not of Christ, but of the devil. At the same time, he pointed out to them how hard a thing it was to die a Christian death; how few entered on a war unsullied by hatred or love of gain; how incompatible a thing it was that a man should have that brotherly love without which no one could see God, and yet bury his sword in his brother's heart.[29]

Commentators have seen this as a turning point in the affairs of Henry VIII in which his absolutism becomes firmly allied with the just war; F. Seebohm, for example, notes that the King 'was not a little afraid that the sermon might damp the zeal of his newly enlisted troops' and that a long conversation ensured between the King and his bishop which ended with Henry

> glad to find that Colet had not intended to declare absolutely that there could be no just war, no doubt persuading himself that his own was one of the very few just ones. The conversation ended with [Henry] expressing a wish that Colet would sometime or other explain himself more clearly, lest the raw soldiers should go away with a mistaken notion, and think he had really said *no* war is lawful to Christians.[30]

As for Thomas More, his Utopians had preferred to smuggle posters into enemy states offering rewards for the assassination of the enemy king, had welcomed Swiss mercenaries to fight their battles for them, and in the last resort of war, had advocated the training of women so that 'in set field the wives do stand every one by their own husband's side'.[31] By the early years of the seventeenth century, the quasi-pacifism of Erasmus, Colet and More is open to little but a charge of 'mere contempletion' by early modern militarists such as Thomas Digges:

> to speake of peace perpetuall in this world of contention is but as ARISTOTLES FOELIX, XENOPHENS CYRUS, QUINTGIANS ORATOR, or Sir Thomas Moors UTOPIA, a matter of mere contemplation, the warre being in this iron age si bien enracinèe qu'il est impossible de l'en oster, si non avec la ruine de l'universe. So well ingrafted that it is impossible to take it away without a universal destruction.[32]

It is the world of Luther and Calvin rather than Aquinas; but the pacifism of the early reformers remained important for the early modern militarists for three reasons. First, it acted as a kind of conceptual link to the idealised period of the fourteenth century and before, when the politics of war expressed in theological terms stood more easily alongside the idea of chivalry. Secondly, and ironically, Erasmus had written the influential *Enchiridion Militis Christiani* in 1516. With its set of rules governing the discipline and training of the Christian soldier, this text's formal links with the later military texts are more compelling than its existence as a pacifist antithesis to their polemic; it is as though the association of Christianity with militarism becomes established as an equation, justifying the militarism espoused on behalf of the absolute state. Thirdly, the early sixteenth-century pacifism can be held responsible, in part, for the decline in military discipline and 'character' which the militarists cite as both destructive of the nation and as opening a door to the excesses of popular unrest.

It was concern for the matters of character and discipline, a knowledge of arms and ethics and ultimately for the relationship between the soldier and the state which led the early modern militarists to speculate on the present decay in terms of an idealised past. As with many of these arguments, the medieval pattern which they glorify had to be tempered by modern conditions and politics. For the purposes of late sixteenth- and early seventeenth-century rhetoric, the past was a place of clear military objectives and success, substantiated by the reputation of knights at home and abroad; the images of the chivalric past are never summoned without indignation at the present decay. Barnaby Rich, writing in 1578, accused the 'carping cavillers' of the court of having distilled and corrupted the English tradition of a militaristic nobility, by growing 'lazy and greedy, wallowing in vice and wickednesse' and by

> neglecting those disciplines which made them both honourable and worshipful – whose magnamitie in the times of warres hath made them famous in forrain countries, and whose nobleness and vertues . . . in times of peace, doe shine coequal with the best.[33]

Rich's *Allarme to England* laments the passing of an age of nobility and virtue when the tournament (as in the *Pas d'Armes*) was actually a display of martial discipline, and scorns its transformation into the courtly jousting games and 'soft and silken wars' which Glynne Wickham confirms as having 'lingered as a Court prerogative . . . conducted in the tiltyard by day and in the banquet hall as the climax to a masquerade by night' into the early years of the seventeenth century.[34] Also at stake is a sense of sexual difference, since in England:

> Gentlemen that are descended of honourable families in these days give themselves rather to become Battalus Knights (effeminate men) than Martiall Knightes, and have better desire to be practised in Carpet Trade than in that kind of virtue. To be shorte . . . in Englande, Gentlemen have robbed our women of their mindes, and our women have bereved us of halfe our apparell.[35]

It would be a mistake, however, to conclude that such texts are simply conservative, recommending a wholesale return to the values of the 'Martiall Knightes'. Rather, these values are to be *renegotiated* in important ways, almost with an awareness of the problems modern historians have associated with the decentralisation of power inherent in a chivalric code which had legitimised private feuding instead of maintaining public order.[36]

The ideological project was to derive an image from the past of chivalric integrity, moral purpose and military discipline which would be appropriate to the creation of a modern army, the purpose of which was not only to represent an increasingly centralised state abroad, but also to provide an internal police force in order to forestall the popular unrest which the early modern writers refer to throughout the canon of military texts. The ideal military structure would overcome the problems associated with the unpopularity of the militia system and its quality as a fighting force. Barnaby Rich cites the case of London where,

> when they set forth soldiers, either they scoure their prisons of thives, or their streets of rogues and vagabonds ... the name of a soldier is become so odious to the common people ... God grant us that we never be given to trie the service of such people.[37]

By close attention to the recommendations of the military theorists, the status of the soldier in society would be fundamentally changed, since, according to Geoffrey Gates, the English in recent time 'hath had that fault of being unnatural and unthankful' to soldiers, for if England were not an island but 'stood in the continent of the world environed with mightie nations ... then it should know the value of the soldier, and lick the dust off the feete of her men of prowesse: then would the lawyer and the merchant humble themselves to the warriers'.[38]

Furthermore, there are a great many examples of the early modern militarists revealing that an established army would allow warfare *abroad*, which in turn would establish internal peace. For Peter Whitehorne, in his introduction to Machiavelli's *The Arte of Warre*, peace is guaranteed only by war, since earlier societies,

> when through long and continued peace, began to bee altogether given to pleasure and delicatnesse, little regardyng Martiall feates, nor such as were expert in the practise thereof: Their dominians and estates, did not so moche before increase and prospere as then by soche meanes and oversight, thei sodainly fell into decaie and utter ruine.[39]

For Thomas Digges war was 'sometimes lesse hurtfull, and more to be wisht in a well governed State than peace', since peace promoted 'ease and pleasure, two seducing Syrens in whose beastly servitude too many are inthralled past recoverie'. And he recommends 'forreine warre, a sovereigne medicine for domesticall inconveniences. Desire warre rather than quitenesse, and thefore fall out at home if forreine foes the wanting.'[40]

In *The Politicke and Militarie Discourses* the idea of war as an insurance against civil unrest is expressed quite openly, since the ideal

> great estate replenished with warlike people, ought still to have some foreine warre wherewith to keepe it occupied, least being at quiet they convert their weapons against each other.[41]

According to texts like this, the 'warlike people' would be inspired by *public* displays of militarism presented in 'publicke places of Exercise' as had been the case in earlier times.[42] An additional demand was, therefore, that the modern military formation would consist of soldiers who had a clear *knowledge* of their own worth in the social formation and the worth of their cause; this knowledge, equivalent to that held *individually* by the idealised medieval knight, would, in the early modern ideal army, be held by each and every private soldier:

> it would seem requisite and necessarie that great regarde shoulde be used in the appointing of lawes, discipline, and orders, the which not only among them selves, but also to their utter enemies ought inviolaby to be kepte according to the iustice and equitie of the cause for which they entred into armes.[43]

The militarists are nostalgic for a concept of the knight, but aware also that if a parallel were to be made between the military formation and the social formation, then the modern soldier was to be a citizen rather than a king-in-miniature. The private, knowing soldier would submit himself willingly to the overall body of the army institution, know his weapons and his cause, be self-motivated and active; he would be at the same time both the autonomous knight *and* the anonymous figure lost within the disciplined ranks of advancing soldiers, so that

> he may well be called a trained soldier that knows by the sound of drum and trumpet, without any voice, when to march, fight, retire, etc; that is able in marching, embattling and fighting; that has some sight in the mathematicals and in geometrical instruments, for the conveying of mines under the ground, to plant and

manage great ordnance, to batter or beat down the walles of any towne or castle; that can measure altitude, lattitudes and longitudes, etc. Such a one may be termed in my opinion an expert soldier.[44]

In this way the early modern militarists forged an ideal of the soldier-as-citizen, an expert and an example to others, able to police his fellow citizens and fight abroad, to *know* himself and his cause, and to strengthen his body so that it can strengthen the overall body of the army.[45] Listing the qualities and skills which the public should expect in the soldiers they were to observe in the 'publicke places of Exercise', *The Souldier Pleading His Own Cause* includes 'Obedient' behaviour, 'Secrecie', 'Sobriety', 'Courage', 'Loyalty'. The public was also to be able to assume that the soldiers were 'Free from Bribes', 'Wise and Politicke' and practised in such 'Artes of Warre' as 'Arithmetick' and 'Geometry', as well as having 'Knowledge in Histories' and the ability 'to speak divers Languages'.[46]

That each soldier should have a 'Knowledge in Histories' is the key to early modern military idealism. It is a condition which makes sense of the disparate forces which underpin the demands of the writers; the chaotic militia system, the threat of popular discontent, the requirement for a national military identity, and the vulnerablity of the absolutist state at the end of the sixteenth century. Early modern militarism, pragmatic, innovative and with a close awareness of technical advance, none the less proposed an ordering of the *past* which we might speak of as a form of 'medievalism'. If the past could be regained, refashioned, revalued, then the future was assured. Typical of this process and, I want to suggest, representing an encoding of the whole sense of early modern 'medievalism', is the treatment of weaponry in the military texts; military idealism, linking images of the past to present demands, most closely reveals the ideological work of these texts.

Whilst acknowledging the considerable impact made upon the military scene in Europe by the invention of gunpowder, the early modern militarists were reluctant to relinquish weapons which they thought of as symbolic of England's triumphant military past. Humfrey Barwick's insistence in 1594 that munitions should be adopted in order to restore the status England had enjoyed in history due to the use of the longbow, brought a swift response from a number of writers; in 1596, the writer known as 'R.S.', whose treatise was 'abstracted out of ancient and modern writers', promoted the particular effectiveness and 'Englishness' of the longbow and *lamented* its recent decline from use.[47] Most texts, however, advocated a synthesis of the old and the new so that the bow could still yield its symbolic national significance, its 'medievalism' *alongside* such modern weapons as the musket. Just such a compromise had been suggested in Thomas Styward's *The Pathwaie to Martiall Discipline*, a book which, in 1581, 'entreateth of sundrie proportions and training of Caleevers, and how to bring Bowes to a great perfection of service'.[48]

It is with the argument for a synthesis of old and new that I return to two of the best examples of this kind of 'medievalism', significantly taken from books which appeared towards the end of the long period of early modern military writing; these texts may be considered mature examples of the form. *The Double-Armed Man* came in 1625 from the pen of William Neade and included a frontispiece illustrating a pikeman who 'stands coucht and charged for the horse, with his sword drawne'. This is the experienced, valued, expert 'citizen soldier', and, in many ways, the figure represents everything that could be desired in the contemporary ideal. The soldier is strong in body, for how else could he maintain the unnatural crouch with one knee bent towards the enemy, his other leg stretched out behind, and his sword raised above his head? He is well-clad and well-shod, and his neat beard and collar are those of a gentleman. He is alert and ready for an oncoming cavalry charge, with his long pike set against his rear foot and extending through his left hand towards the enemy's charge. Yet his is also the medieval Knight; his helmet is plumed, his armour heavy and extending to the knee, and there is even the hint of a spur. And, as if this anachronistic symbolism is not enough, the pikeman is actually 'triple-armed' since he has at his belt a quiver of arrows and his pike is simultaneously a longbow. The accompanying caption suggests that

> This Portraiture of charging for horse, is to shew that the Bow is very materiall for this service; for the five or six first ranks standing coucht at this charge, the middle and the reare may shoot their volleys of arrowes, and therewith both gaule, wound, disorder, and kill the enemy, both man and horse.

In the actual battles of the late sixteenth and early seventeenth centuries, this figure would have been a musketeer, and the accompanying 'words of command' for advancing ranks to alternatively 'crouch low' and 'come up to your order, and shoot your arrows' are those which apply to guns. Yet the Double-Armed Man exactly encodes the 'medievalism' of the period, his bow and arrow aimed with the symbolic force of history.

Still more bizarre (to the point of absurdity) is an illustration from John Cruso's *Military Instructions for the Cavallerie*. This text was produced only a decade or so before the engagements on English soil which motivated the actual introduction of many of the more workable recommendations concerning discipline, knowledge and expertise found in the texts – ironically enough not on the side of absolutism but against it. The Knight illustrated in Cruso's text would have fared ill against the New Model Army, but in 1632 he represents perfectly the medieval aspect of early modern militarism.

He appears in twelve sequential illustrations, each labelled with the 'words of command', which will help the instructor discipline his cavalry as they mount their horses and prepare their weapons for an advance on the enemy. At first glance the elaborate armour, plumed helmet, high saddle and elegant, heavy horse (which trots through the sequence with dressaged discipline equal to that of its rider) is entirely medieval; it is not difficult to image him armed, like Peraldus's Knight, with a shield of faith and an accompanying flight of doves representing the gifts of the Holy Spirit.[49] Yet Cruso's Knight is modern; he has no sword, shield or lance and the 'instructions for the Cavallerie' are to 'draw your pistoll', 'order your pistoll', 'lode your pistoll' and so on.

The medieval images which appeared in early modern military texts are witness to a crisis in the politics of a state determined upon an absolutism which was never furnished with the essential component of a disciplined, equipped, motivated standing army. As a result of this absence, early modern militarism steered an uneasy path between the advocation of a revolution in military thinking (towards a modern, technically sophisticated army supplied with knowing 'citizen soldiers') and the retention of an iconography derived from a peculiar reading of history. The uncertainty of this 'medievalism' in the face of the chaos of actual attempts to participate in campaigns is the source of much examination and parody in early modern literature, particularly that produced for the contemporary stage.[50] Romantic portrayals of medieval chivalry were to survive the upheavals of the mid-seventeenth century, of course, and have been cultivated ever since; but on the actual battlefield the Double-Armed Man found his arrows had little effect against Cromwell's Ironsides.

NOTES

1. William Neade, *The Double-Armed Man* (London, 1625).
2. M. J. D. Cockle, *A Bibliography of Military Books up to 1642* (London, 1900).
3. Niccolo Machiavelli, *The Arte of Warre, Written First in Italia by Niccolo Machiavelli and Set Forthe in Englishe by Peter Whithorne* (London, 1560). Machiavelli's writing had been widely read in Italian before 1560 and *I Discorsi, Istorie Fiorentine, Il Principe* and *Libro dell' Arte della Guella* itself were printed in London in the last two decades of the sixteenth century, fictitiously imprinted with Piacenza or Palermo as their place of origin.
4. Christine de Pisan, *The Boke of the Fayt of Armes and of Chyvalreye* (London, 1498); Barnaby Rich, *A Right Excelant and Pleasant Dialogue betweene Mercury and an English Souldier* (London, 1574), *Allarme to England, foreshewing what Perilles are Procured when People Live Without Regarde to Martiall Lawe* (London, 1578) and Barnaby Rich, *His Farewell to Militarie Profession* (London, 1581).
5. Henry J. Webb, 'Classical Histories and Elizabethan Soldiers', *Notes and Queries*, vol. 200 (November 1955) pp. 468–9.
6. The most productive period for this kind of writing was at the end of the nineteenth century, and some of the best examples are Sir Sibbald Scott, *The British Army: Origin, Programme and Equipment* (London, 1868): Clifford Walton, *History of the British Standing Army* (London, 1894) and C. M. Clode, *The Military Forces of the Crown* (London, 1894). More recently writers include the Renaissance 'enlightenment' in the histories of warfare which seem ever popular, especially at times of war. Examples of such ahistorical thinking are examined in my article 'Images of the Sixteenth and Seventeenth Centuries', in F. A. Barker *et al.*, *Literature, Politics and Theory* (London, Methuen, 1986).
7. Eric Sheppard, *A Short History of the British Army to 1914* (London, 1926) pp. 7–8.
8. Robin Higham, *A Guide to the Sources of British Military History* (London: Routledge & Kegan Paul, 1972) p. 1.
9. Correlli Barnett, *Britain and Her Army* (London: Allen Lane, 1970) pp. 31–2.
10. Ibid., p. 41.
11. John Hale, *The Art of War and Renaissance England* (Washington, DC: Folger 1961) p. 3.
12. *Acts of the Privy Council*, VIII.137.
13. Ibid., IX.182, 187–8, 263 and 373.
14. The events which occured in the Forest of Dean were highly organised, when 'some 500 men "did wilt two drums, two coulers and one fife in a warlike and outragious manner assemble themselves together armed with gunnes, pykes, halberdes and other weapons" and set off to cast down enclosures'. See K. Wrightson, *English Society, 1580–1680* (London: Hutchinson, 1982) pp. 150–1.
15. *Acts of the Privy Council*, X.12, 16, 34, 141, and XXII.537 and 557.

16. Buchanan Sharp, *In Contempt of All Authority* (Berkeley, Cal.: California University Press, 1980) pp. 3–4.
17. Wrightson, *English Society, 1580–1680*, p. 149.
18. Sharp, *In Contempt of All Authority*, p. 6–7.
19. Sir Edward Cheyney, *A History of England*, 2 vols (London, 1926) vol. II, p. 28.
20. In the spring of 1596 fewer than 200 men returned to Essex from the 2000 pressed for military service abroad that year, a statistic which led Sir John Smythe to attempt a rebellion during the muster of a further 1000 men destined for a similar fate – an act of disloyalty explained by Lord Burghley as 'by reason of his drinking in the morning of a great deal of white wine and sack' in the White Hart in Colchester. Smythe was in fact a leading military theorist of his time who 'had discussed the legality of sending, pressed men for service overseas with Manwood, Lord Chief Baron', according to his editor, John Hale. See his edition of Smythe's *Certain Discourses Military* (New York, 1964) first published in 1590.
21. Perry Anderson, *Lineages of the Absolutist State* (London: Verso, 1974) p. 125. See also Lawrence Stone, *The Crisis of the Aristocracy, 1558–1641* (London: Oxford University Press, 1967) pp. 199–270.
22. R. C. Smail, 'The Art of War', in Austin Lane Poole (ed.), *Medieval England* (Oxford: Clarendon Press, 1958) pp. 128–67, esp. pp. 162–3.
23. The best example is Richard Bernard, *The Bible-Battals or The Sacred Art Military* (London, 1629).
24. See K. H. Göller (ed.), D. S. Brewer, *The Alliterative Morte Arthure: A Reassessment of the Poem* (Bury St Edmunds: D. S. Brewer, 1981); Juliet Vale, *Edward III and Chivalry* (Bury St Edmunds: Boydell Press, 1982); and Richard W. Kaeuper, *War, Justice and Public Order* (Oxford: Clarendon Press, 1988).
25. Thomas Trussell, *The Soldier Pleading His Own Cause* (London, 1619) sig. C8.
26. R. W. [Richard Ward?], *The Anatomy of Warre* (London, 1642) pp. 1, 5.
27. Göller (ed.), *The Alliterative Morte Arthure*, p. 16.
28. Desiderius Erasmus, *The Praise of Folly*, trans. Leonard F. Dean (Chicago: Chicago University Press, 1946) pp. 112–13.
29. See E. E. Reynolds, *Thomas More and Erasmus* (London: Longman, 1965) p. 125.
30. F. Seebohm, *The Oxford Reformers* (London, 1887) pp. 265–6. Seebohm continues, 'it has been reported that Colet complied with the King's wish, and preached another sermon in favour of the war against France, of the necessity and justice of which, as strictly defensive, the King had convinced him'.
31. Thomas More, *Utopia*, ed. Edward Surtz SJ (New Haven, Conn.: Yale University Press, 1964) p. 125. For a comparison between Erasmus and More on Warfare see M. M. Philips, *The Adages of Erasmus* (Cambridge: Cambridge University Press, 1965) pp. 114–16.
32. Thomas Digges, *Four Paradoxes, or Politique Discourses concerning Militiarie Discipline* (London, 1604) p. 109.
33. Barnaby Rich, *Allarme to England, foreshewing what perilles are procured*

when people live without regarde to Martiall Lawe (London, 1578) sig. C.iii.
34. Glynne Wickham, *The Medieval Theatre* (Cambridge: Cambridge University Press, 1974) p. 155.
35. Rich, *Allarme to England*, sig. H.
36. See Richard W. Kaeuper, *War, Justice and Public Order* (Oxford: Clarendon Press, 1988).
37. Rich, *Allarme to England*, sig. K iiii.
38. Geoffrey Gates, *The Defence of Militarie Profession* (London, 1598) pp. 9–11.
39. Henry Curt (ed.), *Niccolo Machiavelli: 'The Arte of Warre' and 'The Prince' . . . Englished by P. Whitehorne* (London, 1905) p. 6.
40. Digges, *Four Paradoxes*, p. 104.
41. François De La Noue, *The Politicke and Militarie Discourses* (London, 1587) p. 124.
42. Digges, *Four Paradoxes*, p. 51.
43. Rich. *Allarme to England*, sig. I.
44. Thomas Smith, *The Arte of Gunnerie* (London, 166) sigs. Aii. r–v.
45. These qualities, combined in the individual soldier and with each soldier bound to the larger institution are increasingly referred to through the metaphor of the body. The best example is in James Achesome, *The Military Garden, Or Instructions For All Young Soldiers* (London, 1629).
46. Thomas Trussell, *The Souldier Pleading His Own Cause* (London, 1619) Introduction.
47. Humfrey Barwick, *A Briefe Discourse, Concerning the force and effect of all manuell weapons of fire and the disability of the Long Bowe of Archery, in respect of other of greater force now in use* (London, 1594); R. S., *A Briefe Treatise, To proove the necessitie and excellance of the use of archerie* (London, 1696).
48. Thomas Styward, *The Pathwaie to Martiall Discipline* (London, 1581) title-page.
49. Gulielmus Peraldus, *Summa de Vitiis* (c.1236).
50. See my 'Shakespeare: War, Theatre and the National Landscape', *Arena*, vol. 83 (Victoria, Austrialia, 1988) pp. 103–16, for a discussion of warfare in the plays of Shakespeare's contemporaries; Annabel Patterson, *Shakespeare and the Popular Voice* (Oxford: Basil Blackwell, 1989) for an excellent description of popular unrest in the period; and Catherine Belsey, 'The Illusion of Empire: Elizabethan Expansionism and Shakespeare's Second Tetralogy', *Literature and History*, vol. 1, part 2 (second series) (1990) pp. 13–21, for an account of warfare in Shakespeare's histories.

9

Romance in the Eighteenth-Century Chapbook
JOHN SIMONS

Here are some voices from the eighteenth century:

I was fond of books before I began to write poetry these were such that chance came at – 6py Pamphlets that are in the possession of every door calling hawker and found on every book stall at fairs and markets whose titles are as familiar with every one as his own name shall I repeat some of them 'Little Red Riding Hood' 'Valentine and Orson' 'Jack and the Jiant' 'Tom Long the carrier' 'The king and the cobbler' 'Sawney Bean' 'The seven Sleeper' 'Tom Hickathrift' 'Johnny Armstrong' 'Idle Laurence' ... such were the books that delighted me and I savd all the pence I got to buy them for they were the whole world of literature to me and I knew no other.[1]

Here, in passing through the street my eye as usual was attracted by the bookseller's window. I had not forgotten how rich I was and could not resist. I went in, examined some of the stores the shop contained, and with great difficulty restrained myself to the purchase of the *Seven Champions of Christendom*, which cost me a shilling.... With what eagerness I read the valiant deeds of these valiant knights, as I rode home in my empty cart, I will leave the reader to divine.[2]

Some days ago I went into the old printing-office in Bow Church-yard kept by Dicey whose family have kept it fourscore years. There are ushered into the world of literature *Jack and the Giants*; *The Seven Wise Men of Gotham*, and other story books which in my dawning years amused me as much as *Rasselas* does now, I saw the whole scheme with a kind of pleasing romantic feeling to find myself where all my old darlings were printed. I bought two dozen of the story-books and had them bound up with this title, *Curious Productions*.[3]

I found upon conversation with him, that the child had excelent parts, and was a great master of all learning on the other side eight years old. . . . I found he had turned his studies, for about a twelvemonth past, into the lives and adventures of Don Belianis of Greece, Guy of Warwick, the Seven Champions, and other historians of that age. . . . He would tell you the mismanagements of John Hickerthrift, find fault with the passionate temper in Bevis of Southampton, and loved Saint George for being the champion of England; and by this means had his thoughts insensibly moulded into the notions of discretion, virtue and honour.[4]

From agricultural poet to working-class novelist, from literary biographer to middle-class child we have testimonies to the extraordinary prevalence of the medieval or pseudo-medieval romance in chapbook form throughout the eighteenth century. The purpose of this chapter is to survey the history of the Middle English romances in their late and popular forms and to make some comment on the significance of their continued appearance and on the processes by which they were transformed from verse narratives often running to 5000 lines or more into 24-page prose booklets.

However, before we start to look at the chapbook romance in the eighteenth century we must consider something of the pre-history of the texts which were so savagely abridged. There is little doubt in my mind that the primary form of secular narrative in the thirteenth and fourteenth centuries was the chivalric romance written in couplets or in a variety of stanza forms, most interestingly in tail-rhyme.[5] Though much play has been made of the 'popularity' of these texts any consideration of social structure and opportunity in late medieval England leads inexorably to the conclusion that the audience of romance was courtly or, at the very least, composed of wealthy families whose stake in English society gave them a knowledge of and interest in courtly behaviour and a participatory role in the hierarchies of power of which chivalric ideology is the vehicle.[6] This situation changed little in the fifteenth century as the old romances continued to be copied and new prose romances translated from those in vogue in the Burgundian court or modelled on them came into being.[7] The advent of printing in England found romances among the earliest productions of the London printers. In the early years of book production, when it may be fairly said that the printed text had the status of a curious *de luxe* manuscript, the composition of the audience remained much as it had been in the previous century though, of course, the relationship between the idealised society of the narrative and the society of the reader became less immediate.[8]

As printing developed and as access to books became easier the romances attracted a new readership. Throughout the first three-quarters of the sixteenth century versions of Middle English romances feature as staple productions of the major printers. During this period there was a concentrated effort to produce good copies of the medieval manuscripts with some modernisation of language; attempts to modify the narrative so as to change its emphases and adjust it to modern tastes were not part of the process. By the 1580s, however, the permeation of humanistic ideas and the new theology of the Reformation into courtly culture – and in England at least the Reformation was probably a more significant cultural force than the Renaissance – had led to a rejection of romance on the grounds of its profanity, its crudity and its alleged origins in monastic houses. We find this rejection in figures as diverse as Ascham, Sidney and Nashe and this meant that there was a progressive exclusion of the romance narratives from the powerful circles in which they had previously been welcomed.[9]

In the wider circulation of books between the late sixteenth century and the 1630s the chivalric romances not only found a new audience but they were also developed in two main ways to suit that audience's tastes and interests. In some cases they continued to appear in something like their original form though modernised in language and much modified in content; in other cases completely new texts were produced which retained the deep structures and motifs of the chivalric narratives but replaced their content with contemporary material or with representations of a pseudo-medieval world.[10] At the same time a flow of material translated from Spanish and Portuguese and of new English texts based on these Iberian narratives became an important new element in forming a canon of romance and creating a continued demand for such adventure stories.[11] Italian romance epics such as those by Tasso and Ariosto seemed to have found their place in courtly culture, while the Iberian romances crossed the divide between the courtly readers and the new consumers of whom we must now speak.

The changes in the style, presentation and literary context of medieval romance brought with them a new audience. It has been common to refer to this new readership as a 'middle class'. There is nothing wrong with this as long as a good deal of caution is exercised in understanding what this might mean. First, it would be quite wrong to assume that this 'middle-class' readership was necessarily homogeneous in its political alignments or social connections. Such a reading is doomed to over-simplify the social and political struggles which led up to the England Revolution and will ultimately founder on the rocks of any analysis of support for the Royalist, Parliamentary or Neutralist causes in the 1640s. At the same time it is true that a broad base of literacy in urban and, specifically, metropolitian centres had developed cultural needs in a group which had few immediate connections with the Court, was engaged in commerce and manufacture at a range of levels and enjoyed a high degree of social mobility largely as a result of these activities, which had in common a generally Protestant and patriotic world-view and which was economically distinct from the mass of English people who remained in poverty and illiteracy.[12] From a distance, the group appears to have much in common but detailed analysis soon reveals many distinctions of religious belief and political affiliation. Given the difficulties of the term 'middle-class' but wishing to retain some of the political implications inherent in its use and paying due attention to the urban character of the group as a whole, perhaps the word 'citizen' which precisely translates the attractive but complex term 'bourgeois' is the best general adjective which can be applied to its culture and members.

The form and content of the new romances points very clearly to a citizen audience and what little is known about the new professional romance writers and what might be assumed from evidence such as book dedications suggests readers who were engaged in commerce most usually through connections with a craft guild. The urban connection is particularly important for judging audience composition, especially after 1557 when a statute effectively limited the production of vernacular texts to London: this had the practical effect not only of making the control of opinion and expression easier but also of limiting systematic access to literature to those with access to the capital. The metropolitan environment had a significant impact during the years of the reformulation of romance and, in particular, on the penetration of 'realist' elements into the content.

This should not, however, be pushed too far: quests for the origin of the English novel in Tudor and early Stuart prose fiction have usually seized upon Thomas Deloney and, to a lesser extent, Henry Robarts as the founding fathers.[13] This capture ignores two important points: first, it fails to acknowledge the position of the realist elements in the overall *oeuvre* of these citizen writers where they will be found in the midst of a plethora of highly traditional elements from romance; secondly, critics who locate the origins of the novel in the sporadic realism of citizen romance ignore the social descriptions which had been a feature of English romance between the twelfth and the fifteenth centuries and which were inherited from the traditions of Anglo-Norman chivalric narrative. My view is that the novel and the romance constitute separate though related evolutionary pathways in the development of prose fiction and, if we are to find the modern novel embryonic in the early modern period, we should look not to professional romance writers like Robarts but to the collections of novellas based on Italian, French and, occasionally, Spanish models produced by figures such as Thomas Painter, Barnabe Riche and George Pettie or to the translations of European fiction by David Rowland, Thomas Mabbe and, later, Sir Thomas Urqhart.[14]

By the end of the seventeenth century the urban audience had undergone a change of taste and, arguably, fortune so that the chivalric romances described above were now rejected for more 'polite' productions. It is at this point that the main focus of this chapter, the chapbook, makes its appearance. The romances which had been reprinted from medieval originals over the past 200 years and the new citizen romances of the later sixteenth century were now becoming available (with some exceptions) in chapbook form. The classic chapbook was a small booklet, most commonly of 24 pages, which sold very cheaply and, crucially for any comprehension of its significance, was distributed not only through printers and booksellers but also through the network of commercial pedlars, or chapmen, which threaded its way through the English countryside.[15] Furthermore, relaxations of restrictions on printing in the vernacular meant that, as far as chapbooks went at least, other centres grew up to rival London and to service cultural demands of distinctively regional character. Newcastle was particularly important in this respect but other towns such as York and Banbury made valuable contributions to the chapbook industry.[16] Furthermore, the American colonies which at this time must still be considered in the context of mainstream English literary culture generated their own demand for chapbooks which will be considered separately below.

Much of the material on early popular literature has been painted with a broad brush and while it has put popular culture on the academic agenda, it has tended to obscure some of the distinctions which need to be upheld if the chapbook romances are to be properly understood. First, we need to separate out the broadside ballads which circulated in the countryside, either singly or in collections, from the later sixteenth century. The early productions of figures such as Thomas Deloney, William Elderton and Martin Parker gave way in the eighteenth century and, spectacularly, in the nineteenth century to an enormous volume of broadsides either on traditional themes or exploitative of some recent sensational or scandalous event.[17] These productions, popular as they were and often distributed by chapmen, must be kept quite distinct from the chapbooks, which represent a wholly different layer of taste and contain wholly different strata of literary and cultural history.

The range of chapbooks comprehended far more than just romances. Again, some work needs to be done to distinguish the layers of texts which were available to a humble audience in the eighteenth century in order to see how one such layer represented a genuine survival of medieval court culture. There was a wide range of religious and quasi-religious chapbooks which developed either from older sources or from the conscious efforts of particular groups to disseminate their message in print.[18] These books are, to an extent, the popular legacy of the godly culture of the seventeenth century. Anyone who studies records of book ownership in the early modern period will be struck by the near-universality in surviving inventories of Bibles as possessions, with prayer-books and religious tracts coming a close second.[19] However, the ownership of religious books does not necessarily guarantee an informed or godly interest in religious matters. There is, for example, the story of a *Guy of Warwick* chapbook being used for the ceremony of divination by key for which a Bible was more usually appropriate.[20] The material also suggests that in rural England a culture of superstition and magic still existed and this potentially pulled the community back into past world views and cultural orientations.[21] I have an almost somatic scepticism towards positions which attempt to over-elaborate the potential coherence and power of systems of folk belief but we should accept the existence of such beliefs and the possibility of their influence on rural culture.

I shall go on to argue that the chapbook romances represent an important strand in the transmission of medieval culture and in the production of the Middle Ages as a new discourse; but it is worth looking briefly now at other eighteenth-century interests in medieval culture. This digression is necessary to show an increasing division between popular and polite culture in the eighteenth century and thus further isolate the chapbook romances; but it will also demonstrate the way in which the discourse of the Middle Ages can penetrate a cultural formation at various levels and in different configurations. Throughout the latter half of the century antiquarians, scholars and poets were becoming increasingly interested in the Middle Ages as a period the manners and society of which could be used to serve the dual purpose of validating the progress of the Enlightenment and of providing a location in which the repressive force of Reason could be relaxed. Plainly the vogue of MacPherson's 'Ossian' or the poems of Thomas Chatterton represent one aspect of this moment and, more seriously, the careful scholarship of Richard Hurd, Thomas Warton and Joseph Ritson is another.[22] We can also point to the somewhat more flamboyant intervention of Bishop Percy whose *Reliques of Ancient English Poetry* (which included some ballads very closely related to romances) has been characterised as 'unquestionably the most influential and important book of the late eighteenth century'[23] and to the ambiguously valuable work of Sir Walter Scott in collecting ballads in the Highlands of Scotland.[24] In Wales Iolo Morganwg was also busy improving on medieval heritage in the *Trioedd Ynys Prydain*.[25] On the European mainland British activity was paralleled in the work of the Grimms and Herder.[26]

This scholarly and artistic activity is closely related to the roots of Romanticism and the Gothic. It had little to do with the unchecked transmission of medieval material through the chapbooks, but we can note that while the cottages of rural labourers often housed sets of books which contained large elements of the traditional chivalric romances, this same tradition was being rediscovered in the studies of gentleman scholars. However the tradition here was no longer an aspect of a living culture – until it broke out of the study via Romantic poetry – but was fixed by the new disciplines (new in secular vernacular scholarship at least) of philology and textual criticism.

However, if some of the gentry were becoming interested in the Middle Ages for scholarly practice or for the guilty *frisson* of the Gothic and its pornographic thrill, other members of polite households were deriving great pleasure from the chapbook romances which were consumed by their humbler compatriots. This audience was, of course, composed of children who are all too often left out when literary histories come to be written.[27] We have already seen how Boswell mourned the loss of his childhood in the innocent pleasures of the chapbook romance; and evidence of chapbook readership by polite children is furnished by Steele. Testimony of such readership is found in figures as eminent and diverse as Coleridge[28] and Goethe who left a tantalising memory:

> We children therefore had the good fortune to find daily on the little table in front of the second-hand bookseller's doorway these precious remnants of the Middle Ages: *Eulenspiegel, The Four Sons of Aymon, Fair Melusine, Kaiser Octavian, Fortunatus.*[29]

Meanwhile in France, the *bibliothèque bleue*, which included a large number of chapbook romances enjoyed a wider audience than the agricultural one at which it seems to have been primarily aimed. The taste for chapbooks may even have seemed dangerous to those who once had it and the development of books specifically for the delectation and improvement of children such as the productions of John Boreman and, especially, John Newbury's *Little Pretty Pocket Book* may have been a result of attempts to neutralise the threat which children posed to the order of a rational household by diverting their tastes away from the unsuitable sensationalism and violence of the romances.[30] This process reached a culmination, of a kind, in the ironic perspectives of William Blake.[31]

While it is plain that the purveyors, consumers and sponsors of polite culture read chapbooks in their childhood and often maintained an interested in them into adulthood we may also point to a penetration of polite culture into the world of the humbler chapbook readership. It is important to understand that this was so in order fully to savour the complexities of cultural networks in the eighteenth century and to avoid the pitfall of over-simplification through a misleading compartmentalisation. The *locus classicus* for this phenomenon is to be found in the memoirs of the bookseller James Lackington who noted in 1792 that:

> The poorer sort of farmers and even the poor country people in general, who before that spent their evenings in relating stories of witches, ghosts hobgoblins etc., now shorten the winter nights by hearing their sons and daughters read tales, romances etc., and on

entering their houses you may see *Tom Jones* and *Rasselas*, and other entertaing books stuck up on their bacon racks.[32]

Now, Lackington may be referring to chapbooks here in his mention of romances and he may have in mind chapbook versions of some novels which did become available as the century progressed. However, I think that we should take this somewhat colourful account at face value and assume that where there was money for books and the means to read them the rural audience did not observe the protocols of classification into 'polite' and 'popular' which modern scholars are all too apt to do. One is struck, for example, by the figure of the young William Cobbett who, although from labouring stock, has not left any records of chapbook readership but did settle down in a hedge outside Kew Gardens entranced by, of all things, Swift's *Tale of a Tub* on which he had spent all of his worldly wealth.[33] The chapbook and the polite novel could occasionally meet head on. There were chapbook versions of *Moll Flanders* and *Robinson Crusoe*[34] but Samuel Richardson was well acquainted with chapbooks through his apprenticeship to the printer John Wilde and I do no believe that it has been pointed out that the villainous figure of Colbrand in *Pamela* takes his name from one of the enemies of that most durable hero of chapbook romance, Guy of Warwick.[35] We may now turn to a consideration of some of the forms of medieval romance as it appeared in the chapbooks.

Most chapbook scholarship has concentrated on clearing pathways through the thicket of bibliographical problems which surrounds these small and fragile artefacts. We are fortunate in having good annotated material on the stock-holdings and production records of some major producers and sellers. Stock-lists, most notably that of Cluer Dicey and Richard Marshall,[36] show us clearly that romances, either medieval or Elizabethan pseudo-medieval, formed a major part of any collection and there is much truth in F. J. Darton's remark that 'the chapbook from 1700 to 1840 or thereabouts, contained all the popular literature of four centuries in a reduced and degenerate form'.[37] We may argue with the term 'degenerate' but any perusal of stock-lists and other records will confirm the prevalence of romance material in the chapbook library.[38] The concentration on bibliography has to some extent been at the expense of more critical attention to individual chapbooks and I would now like to look in some small detail at the ways in which chapbook compilers treated their material.

Romance in the Eighteenth-Century Chapbook

It would be impossible to perform any analysis of chapbooks without consideration of *Guy of Warwick*.[39] The Middle English form of this romance exists in several manuscript versions which derive from Anglo-Norman originals. *Guy* was one of the earliest romances to be printed (first by Pynson in 1500 and finally by Copland in 1560) and in 1613 Samuel Rowlands, a prolific citizen-writer, recast the story both to modernise the increasingly unfamiliar language and to add some elements which placed the legend more comfortably within the bounds of Jacobean sensibilities.[40] Rowlands's method, however, was largely one of selective abridgement and it was his shortened version that formed the core of the texts from which chapbook versions were derived in the eighteenth century. The chapbook to which I shall refer was printed in London in the middle of the eighteenth century, has the common 24 pages, and is decorated with a variety of illustrations showing Guy in his full armour or, together with his lover Phillis, dressed as a Georgian gentleman.[41]

The chapbook reduces the bulk of Rowlands's (already reduced) poem to a manageable size but retains the broad outlines of Guy's exciting adventures without lapsing into incoherence. The text retains at least one of Rowlands's major additions in Guy's Hamlet-like address to a skull. This passage is worth quoting in full as it gives an excellent sense of the tone of chapbooks and also shows how chapbooks could achieve a distinctive voice even in a limited compass:

> Guy pursued his intended journey and coming to a grave, he took up a worm-eaten Skull, which he thus addressed – Perhaps thou wert a Prince, or a mighty Monarch, a King, a Duke, or a Lord! – But the King and the Beggar must all return to the earth; and therefore man had need to remember his dying hour. Perhaps thou mightest been a Queen or a Dutchess, or a Lady varnished with much beauty; but now thou art worms-meat, lying in the grave, the Sepolchre of all creatures.

The chapbook does not attempt to abridge everything but makes bold cuts in the longer and more complex adventures. Only the highlights of Guy's legend remain: his first meeting with Phillis and the adventures by which he wins her hand, the battle with a dragon, his religious conversion and penitential journey and return, the battle with the giant Colborn (*sic*) at Winchester, his saintly death. To give an example here is the moment of Guy's conversion:

> In the very height of Guy's glory, being exalted to his fathers dignities, Conscience biddeth him repent of all his former sins, and of his youthful time spent in the behalf of women; so Guy resolved to travel to the Holy Land like a Pilgrim.

This episode occupies a proportionally small space in the long verse texts of the Guy story. In the chapbook it achieves a proportional prominence which matches its pivotal importance in Guy's life. Here are the complex series of adventures which Guy has in association with Earl Terry:

> Soon after Guy met with the Earl of Terry, whose father was confined in his castle by Duke Otto; but he and that Lord posted thither, and freed the castle immediately; and Guy in an open field slew Duke Otto hand to hand; but his dying words of repentance moved Guy to remorse and pity.

Whereas the long versions describe these at leisure, the chapbook slims them down in order to make space for events which readers expected to find in the romance of Guy.

What I am suggesting is that the compiler of the Guy chapbook went carefully about his or her work. The reader is taken through the narrative by stepping from emotional peak to emotional peak. Far from being a brutal and unreflective assault on a complex narrative, there has been a real effort to identify and preserve a central core of experience in the romance which is now made the subject matter of the chapbook. The series of complicated but, ultimately, rather similar adventures which in the extended poems form a vehicle for transporting Guy from one important event to another, are stripped away so that the heart of the text is exposed. This sensible approach to the business of chapbook compilation which leaves only the affective bones of the story may go some way to explaining how it was that such apparently simple texts could achieve such emotional power over their readership.

The compiler of a *Seven Champions of Christendom* chapbook produced in Newcastle in 1834 went about the task of abridging an extremely long and complex narrative in a similar way.[42] The major section of the *Seven Champions*, which was a text first produced by the citizen-writer Richard Johnson in 1596, with a second part in 1597, concerns the adventures of St George and these are derived almost wholly from the Middle English romance of *Sir Bevis of Hamton* which was printed by de Worde in 1500, Pynson in 1503 and Copland in 1565.[43] Grafted on to St George's legend are stories of St Andrew, St Patrick, St David, St James, St Antony and St Dennis which derive from a range of sources including other Middle English romances. While *Guy of Warwick* exemplifies the potential of Middle English romance for presenting a hero who has a contemplative side *Bevis of Hamton* chronicles the doings of a violent and thuggish hero who is redeemed by his patriotism and muscular piety. This robust godliness was, of course, attractive to the citizen audience of the later sixteenth century and has continued to be so almost up to the present day. The latest editions of nearly full versions of the story that I have seen are undated illustrated volumes for children which appear to come from the 1920s, while as late as 1972 a toy-theatre version was newly produced.[44]

The *Seven Champions* chapbook attempts to do for St George what the *Guy* chapbook had done for its eponymous hero. Instead of going in for a wholesale compression it attempts to abridge the complex adventures of St George so that the main elements stand out: the imprisonment by Kalyb, the rescue of Sabra from the dragon, the imprisonment by the Sultan of Persia, the final destruction of the pagan army. However, the original text is so complex and full of action that the narrative is not so easily brought together by a chain of emotional links. Here is an example:

> The heralds sounded a charge, and the two knights engaged. At the first onset, their spears were broken into pieces, and men and horses were thrown to the ground. The accuser leaped up, and struck so fiercely, that he cleft the enemy's shield in two, St George then put forth his strength, and smote off the accuser's right arm, so that he sank to earth and died.
>
> St George now set sail with his beloved Sabra for Persia, which on reaching, he found the other six champions had conquered. After completing their conquest, the seven champions took shipping for England where they were received with every mark of joy.

Even so the chapbook, fairly late in the tradition, does show how a valid attempt could be made to retain a credible narrative in a short space by stressing the more easily recognisable and thrilling elements in the original. It is noteworthy that *Seven Champions* material, perhaps from chapbooks, made its way into a range of English mummers' plays and, although the pathways by which the texts were transmitted are subject to great speculation, this is a good testimony to the availability of romance in the English countryside.[45]

In both cases it would be difficult to argue that the chapbooks are attempting to promote any particular world-view. I shall later outline two ways in which the French *bibliothèque bleue* has been read and see to what extent these positions can be related to the English chapbook. Provisionally though, I would suggest that in the two representative texts which I have briefly discussed here a far from thoughtless attempt has been made to make two major works of medieval/Elizabethan literature available to an eighteenth-century audience in an affordable and coherent form. The pleasures of such texts derive from the potent combination of a tightly packed narrative and, I would guess, from the sense that the reader has of participating in an old and valued literary tradition. The extent to which this sense of participation, with all the values of self-improvement which it potentially carries, may be seen as ideologically loaded either for or against the audience needs to be debated closely.

Before we make a further assessment of the role of chapbooks among the English reading public we might pause to consider the American picture, from which we can learn much. It has been said that 'English chapbboks . . . began to deluge America about the beginning of the eighteenth century'[46] and that 'chapbooks, imported from Europe and widely imitated in the colonies, were the principal medium for popular literature in early America'.[47] However, these positions may be over-statements as a mass of evidence exists to show that, just as in England, the lack of systematic access to the book market led to wide-ranging reading with an emphasis on religious materials. For instance, the 1780s found Abner Sanger, who resided on the frontier and had little access to books, reading a copy of Bishops Butler's *Analogy of Religion* which he had been given by a local doctor as payment for agricultural labour. By the turn of the century Candace Roberts, an itinerant painter of clock-faces and tinware was immersing herself in Romantic novels.[48] Both these figures were potential chapbook readers but, as R. D. Brown has shown, proximity to a port went hand-in-hand with 'the ready availability of printed goods, especially books'.[49] When we look at the colonies and the early USA we are struck by the existence of libraries which would have done credit to the polite *salons* of the Old World but, at the same time, we find good evidence for the popularity of chapbook romances.[50] In 1757 the Philadelphia bookseller David

Hall ordered 24 *Robin Hood* chapbooks and twelves copies of the *Seven Champions* from London, while in 1760 William Bradford's list included both the *Seven Champions* and *Guy of Warwick*.[51] In the 1680s John Usher's establishment in Boston imported 3421 books and sold six copies each of the pseudo-medieval texts *Tom a Lincolne* and *Jack of Newbury* as well as carrying stocks of *Guy of Warwick*.[52] The New World obviously had its own needs but we can see in these figures a basic homogeneity between English and American culture which expresses itself in the popularity and prevalence of the chapbook romance as an element in the fundamental texture of the eighteenth-century mind. Furthermore, the American example teaches us that, given the different physical and social conditions in the two continents, the chapbooks could not have been subject to uniform uses or interpretation.

That the romance chapbooks formed an important part of the mental world of the eighteenth-century humble reader cannot be doubted. The chapbooks were also an important possession. We know enough about the economy of the book trade and deduce enough about patterns of ownership to reject the view that chapbooks were ephemeral articles of low value and transitory possession. Both Darton and Vincent make this point, though in different ways:

> They *were* preserved because they were not so numerous or easily procured as to be thrown away lightly.[53]

> Print was still too rare a commodity to be read and thrown away at one sitting. The precious dog-eared pages were read and re-read, borrowed re-borrowed until imperceptibly they merged back into the communal oral tradition whence most had originally come.[54]

We should not underestimate chapbooks. At the same time we would be making a grave error if we attempted to cast all the texts in one mould. For example, there ought to be due attention paid, especially for the earlier eighteenth century, to the determinations of regional difference. Similarly, it is clear that the role of chapbooks as children's literature as discussed above would have been very different to that of reading for adults. We do not find in English, at least not in developed forms, story-telling traditions such as the *veillée* (but does the quotation from Lackington cited above hint at such?) where in France – and also in Italy – communal recitations formed a part of village life in the evenings. The material from these gatherings was raided for the polite tales of Perrault which have no near English equivalent.[55] Nor do we find that complex interpenetration of the learned and the popular which is represented by the Provençal writings of the Abbé Fabre.[56] This suggests strongly to me that an oral tradition in England existed only relatively weakly in association with the popular versions of once courtly or urban texts contained in the chapbooks, or had been significantly attenuated by the godly attitudes which were associated with the so-called reform of popular culture in the seventeenth century.[57] Thus the Middle Ages passed into the Enlightenment not, as we might expect, through layers of oral traditional and folk-memory but through authentic versions of literate medieval culture. The precise relationship between the oral-traditional and the literate must surely have been subject to strong regional fluctuations. We should also note the strength of the continuing distinction between urban and rural.

However, while we must acknowledge the sharp distinctions between, say, Oxfordshire and Yorkshire, and the sharper distinctions between town and country, we must also acknowledge the role of chapbooks as a relatively homogeneous body of print which flowed through all areas via the publishers and the chapmen, in diminishing the importance of these variations and in building cultural bridges. These bridges not only enabled regions to share in a common culture in spite of the difficulties of communication but also provided an extraordinary continuity of cultural provision. The romances had a special role to play here, for they both represented the latest stage of a tradition which had existed since at least the thirteenth century and internalised and thus validated scraps of the oral and traditional culture that they were helping to replace.

The study of chapbooks poses some important questions for traditional models of periodisation or to any conventional model of audience structure which conveniently aligns class or age with specific reading materials. Chapbook studies also tend to provide evidence of cultural continuities which unsettle attempts to present the transitions from the Middle Ages to the Enlightenment as a series of decisive political ruptures. On the other hand, these very continuities also unsettle Romantic scholars who wish to find networks of rural culture distinct from the alienating pressure of the Industrial Revolution and even the 'march of intellect'. Plainly, certain historical events, for example the Revolution of 1688, do set decisive new social agendas and determine political paradigms which will be incommensurate with those of the past; and evidence certainly does exist of particularised regional cultures. However, it cannot be ignored that the chapbooks appear to evade both immediate determination and local signification. The point is that time, in so far as it is a dimension of political change, does not move at a uniform rate. The ultimately determining power of large shifts in the macro-structure of the economy does not necessarily exert a uniform force across all levels of the cultural superstructures. While events of, say, 1640, 1688 and 1745 accelerated movement in every political detail, none but a limited section of literate culture could respond at the same rate.[58] The world may have changed decisively for the English in 1688 but that does not mean that they threw away their libraries nor that they became disposed to read their books in very different ways. Obviously changes will take place over time but it should also be remembered that the perception of significance in the literary text has as much to do with its reception within the context of a complex cultural tradition as with any unmediated confrontation of reader and narrative. In other words, meaning as it inheres in texts such as chapbook romances is an inheritance which is not easily alienated whatever the changing face of the political economy.

In France the *bibliothèque bleue* has been seen in two contrasting ways. On the one hand, Mandrou maintains that the texts represent escapist fantasy; on the other, Muchembled sees an attempt actively to promote a climate of cultural conformity and, therefore, political docility.[59] Peter Burke has attempted to mediate between these positions by proposing that the booklets of the *bibliothèque bleue* 'appealed particularly to the more prosperous peasant families within a given community, the "brokers" between that community and the outside world who bought them as a status symbol and a means of reinforcing their position in the community with the prestige of print'.[60] I believe that this view is probably substantially correct for France but that it is not fully applicable to England where there was no peasantry in the French sense nor was rural society organised along anything like similar lines.

Work on chapbooks must, however, learn from work on the *bibliothèque bleue*. We have already seen that there was a complex interpenetration of popular and polite cultures during the eighteenth century. We can also imagine that, although chapbooks were the most inexpensive form of literature, in a society where money was short only limited funds were available for their purchase and that only families who had some surplus income from time to time could buy them. This gives some value to Burke's hypothesis. Although Mandrou has done valuable work on classifying and describing early popular literature, I find his conclusions difficult to understand or, rather, less than useful: surely 'escapism' is a position which can only be subjectively identified from within a given social condition and which also implies a scale of comparative values to which the French peasantry probably had very limited access. Muchembled's hypothesis tends to fall because there is absolutely no evidence that any chapbook publisher or distributor sought to inculcate any world view (except in so far as such tradition materials will appear to contain ostensibly conservative ideologies), nor, at a higher level, is there any evidence of any interest in the control of popular literature of its potential role as propaganda. If anything the position was precisely the opposite, and thinkers from Locke onwards who bothered about these things at all saw the traditional values of chapbooks as obstructive to progress and, where chapbooks were used as the vehicle of specific messages, it was for radical evangelical and temperance purposes.[61]

In spite of the absence of any evidence to the contrary, I find it hard to assent to any position which argues that the chapbooks represented a coherent world-view which was imposed upon a reading public. It would, in any case, be silly to believe that people accept everything they read simply because it is traditional. One should surely assume that some attempts were made to understand the doings of Guy of Warwick in the context of the world as the reader found it. It is impossible, though, to speculate on the form that these attempts may have taken: what we can say is that the chapbooks provided readers with representations of a world which contrasted with their own, enabled them to develop some sense of a history in which they themselves were caught up and to explore value systems which were, perhaps new to them. In other words, chapbook romances provided some basic intellectual and educational pleasures which were enacted within a more general reading of secular and religious material. An overview of the range of chapbooks available to the eighteenth-century reader and, indeed, of the categories which modern scholars have used to describe them, suggests that a careful collector could assemble a compendious array of popular knowledge in which the romances provided both literature and history.

If the chapbooks had any other role it was in the process of cultural bridge-building described above and it is not impossible that the permeation of popular reading material throughout the country did have a small part to play in the hardening sense of the United Kingdom as a nation state.[62] I believe that chapbooks did, in fact, have such a role not by design but by the nature of the industry which was able to distribute them and thus bridge some of the gaps in easy communication between communities which tend to characterise pre-industrial societies. The political and ideological changes which were needed to ensure the success of new mercantile, industrial and imperial nations could take place more easily within a state which recognised the bonds of association between its constituent territories. However, my project here has been to survey the field of the chapbook romance and to demonstrate some ways in which it preserved the traditions of medieval narrative well into the nineteenth century; discussion on the function of these small books in history will be left as suggestion and speculation.

NOTES

1. John Clare, *Autobiographical Fragments*, ed. E. Robinson (Oxford: Oxford University Press, 1986) pp. 56–7.
2. Thomas Holcroft, *Hugh Trevor*, ed. S. Deanes (Oxford: Oxford University Press, 1973) p. 41.
3. James Boswell, *Boswell's London Journal*, ed. W. A. Pottle (London: Heinemann, 1950) p. 299.
4. Richard Steele, *The Tatler*, no. 95.
5. The most recent general survey of the Middle English romances is by R. W. Barron, *Medieval English Romance* (London: Longman, 1988).
6. See, for example, V. B. Richmond, *The Popularity of Middle English Romance* (Bowling Green, Ohio: Bowling Green University Popular Press, 1975).
7. For a survey of these, see N. F. Blake, 'William Caxton's Chivalric Romances and the Burgundian Renaissance in England', *Essays and Studies*, vol. 57 (1976) pp. 1–10.
8. R. S. Crane, *The Vogue of Medieval Chivalric Romance in the English Renaissance* (Menasha, Wis., 1917) surveys this field.
9. On this rejection, see R. P. Adams, 'Bold Bawdry and Open Manslaughter', *Huntington Library Quarterly*, vol. 23 (1960).
10. For studies of two authors of such texts see J. Simons, 'Realistic Romance: the Prose Fiction of Thomas Deloney', *Contexts and Connections*, vol. 12 (1983); and 'Open and Closed Books: a Semiotic Approach to the History of Jacobean Popular Fiction', in C. Bloom (ed.), *Jacobean Poetry and Prose* (London: Macmillan, 1988) pp. 8–24. See also L. B. Wright, *Middle Class Culture in Elizabethan England* (Chapel Hill, N. C.: University of North Carolina Press, 1935).

11. A full account of these texts is given by H. Thomas, *Spanish and Portuguese Romances of Chivalry* (Cambridge: Cambridge University Press, 1920); and D. O'Connor, *Amadis de Gaulle* (New Brunswick, N. J.: Rutger State University Press, 1970).
12. The best analysis of this area remains that by D. Cressey, *Literacy and the Social Order* (Cambridge: Cambridge University Press, 1980).
13. See, for example, M. Spufford, *Small Books and Pleasant Histories* (Cambridge: Cambridge University Press, 1981); M. Schlauch, *Antecedents of the English Novel* (London: Oxford University Press, 1963); J. J. Jusserand, *The English Novel in the Time of Shakespeare* (London: Benn, 1966); and P. Salzmann, *English Prose Fiction, 1588–1700* (Oxford: Clasendon Press, 1985).
14. Rowland's translation of *Lazarillo de Tormes* was published in 1586; Mabbe's *The Rogue*, a translation of *Guzman de Alfarache* appeared in 1622; Urquhart's translation of Rabelais was not printed until 1708 but was probably composed during the 1650s.
15. On chapmen see Spufford, *Small Books*, and also her study *The Great Reclothing of Rural England* (London: Hambledon Press, 1984).
16. The fundamental work for any study of chapbooks in Victor Neuburg's *Chapbook Bibliography* (London: Vine Press, 1964). Neuburg's *The Penny Histories* (London: Oxford University Press, 1968) gives facsimiles of seven chapbooks. John Ashton's *Chapbooks of the Eighteenth Century* (London: Chatto & Windus, 1882) is sometimes eccentric but still valuable. Studies of local chapbooks include C. A. Federer, *Yorkshire Chapbooks* (London, 1899); F. M. Thomson, *Newcastle Chapbooks* (Newcastle: Oriel Press, 1969); E. Pearson, *Banbury Chapbooks* (Welwyn Garden City: Seven Dials Press, 1970); and P. G. Isaac, *Halfpenny Chapbooks by William Davison* (Newcastle: Frank Graham, 1971).
17. The basic study of these ballads in the early period is by H. E. Rollins, 'The Black-Letter Broadside Ballad', *PMLA*, vol. 34, (1919) pp. 258–341. Work on later periods may be found in C. Hindley, *Curiosities of Street Literature* (Welwyn Garden City: Seven Dials Press, 1970); L. Shepard, *The History of Street Literature* (Newton Abbot: David & Charles, 1973); L. James, *Print and the People* (Harmondsworth, Middx: Penguin, 1978); M. Vicinus, *The Industrial Muse* (London: Croom Helm, 1974); C. M. Simpson, *The British Broadside Ballad and its Music* (New Brunswick, N. J.: Rutgers State University Press, 1986); and L. Shepard, *The Broadside Ballad* (Wakefield, W. Yorks.: E. P. Publishers, 1978).
18. On religious chapbooks, see D. M. Valenze, 'Prophecy and Popular Literature in the Eighteenth Century', *Journal of Ecclesiastical History*, vol. 29 (1978) pp. 75–92; B. Capp, *Astrology and the Popular Press* (London: Faber & Faber, 1979); and two works by D. Vincent, *Bread, Knowledge and Freedom* (London: Methuen 1981), and *Literacy and Popular Culture* (Cambridge: Cambridge University Press, 1989).
19. For the earlier period, see P. Clark, 'The Ownership of Books in England, 1560–1640', in L. Stone, *Schooling and Society* (London: Johns Hopkins University Press, 1976); for general surveys, see R. D. Altick,

Romance in the Eighteenth-Century Chapbook 141

The English Common Reader (Berkeley, Cal.: University of California Press, 1963); and R. K. Webb, *The English Working Class Reader* (London: George Allen & Unwin, 1955). See also J. P. Klancher, *The Making of English Reading Audiences, 1790–1832* (Madison: University of Wisconsin Press, 1987).
20. Vincent, *Literacy and Popular Culture*, p. 177.
21. The best study of folk beliefs in this period is K. Thomas, *Religion and the Decline of Magic* (Harmondsworth, Middx: Penguin, 1975). R. de V. Renwick, *English Folk Poetry* (London: Batsford, 1980) is also valuable.
22. On Hurd *et al.*, see A. Johnston, *Enchanted Ground* (London: Athlone Press, 1964).
23. D. Dugaw, *Warrior Women and Popular Balladry, 1650–1850* (Cambridge: Cambridge University Press, 1989) p. 50.
24. On Scott, see D. Vincent, 'The Decline of the Oral Tradition in Popular Culture', in R. D. Storch, *Popular Culture and Custom in Nineteenth-Century England* (London: Croom Helm, 1982) pp. 20–47.
25. Morganwg is dealt with in Rachel Bromwich, *Trioedd Ynys Prydain and Welsh Scholarship* (Cardiff: University of Wales, 1968).
26. See J. Zipes, *The Brothers Grimm* (London: Routledge, 1988); and I. Berlin, *Vico and Herder* (London: Hogarth, 1976).
27. F. J. H. Darton, *Children's Books in England*, 3rd edn (Cambridge: Cambridge University Press, 1982) remains the standard work but V. Neuburg, *Popular Education in Eighteenth-Century England* (London: Woburn Press, 1971) is especially valuable in this context.
28. On Coleridge see J. L. Lowes, *The Road to Xanadu* (London: Picador, 1978) pp. 416–17.
29. Quoted in B. Hurlimann, *Three Centuries of Children's Books in Europe* (London: Oxford University Press, 1967) pp. xiii–xv.
30. John Newbury's *Little Pretty Pocket Book* book has been given a modern edition by M. P. Thwait (London: Oxford University Press, 1966). While Newbury is usually given the credit for being the first author to cater specifically for children, a strong case for giving this honour to John Boreman is made by P. Muir in his *English Children's Books* (London: Batsford, 1954) p. 60.
31. Blake and the chapbook is discussed by G. Summerfield, *Fantasy and Reason: Children's Literature in the Eighteenth Century* (London: Methuen, 1983).
32. Cited by R. Porter, *English Society in the Eighteenth Century* (Harmondsworth, Middx: Penguin, 1982) p. 253. This passage is also cited with some commentary by L. Lowenthal in his essay 'Eighteenth-Century England: a Case Study', in his *Literature and Mass Culture* (New Brunswick, N. J.: Transaction, 1983) pp. 75–152.
33. William Cobbett, *The Political Register*, 19 February 1820.
34. On novels in chapbook form see two essays by P. Rogers: 'Moll in the Chapbooks', in his *Literature and Popular Culture in Eighteenth-Century England* (Brighton, Sussex: Harvester, 1985) pp. 183–197, and 'Classics and Chapbooks', in I. Rivers (ed.), *Books and their Readers in Eighteenth-Century England* (Leicester: Leicester University Press, 1982) pp. 27–46.

35. Richardson's apprenticeship to Wilde is dealt with in C. H. Flynn, *Samuel Richardson: Man of Letters* (Princeton, N. J.: Princeton University Press, 1982) p. 153.
36. This is reproduced in Neuburg's *Chapbook Bibliography*, pp. 75–80.
37. Darton, *Children's Books in England*, p. 81.
38. A survey of material which shows how some texts existed alongside the chapbooks is E. R. Wasserman, *Elizabethan Poetry in the Eighteenth Century* (Urbana, Ill.: University of Illinois, 1948) Appendix, 'The Popularity of Elizabethan Prose Fiction in the Eighteenth Century', pp. 253–9.
39. R. S. Crane, 'The Vogue of *Guy of Warwick* from the Middle Ages to the Romantic Revival', *PMLA*, vol. 30 (1915) pp. 125–94 is a magisterial study of this topic.
40. Rowlands's works have not had a modern editor. They are available in the limited edition produced by E. Gosse for the Hunterian Club (Glasgow, 1880). F. O. Waage has edited Rowlands' *Uncollected Poems* (Gainesville, Fla: Scholars' Facsimiles and Reprints, 1970).
41. See Ashton, *Chapbooks of the Eighteenth Century*, and Neuburg, *The Penny Histories*, from which my quotations are taken.
42. An abridged version of this chapbook, from which I have quoted, is to be found in James, *Print and the People*, pp. 195–8.
43. See Darton, *Children's Books in England*, and J. Simons, 'Medieval Chivalric Romance and Elizabethan Popular Literature' (unpublished thesis, Exeter University, 1982).
44. *The Seven Champions of Christendom* (London: Pollock's Toy Museum, 1972).
45. See E. K. Chambers, *The English Folk Play* (Oxford: Oxford University Press, 1933) and E. Tiddy, *The English Mummers' Plays* (Chicheley, Bucks.: Paul P. B. Minet, 1972).
46. M. Kiefer, *American Children through their Books* (Philadelphia: University of Pennsylvania, 1948) p. 10.
47. R. Nye, *The Unembarrassed Muse* (New York: Dial Press, 1970) p. 23.
48. R. D. Brown, *Knowledge is Power* (Oxford: Oxford University Press, 1989) on Sanger, p. 148; on Roberts, pp. 168–9.
49. Ibid., p. 127.
50. 'Polite' libraries are studied by R. B. Davis in his *A Colonial Southern Bookshelf* (Athens: University of Georgia, 1979).
51. E. Wolf II, *The Book Culture of a Colonial American City* (Oxford: Clarendon Press, 1988) p. 69.
52. J. D. Hart, *The Popular Book* (Berkeley, Cal.: University of California Press, 1961) pp. 15–17.
53. Darton, *Children's Books in England*, p. 70.
54. Vincent, *Literacy and Popular Culture*, p. 198.
55. See R. Darnton, *The Great Cat Massacre* (Harmondsworth, Middx: Penguin, 1985).
56. See J. Ladurie, *Love, Death and Money in the Pays d'Oc* (Harmondsworth, Middx: Penguin, 1984). Relevant comparative materials from very different cultures and very different times may be found in G. Armistead and J. Silvermann (eds), *The Judaeo-Spanish Ballad*

Chapbooks of Yacob Abraham Yona (Berkeley, Cal.: University of California Press, 1971), and F. J. Norton and E. M. Wilson (eds), *Two Spanish Verse Chap-books* (Cambridge: Cambridge University Press, 1969). Both of these collections include chivalric material.

57. On this, see P. Burke, *Popular Culture in Early Modern Europe* (London: Temple Smith, 1978); B. Reay, *Popular Culture in Seventeenth-Century England* (London: Routledge, 1988); D. Underdowne, *Revel, Riot and Rebellion* (Oxford: Clarendon Press, 1985); J. M. Golby and A. W. Purdue, *The Civilisation of the Crowd* (London: Batsford, 1984); and S. Easton, *Disorder and Discipline* (London: Temple Smith, 1988).

58. My ideas about the nature of historical time owe much to those of F. Braudel, especially as worked out in his *The Mediterranean in the Age of Philip II* (London: Fontana, 1975). See also his collection of essays: *On History* (London: Weidenfeld & Nicolson, 1980).

59. R. Mandrou, *De la culture populaire au dix-huitième siècle* (Paris: Imago, 1985); R. Muchembled, *Culture populaire et culture des élites* (Paris: 1971).

60. Peter Burke, 'The "Discovery" of Popular Culture', in R. Samuel (ed.), *People's History and Socialist Theory* (London: Routledge & Kegan Paul, 1981) pp. 216–21.

61. See V. Neuburg, *Popular Literature* (Harmondsworth, Middx: Penguin, 1977) pp. 249–64 for an excellent survey of tracts.

62. P. Womack, *Improvement and Romance* (London: Macmillan, 1989) discusses the ways in which the Scottish Highlands were 'constructed' so as to be capable of integration into the United Kingdom.

10

'The Paths of Virtue and Early English': F. J. Furnivall and Victorian Medievalism
PETER FAULKNER

In 1893 William Morris published an edition of Robert Steele's *Medieval Lore* at the Kelmscott Press. In his Preface he remarked on the changing attitudes to the Middle Ages in the nineteenth century. The early enthusiasts for the period had been *'laudatores temporis acti'*, looking back with nostalgia to a simpler world; by contrast:

> at the present time those who take pleasure in studying the life of the Middle Ages are more commonly to be found in the ranks of those who are pledged to the forward movement of modern life; while those who are vainly striving to stem the progress of the world are as careless of the past as they are fearful of the future.[1]

Although F. J. Furnivall did not share Morris's commitment to Socialism, he was certainly a 'progressive' thinker in that he wanted a knowledge of England's past to energise the creation of a better future for all her citizens. His life-long commitment to the Working Men's College went along with his interest in English culture and history in ways that were positive and creative. His work should be known in the context of the general theories of culture and society put forward by Carlyle, Ruskin and Morris. He was not a major shaper of social ideas, as they were, but an energetic and productive worker whose activities helped to give substance to his contemporaries' (and so our) view of the English past, with obvious ideological implications. He was also an ebullient and sometimes belligerent character, one of a group amusingly criticised by Quiller-Couch in 1916 as 'wonderful fighters in a cause that at first seemed hopeless', but also 'extremely irascible men': 'If you happened to disagree with them, their answer was a sturdy Anglo-Saxon brick.'[2]

Born in 1825, the son of a prosperous medical man, Frederick James Furnivall was educated at University College, London, and Trinity Hall, Cambridge (where he devoted much of his time and energy to sculling). He then entered Lincoln's Inn, and was called to the Bar at Gray's Inn early in 1849. He established a conveyancing business in the same year but soon found himself involved in quite other activities, namely, the study of the English language, and workers' education, which together became his life's work.

Furnivall joined the Philological Society in 1847 on coming to London, and by 1853 was committed enough to its activities to become one of its Secretaries. In the same period he was strongly influenced by J. M. Ludlow and C. E. Maurice, whose Christian Socialism was an attempt to bridge the appalling gap between the privileged and the underprivileged in Victorian society. This led in 1849 to the opening of a school in Bloomsbury for boys and men, and in 1852 to holding classes near Oxford Street for working men. But the main educational achievement of the group was their establishment of the Working Men's College in Red Lion Square in October 1854, with Maurice as principal. Furnivall spent much of his time at the College, teaching English grammar and literature (a comparatively new activity at the time) and contributing a great deal to the social life of the College by organising concerts, dances and Sunday rambles, as well as botanical walks and outings on the river. All this was not uncontroversial, because Maurice believed that Sundays should be reserved for religious activities. Furnivall carried the day, but his relationship with Maurice became purely formal. He remained enthusiastically devoted to the College throughout his life, and is one of the strongest presences in the account of the College edited by J. Llewelyn Davies in 1904.

As his disagreement with Maurice suggests, Furnivall was one of the many Victorians to lose his early faith in Christianity. He became an outspoken agnostic and what we may term a missionary for Early English. Dr Benzie, in the only recent book on Furnivall, gives an illuminating account of this phase of his development:

> the buoyant fervor and piety with which he had lived the evangelical life was now redirected with fresh, optimistic and compensatory energy to more secular ends: the celebration and reclamation of the golden ages of England peopled with noble, heroic ancestors.[3]

This exaggerates the extent of Furnivall's idealisation of the past, but it does catch something of his tone. John Munro's account of 1911 (quoted by Benzie) makes a parallel point:

> Tennyson's *Idylls* had already turned his attention to that distant past wherefrom faint but audible voices called to him, sometimes in the very accent of his own warmhearted humanism and his own comprehensive democracy; and he grew more and more convinced that these forefathers' voices should be made audible and significant to modern men.[4]

This motivation certainly lies behind the commitments of these years, and was actually to sustain the efforts of a whole lifetime. Involvement with the Philological Society led, via the suggestion of R. C. Trench, to the idea of a great new dictionary, and in 1861 Furnivall was appointed editor. He accumulated material and encouraged many others to do so, but could never bring the necessary time or discipline to the work, which was taken over by the Oxford University Press in 1876. Only with the appointment of James Murray as editor did the great project proceed towards the triumphant conclusion recently celebrated in Katharine Murray's *Caught in the Web of Words*.[5] But it should be noted that both Murray and W. W. Skeat were prepared to praise Furnivall's contribution to the conception and achievement of the dictionary, despite Katharine Murray's evidence for his shortcomings. Next he began what was to become his life's work, the publication of early texts. The first of these was the Authurian epic of the fifteenth century, the *Seynte Graal*, which he prepared for the Roxburghe Club in 1861. This was followed in 1862 by Robert of Brunne's *Handlyng Synne*, to which he added William of Waddington's *Manuel des Peschiez*. In 1862 he also produced a collection of early English manuscript poems for the Philological Society. But it was characteristic of his enthusiasm – and impatience – that he decided that the process of publication needed to be much swifter than the existing organisations allowed and so created, largely by his own efforts, though sweeping many others along with him, the Early English Text Society. Its rationale is clearly expressed in the formulation to be found inside the cover of the Society's publications from 1892:

> The Early English Text Society was started by Dr. Furnivall in 1864 for the purpose of bringing the mass of Old English Litera-

ture within the reach of the ordinary student, and of wiping away the reproach under which England had long rested, of having felt little interest in the monuments of her early language and life.

The 'reproach' was one felt by few of Furnivall's contemporaries, but by the end of his life 46 years later his efforts had made it irrelevant.

It remains to consider more carefully Furnivall's motivations and intentions in his mission. This is harder to do than might be expected, because to him it was so much a matter of commonsense, of an unquestioned assumption, that he was not explicit about it. It is far more characteristic of him to suggest that it needed to be done. This raises the important question of when and why national cultures need to articulate themselves in detail. For the Victorians it seems to have become necessary in the mid-nineteenth century, as the definition of the nation moved into question, with ever-increasing awareness of class divisions. It was felt that an increased knowledge of the past would help unity in the future – a romantic and simplifying view. Munro's comment about Furnivall is relevant here: if the voices of the past called him 'sometimes in the very accents of his own warmhearted humanism and his own comprehensive democracy', it was because this was the music that he wished to hear. His evident confidence in the progress of humanism and democracy led him to believe that any knowledge of the English past would contribute to the creation of a healthier future. Whereas the great medieval historians of the period drew attention to such institutions as the guilds or the Parliament, Furnivall subsumed everything under the general heading 'life'. He would certainly 'take sides' in reading history, always sympathising with the underdog, but he shows little sense of historical development. Thus it is that although we can reasonably consider him as contributing much to Victorian medievalism, he himself used the term 'Early English' to cover the whole range from before the Conquest to the reign of Elizabeth. No one was ever less addicted to rigid compartmentalisation. It is consistent with this eclecticism that he should have gone on to found not only the Chaucer Society but also the New Shakspere Society – and the Browning Society.

The Early English Text Society, founded in 1864, is, however, Furnivall's greatest achievement. By the time he died in 1910 it had issued well over 100 texts in the Ordinary Series derived from manuscript sources, and almost as many in the Extra Series from early printed sources. No one did as much to make available material about Early English life. What he saw as the achievement of the Series is made clear in the note which appears in the inside cover of Early English Text Society publications from 1892:

> During the twenty-eight years of the Society's existence, it has produced, with whatever shortcomings, an amount of good solid work for which all students of our Language, and some of our Literature, must be grateful, and which has rendered possible the beginnings (at least) of proper Histories and Dictionaries of that Language and Literature, and illustrated the thoughts, the life, the manners and customs of our forefathers and foremothers.

The last phrase in particular explains the focus of Furnivall's interest, and incidentally also illustrates an attractive lack of gender bias (though forefathers do precede foremothers).

A consideration of one of the early texts will show a good deal that is characteristic of all those with which Furnivall was personally involved, though of course many other participated in the editorial work. In 1868 Furnivall edited for the Society a book given the title *Manners and Meals in Olden Time* (though it is often referred to as *The Babees Book*, from one of its texts). The book is dedicated to the historian Charles Pearson, and consists of a number of late medieval and Tudor texts, in both prose and verse, bearing on contemporary manners, especially at table, the main ones being Hugh Rhodes's *Boke of Nurture* (first published before 1554) and John Russell's similarly named *Boke* (of about 1452).

Furnivall opens with a section entitled 'Forewords, or General Preface', followed by Prefaces to the two texts named above. His idiosyncratic liking for the plural form 'Forewords' shows his literal-mindedness, but does not supersede (as is sometimes alleged) the alternative Romance form. The Forewords begin with a pronouncement referring in medieval fashion to the authority of Aristotle, and explaining the book's rationale:

> [I have] gathered together divers treatises touching the Manners & Meals of Englishmen in former days, & have added therto divers figures of men of old, at meat and in bed [a footnote informs us that 'The Woodcuts are Messrs Virtue's, and have been used in Mr. Thomas Wright's *History of Domestic Manners*

'The Paths of Virtue and Early English' 149

and Customs, &c.] to the end that, to my fellows here & to come, the home life of their forefathers may be somewhat more plain, & their own minds somewhat rejoiced.[6]

This makes clear the ethos of the whole project: to provide information about the past which will give pleasure to modern readers, who are assumed to share the editor's enthusiasm for such information. The Forewords show qualities to be found in most early texts of the Society, including an excessive use of footnotes which constantly hinders the reader's search for coherence. One of the most amusing of these occurs on the first page, and refers to the separate Prefaces provided to Rhodes and Russell:

> If anyone thinks it a bore to read these Prefaces, I can assure him it was a much greater bore to have to hunt up the material for them, and set aside other pressing business for it. But the Boke of Curtasye binding on editors does not allow them to present to their readers a text with no coat and trowsers on. If any Member should take offence at my expressions in this or any future Preface of mine, as a few did at some words in the last I wrote, I ask such Members to consider the first maxim in their Boke of Curtasye, *Don't look a gift horse in the mouth*. Prefaces are gift horses; and if mine buck or shy now and then, I ask their riders to sit steady, and take it easy. On the present one at least they'll be carried across some fresh country worth seeing.[7]

The sporting metaphor seems entirely appropriate for an enterprise conducted with high spirits and pugnacious humanity but in a typographical layout that does nothing to make things easy.

Furnivall's footnotes often take the form of commentary on his own enterprise, as on p. iv where he glosses the remark that 'the whole subject of upper-class education in early times in England' has 'never yet been separately treated', with a frank note stating that he had forgotten Warton's *English Poetry*, and that friends have also drawn his attention to the relevant sections of the volumes of Henry's *History of England*. He concludes:

> Had I seen these earlier I should not have got the following extracts together; but as they are for the most part not in Henry, they will serve as a supplement to him.[8]

There is a sense of a shared enterprise, though one being carried through with more determination than co-ordination. Furnivall is always prepared to admit his mistakes and to name those who have advised him better; it was the enterprise that mattered to him. Hence the generous dedications of many of his editions.

Here as elsewhere Furnivall offers an introductory plan for the Forewords, beginning with some comments on the kinds of young people to whom the *Bokes* are addressed, and then using six further headings, each of which is discussed with many quotations (and a large number of awkward footnotes). The discussion considers education in a series of locales: 'In Nobles' houses'; 'At Home and at Private Tutors'; 'At English Universities'; 'At Foreign Universities'; 'At Monastic and Cathedral Schools'; and 'At Grammar Schools'. Furnivall emphasises the importance of the education of the nobility and gentry in the houses of other nobles, giving many examples – and also noting the severity of punishment often inflicted. Home and private education is then outlined, again with examples – which leads to an enquiring footnote, 'When did *breakfast* get its name, and its first notice as a regular meal?'[9] He includes attention to the education of girls, finding the first governess in the reign of Stephen.[10] The account of English university education focuses on Oxford, and Furnivall notes with indignation the changes of the sixteenth century:

> By Harrison's time, A.D. 1577, rich men's sons had not only pressed into the Universities, but were scrooging poor men's sons out of the endowments meant only for the poor. . . . The law of 'natural selection' prevails.[11]

Indignation came readily to Furnivall, usually on behalf of the under-privileged, and often gave vigour to his prose: the verb 'scrooging' is an energetic coinage. Education in foreign universities is treated briefly, with a reference to the later habit of sending young noblemen on their travels to Italy. The monastic and cathedral schools are discussed with quotations from Lydgate and Langland. The use of the Langland quotation is deliberately extended beyond its immediate relevance with an explanatory remark:

> Here I might stop the quotation, but I go on, for justice has never yet been done to this noble *Crede* and William's *Vision* as pictures of the life of their times, – chiefly from the profound ignorance of

us English of our own language; partly from the grace, the freshness, and the brilliance of Chaucer's easier and inimitable verse.[12]

And having quoted a vigorous passage about the undeserved promotion of some worthless young men of the lower class to positions of power in the Church, Furnivall feels it necessary to turn to 'the other side'. Typically, he is concerned with

> the ploughman's son who didn't turn monk, whose head *was* 'shet' in the straw [unlike the privileged young men chosen for the Church], who delved and ditched, and dunged the earth, eat bread of corn and bran, worts fleshless (vegetables, but no meat), drank water, and went miserably (*Crede*, 1, 1565–71). What education did he get? To whom could he be apprenticed? What was his chance in life?[13]

That final question comes with all the force of Furnivall's Victorian Radicalism. He answers it from the Statute Books forbidding the apprenticeship of any children who have worked at the 'Plough and Cart' until the age of twelve, and this leads him into direct commentary on contemporary politics at the time of the Second Reform Act:

> These Acts I came across when hunting for the Statutes referred to in the *Boke of Curtasye* as fixing the hire of horses for carriage at fourpence a piece, and they caused me some surprise.[14]

It is part of Furnivall's attractive simplicity that this should have been possible; he was not a detached historian, but a man who could be 'surprised' (and disturbed) by what he found out about the past because he saw it as relevant to the present. He therefore continues:

> They made me wonder less at the energy with which some people now are trying to erect 'barriers against democracy' to prevent the return match for the old game coming off. – However improving, and however justly retributive, future legislation for the rich by the poor in the spirit of past legislation for the poor by the rich might be, it could hardly be considered pleasant, and is surely worth putting up the barrier against, one of education in each poor man's mind. (He who americanizes us that far will be the greatest benefactor England has had for some ages).[15]

The position taken here is that of non-revolutionary Radicalism: the injustice of the past is admitted, but as full restitution would not be pleasant (presumably for the rich), they should put up 'the true barrier' of education. This formulation shows some confusion, for Furnivall did not really see education as a barrier against democracy, but as a pre-condition of it. His impatience with the anti-democrats leads him into a formulation that does not do justice to his own Radicalism – except by its admiring reference to the American education system, known to be far more democratic, then as now.

The account of the cathedral schools draws freely on Robert Whiston's *Cathedral Trusts and their Fulfilment*, which is quoted at length, with a concluding comment on its evidence for the 'scandalous way in which the choristers and poor boys were done out of their proportion of the endowments by the Cathedral clergy'.[16] The endowed grammar schools for 'citizens' and townsmen's children' are then considered, using a list of schools founded before 1545 'compiled for me by Mr. Brock from Carlisle's *Concise Description*'[17] (further evidence of the shared nature of the research), and accounts quoted going back to Fitzstephen in about 1174 ('I use Pegge's translation, 1772, to which Mr. Chappell referred me').[18] The account of the boys' activities is enthusiastic:

> In the winter holidays, the boys saw boar-fights, hog-fights, bull and bear-baiting, and when ice came they slid, and skated on the leg-bones of some animal, punting themselves along with an iron-shod pole, and charging one another. A set of merry scenes indeed.[19]

This relishing of vigorous physical activity – with no apparent qualms about the cruel use of animals for sport – reminds us of the element of 'boyishness' to be found in many Victorian masculinist writers, among whom Furnivall must here be numbered. For him, physical exertion was inherently healthy and good.

In discussing public-school education, Furnivall quotes extensively from Richard Mulcaster, headmaster of Merchant Taylors' School in 1561, honoured as the 'first schoolmaster who stood up for the study of English'.[20] This leads on to the observation that the situation is very similar in 1867: 'there is just one public school at which English is studied historically. . . . This neglect of English as a subject of study is due no doubt to tutors' and parents' ignorance. None of them know the subject historically; the former can't teach it,

'The Paths of Virtue and Early English'   153

the latter don't care about it; why should their boys learn it? Oh tutors and parents, there are such things as asses in the world.'[21] Furnivall then goes on to reflect that the young people to whom the *Bokes of Nurture* were addressed must have been 'dirty, ill-mannered, awkward young gawkes . . . to modern notions'.[22] But he does not want to suggest the superiority of the modern:

> [R]eflections on the good deeds done, and the high thoughts thought, by men of old dirtier than some now, may prevent us concluding that because other people now talk though their noses, and have manners different from our own, they and their institutions must be wholly abominable; that because others smell when heated they ought to be slaves; or that eating peas with a knife renders men unworthy of the franchise. The temptation to value manners above morals, and pleasantness above honesty, is one that all of us have to guard against.[23]

Victorian society may often have succumbed to the temptation, but the evidence suggests that Furnivall did not: no one complained that *his* manners were too fine. He defends the attention here paid to the dirtiness of earlier times by stating that plenty of evidence of 'the riches and luxury in England' has been provided, and that 'to me, as foolometer of the Society, this dark side seemed to need showing'.[24] Presumably the foolometer's duty is to draw attention to whatever superficial reading fails to notice. Furnivall resists a too easy idealisation of the past.

Furnivall ends by commenting briefly on the individual texts, and justifies the second part of the volume which contains French and Latin poems on the same subjects as the English poems. He notes ruefully, however, that 'punishment came for one's wandering from the paths of virtue and Early English'[25] – a natural conjunction for him – in the difficulties he has had with the manuscript of the Latin *Modus Cenandi*, for which J. R. Seeley the historian provided a translation. Other co-workers are thanked, with the heartened conclusion that 'The ready way in which help is given to one, whenever it is asked for, is one of the pleasantest incidents of one's work'.[26] His last words turn towards future projects:

> It is . . . the fullest verse one [i.e. collection] that has yet appeared on its subject, and will serve as the beginning of the Society's store of this kind of material. If we can do all the English part of the

work, and the Master of the Rolls will commission one of his Editors to do the Latin part, we shall then get a fairly complete picture of that Early English Home which, with all its shortcomings, should be dear to every Englishman now.[27]

The final phrase makes clear the patriotic motivation of the whole project – though other parts of the Forewords have shown that by no means all Englishmen live up to Furnivall's expectations of their interest in the national past.

The whole of these Forewords is characteristic. To the modern academic there is an odd mixture of scholarship and informality, and a marked tendency to move backwards and forwards in time. What is unquestionable is the enthusiasm exhibited and communicated for the English past, though this is presented more as a series of lively scenes than as a developing history. Even if the reader is not a scholar, he feels that he is to some extent participating in an historic enterprise – reclaiming the past – and one in which a number of other people are participating.[28] It is that sense of being invited to take part in an important common cultural project that can still carry a modern reader along, and must have been very attractive at the time.

Furnivall's next important, and of course overlapping, activity was the formation of the Chaucer Society in 1868, with the publication of the *Six-Text Print of Chaucer's Canterbury Tales* in the same year. This has recently been discussed by Donald Baker in Paul Ruggiers's *Editing Chaucer: The Great Tradition*, who concludes that Furnivall 'made all modern editions possible'.[29] For what he decided to do was to produce a parallel-text edition of what he saw as the six most important manuscripts, Hengwrt, Ellesmere, Cambridge Gg 4.27, Corpus Christi, Petworth and Lansdowne. In Baker's words:

> Furnivall's chief contributions must be said to have lain in the selection of the texts, seeing to it that they were well copied, printed (Furnivall raising the money), and well proof-read (most of which work Furnivall did himself). Furnivall was clearly not a textual scholar, in the sense that Henry Bradshaw was, but he was fully aware of this, and at every step he generously gave credit to his chief advisers, Bradshaw, Morris, Ellis and others.[30]

Again we have the sense of a corporate enterprise with Furnivall at its head, and one in which the intention is to make texts available rather than to offer any particular interpretation of them. His 'Temporary Preface to the Six-Text Edition' (temporary in the sense that he was always prepared to expect more recent scholarship to overtake his findings) makes this clear. Walter Skeat's edition of 1894–5 drew on Furnivall's work, and it was Furnivall himself who had brought Skeat into editorial work by assigning to him in 1864 the re-editing of *Lancelot of the Laik*. Skeat's recollection of this in his autobiography gives the flavour of Furnivall's force of character:

> My name was mentioned to him as one who was fond of Early English and had some leisure. . . . My objection, that I was unable to read a MS., was over-ruled on the grounds, first, that the sole MS. was always at hand in the Cambridge University Library; and secondly, that I could learn.[31]

Perhaps Furnivall's greatest talent was for drawing in participants for his great enterprise – just as his greatest limitation was an inability to control his exasperation with those who could not, or did not wish to, participate. The Chaucer Society went on after *The Canterbury Tales* to produce the *Minor Poems* (1871–9) and *Troilus and Cressida* (1881–2), also in parallel-text editions which have facilitated later scholarship, so that Furnivall came to deserve Baker's description of him as

> the most important of all Chaucerians – not the best scholar, etc., but the most important – highly personal and yet curiously anonymous, who was able to devote only a small portion of his total working time to Chaucer but who shames us all who, in our serried ranks, minutely ponder the works of that highly personal and yet curiously anonymous poet.[32]

The emphasis here is on Furnivall as a medievalist, so there is no need to follow him into the New Shakspere Society (with its dogmatically old-spelt editions), the Ballad Society, or the Browning Society, to which his contribution has been thoroughly and entertainingly discussed by William Peterson.[33] What has been emphasised as Furnivall's main contribution to Victorian medievalism is, above all, an energy and enthusiasm which went towards the publication of many texts that would otherwise have remained unavailable: the 1892 Early English Text Society cover-note asserts:

'Let the dead past bury its dead' is still the cry of Great Britian and her Colonies, and of America, in the matter of language.

Furnivall, however, would not let the dead remain buried, and was a very successful resurrection-man at a time when there was little institutional support for medieval scholarship. The German academic Alois Brandl, writing in the 1911 tribute volume, remarked that he was 'a scholar with a large range of vision, and an excellent example of those strong personalities which in England make up for the national lack of adequate system'.[34] How adequate such individual effort can be is open to discussion; Furnivall himself, as we have seen, always aimed to be part of a group activity. He excelled as what is now called a facilitator.

The problem of assessing his achievement is closely related to his consistent refusal or failure to explain the reasons for his overall project. Time and again in his numerous Forewords we are led to share Furnivall's excitement about reading a text which leads him 'into the life of its time', as do the Chester Depositions about child-marriages.[35] His writing can convey this excitement, as in his account of Hoccleve in 1892:

> When he got free, and was his own master, he naturally kickt up his heels, and at 18 he seems to have turned into a smart Government-Clerk while waiting for a benefice that he never got. He no doubt jetted along the Strand in fine weather in the fashionable wide-sleeved cloak of the time, down to the Privy-Seal Office in the Palace of Westminster, where he would see the Prince of Wales and the nobles he mentions in his works, and have a chance of talking to them. . . . When young, he was free with his money, stuft and drank at the cook-shops and taverns in Westminster – paying whatever was askt – and instead of going back to the office after dinner, went for an outing on the river.[36]

Although Furnivall conscientiously gives references to Hoccleve's writings for each item of information about his way of life, the effect is undeniably romantic. Here as elsewhere he exhibits what is now criticised as humanism, an emphasis on 'people' from the past which gives them the full force of attention while nothing is said about historical development or civic institutions. This goes with his energetic eclecticism, his preparedness to print all sorts of documents, and to be as excited about wills and testimonies as about works of literature. According to Roman Dyboski in 1911, when Furnivall was praised for his work for English philology, he replied, 'I never cared a bit for philology; my chief aim has been throughout to illustrate the social conditions of the English people in the past.'[37] What did Furnivall's influence contribute to a brand of scholarship that had already offered a powerful critique of Victorian capitalism in the works of Carlyle, Ruskin and Morris? It seems to me that Furnivall's eclecticism had the valuable effect of strengthening the 'democractic' implications of some of the thinking in that tradition, not by drawing attention to important events such as the Peasants' Revolt (the inspiration for Morris's *Dream of John Ball*), but by moving away from the idea of a canon of central texts to a wider range of materials. 'The social conditions of the English people in the past' constitute too wide a field of study for any narrowly defined politics confidently to take over.

Furnivall's period of activity, which ceased only with his death in 1910, coincided with the professionalisation of much academic work; and he was himself continuously involved in editing and publishing. What he managed to retain for Medievalism, as it became incorporated into academic life and lost much of its political edge, was a generous concern for the lives of ordinary people. If this strikes us today as naïve, we may find it useful to interrogate the politics of our own sophistication.

NOTES

1. William Morris, quoted in May Morris (ed.), *William Morris: Artist, Writer, Socialist*, 2 vols (Oxford: Clarendon Press, 1936) vol. I, pp. 287–8.
2. Sir Arthur Quiller-Couch, *On the Art of Reading* (1920; Cambridge: Cambridge University Press, 1947) p. 84.
3. W. Benzie, *Frederick James Furnivall: A Victorian Scholar Adventurer* (Norman, Okla: Pilgrim Books, 1983) p. 22.
4. J. Munro, in *Frederick James Furnivall: A Volume of Personal Record* (London: Oxford University Press, 1911) p. xliii. (The text has *English Idylls*, but the reference seems to be to the *Idylls of the King*.)
5. K. M. E. Murray, *Caught in the Web of Words* (New Haven, Conn.: Yale University Press, 1977).
6. F. J. Furnivall (ed.), *Manners and Meals in Olden Time* (London: N. Trübner, for Early English Text Society, 1868) p. i.
7. Ibid., fn. 4.
8. Ibid., p. iv, fn. 1.

9. Ibid., p. xxiii, fn. 1.
10. Ibid., p. xxv.
11. Ibid., pp. xxxvi–vii.
12. Ibid., p. xlv.
13. Ibid., p. xlvi.
14. Ibid., p. xlvii.
15. Ibid.
16. Ibid., p. lii.
17. Ibid., p. liii.
18. Ibid., p. liv.
19. Ibid., p. lv.
20. Ibid., p. lix, quoting Mulcaster's *Elementairie*, 1582.
21. Ibid., p. lxi.
22. Ibid., p. lxii.
23. Ibid., p. lxiii.
24. Ibid., p. lxvii.
25. Ibid., p. lxviii.
26. Ibid., p. lxxiv.
27. Ibid.
28. See the final footnote to ibid., p. lxxiv: 'If any member or reader can refer me to any other verse or prose pieces of like kind, unprinted, or that deserve reprinting, I shall be much obliged to him, and will try and put them in type.'
29. In Paul G. Ruggiers (ed.), *Editing Chaucer: The Great Tradition* (Norman, Okla: Pilgrim Books, 1984) p. 169.
30. Ibid., p. 158.
31. W. W. Skeat, *A Student's Pastime* (Oxford: Clarendon Press, 1896) p. xxv.
32. Baker, in Ruggiers, *Editing Chaucer*, p. 169.
33. W. S. Peterson, *Interrogating the Oracle: A History of the London Browning Society* (Athens, Ohio: Ohio University Press, 1969).
34. Alois Brandl in Benzie, *Frederick James Furnivall*, p. 13. Brandl describes England on the same page as 'a country unprovided with *Seminare*, and even without a system of modern philological instruction'.
35. F. J. Furnivall (ed.), *Child-Marriages, Divorces and Ratifications, &c in the Diocese of Chester, A.D.1561–6*. (London: Kegan Paul, Trench, Trübner, for Early English Text Society, 1897) p. xv. The dedication of the volume is to 'The Antiquaries of Cheshire in the hope that they will at once hang one of their number, to encourage the rest forthwith to print all the depositions and other valuable-material in the diocesan registry at Chester which they have so long and so culpably left in Ms. only.'
36. F. J. Furnivall (ed.), *Hoccleve's Works. I: The Minor Poems* (London: Oxford University Press, for Early English Text Society, 1892) pp. xxxv–vi. Furnivall used an 'Early English' form of spelling, contracting the final syllable of past participles. His style should be seen in context with that of William Barnes, Gerard Manley Hopkins, and William Morris in his late romances.
37. Roman Dyboski, in Benzie, *Frederick James Furnivall*, p. 43.

Index

Adorno, Theodor, 25
Amadas et Ydoine, 63
Anderson, Perry, 108
Ascham, Robert, 124
Audelay, John, 89
Awentyrs of Arthure, The, 17

Bakhtin, *see* Volosinov
Barnett, Correlli, 103
Barriffe, William, 103
Barwick, Humfrey, 116
Blake, Norman, 1, 7
Blake, William, 129
Boethius, 72–5
Boffey, Julia, 11
Boreman, John, 129
Boswell, James, 129
Bradley, S. A. J., 3, 7
Brampton, Thomas, 89
Burke, Peter, 7, 137–8
Burrow, John, 3, 7

Calvin, John, 112
Canterbury Tales, 1, 9, 83, 154–5
Carlyle, Thomas, 144, 157
Caxton, William, 84, 90, 92–3, 95
Chatterton, Thomas, 128
Chaucer, Geoffrey, 9, 13, 24–40, 69–78, 92, 147, 154–5
Cleanness, 42–3, 45–6
Clerk's Tale, 69, 75, 77, 80
Cobbett, William, 130
Cockle, M. J. D., 101
Coleridge, Samuel Taylor, 129
Colet, John, 111
Collier, J. P., 6–7
Consolation of Philosophy, 73
Copland, Robert, 83, 90
Copland, William, 131, 133
Cromwell, Oliver, 118
Crowley, Robert, 95
Cruso, John, 118
Cursor Mundi, 85–7, 89, 93

Davies, John, 145
Deloney, Thomas, 126–7
Derrida, Jacques, 24–31, 34, 36, 38
Descartes, René, 35, 37
Dicey, Cluer, 122
Digges, Thomas, 114
Doyle, Ian, 1, 12, 19

Eagleton, Terry, 32
Earl of Tolous, 15
Elderton, William, 127
Elizabeth I, 1, 95
Erasmus, 110–11

Fabre, Abbé, 136
Fish, Stanley, 31
Floris and Blauncheflour, 10
Freud, Sigmund, 26
Furnivall, F. J., 6, 144–58

Gates, Geoffrey, 114
Girouard, M., 7
Goldberg, Jonathan, 28–9, 39
Gower, John, 9, 84
Greenblatt, Stephen, 28–9
Guddat-Figges, Gisela, 13–14

Hanna, Ralph, 14, 17
Hardman, Phillipa, 18
Henry VIII, 111
Henry, Prince of Wales, 6
Hilton, Walter, 94
Hoccleve, Thomas, 84, 156
Horall, Sally, 17
Horkheimer, Max, 25
Hurd, Richard, 128

Johnson, Richard, 132

King Horn, 15, 55–6, 58, 61–4
Knight's Tale, 69, 74, 77, 80
Konig Rother, 56, 58

159

Lackington, John, 129, 135
Lancelot of the Laik, 155
Langland, William, 24, 35, 86, 95, 150
Lewis, C. S., 6
Libeaus Desconus, 15
Lichfield, William, 10
Lombard, Peter, 9
Love, Nicholas, 87–8, 93
Ludlow, J. M., 145
Luther, Martin, 112
Luxemburg, Rosa, 34
Lydgate, John, 13, 89, 150

Mabbe, Thomas, 126
MacIntyre, Alasdair, 34, 36
Machiavelli, N., 101
Maidstone, Richard, 89
Malory, Sir Thomas, 2, 13, 18
Mandrou, Robert, 137–8
Marcuse, Herbert, 25–6
Marshall, Richard, 130
Marx, Karl, 26
Maurice, C. E., 145
McSparran, Frances, 10–11
Meale, Carol, 16
Mehl, Dieter, 13–14
Merchant's Tale, 74, 80
Merleau-Ponty, Maurice, 25
Milton, John, 34
More, Sir Thomas, 110, 112
Morganwg, Iolo, 128
Morris, William, 144, 154, 157
Morte Arthure, 17, 110
Muchembled, R., 137–8
Mulcaster, Richard, 152
Murray, Katharine, 146

Nashe, Thomas, 124
Nassyngton, William, 87–8
Neade, William, 101, 117, 119
Newbury, John, 129
Nietzsche, Friedrich, 31

Octavian, 15
Ossian, 128

Painter, Thomas, 126
Parker, Martin, 127

Parkes, Malcolm, 8–9, 12–14
Patience, 43, 46
Patterson, Lee, 7, 24–5, 38
Pearl, 43–4, 46, 89
Pearsall, Derek, 10–13, 15–16, 38
Percy, Thomas, 128
Pettie, George, 126
Pisan, Christine de, 101
Pynson, Richard, 93, 131, 133

Quiller-Couch, Sir Arthur, 144

Rasselas, 122, 130
Richardson, Samuel, 130
Riche, Barnabe, 101, 113, 126
Ricoeur, Paul, 25
Ritson, Joseph, 128
Robarts, Henry, 126
Robinson, Pamela, 13–15
Rolle, Richard, 84, 87
Roman de la Rose, 43, 63
Romance of Horn, see King Horn
Rowland, David, 126
Rowlands, Samuel, 131
Ruskin, John, 144, 157
Ryckes, John, 94

Salisbury, John of, 42, 44, 50
Salter, Elizabeth, 26
Scott, Sir Walter, 128
Seeley, J. R., 153
Seven Champions of Christendom, The, 122–3, 132–3, 135
Seven Sages, The, 10
Shirley, John, 11, 84
Shonk, Timothy, 12
Shoreham, William of, 89
Sidney, Sir Philip, 124
Sir Amadace, 16, 18
Sir Beves of Hamtoun, 55–6, 58–9, 61–4, 132
Sir Degrevant, 17
Sir Eglamour, 15, 17
Sir Gawain and the Green Knight, 41–2, 44, 46, 51
Sir Gowther, 16, 18
Sir Guy of Warwick, 4, 10, 54–68, 123, 127, 130–3, 135, 138

Index

Sir *Isumbras*, 14–16, 18
Sir Perceval, 17
Skeat, W. W., 155
Skelton, John, 84
Spearing, A. C., 1, 7
Steele, Sir Richard, 129
St Erkenwald, 49–50
Styward, Thomas, 117

Thompson, John, 12, 16–17
Thornton, John, 16–18, 88
Tolkien, J. R. R., 5
Trench, R. C., 146
Troilus and Criseyde, 80, 83, 155
Troyes, Chretien de, 41, 45

Turville-Petre, Thorlac, 15

Urquart, Sir Thomas, 126

Vance, Eugene, 41, 45, 52
Volosinov, 26

Warton, Thomas, 128, 149
Webb, Henry, 102
Whiston, Robert, 152
Whitehorne, Peter, 101
Worde, Wynkyn de, 90–5, 133
Wynnere and Wastoure, 110

Yates, Frances, 7